COOKING WITH
Bon Appétit

COOKING WITH

Bon Appétit

Recipe Yearbook 1990

Editors' Choice of Recipes from 1989

THE KNAPP PRESS
Publishers
Los Angeles

Copyright © 1990 by Knapp Communications Corporation

Published by The Knapp Press
5900 Wilshire Boulevard, Los Angeles, California 90036

Library of Congress Catalog Number: 83-643303

ISBN: 0-89535-221-4

Bon Appétit Books offers cookbook stands. For details on ordering please write:
    Bon Appétit Books
    Premium Department
    Sherman Turnpike
    Danbury, CT 06816

On the Cover: *Aspen Chocolate Cream Cake* and *Visions of Sugarplums.*
Photographed by Victor Scocozza.

Printed and bound in the United States of America
10 9 8 7 6 5 4 3 2 1

❧ Contents

Foreword .... *vii*

1 Appetizers 1

2 Soups and Salads 9
Soups 10
Side-Dish Salads 15
Main-Dish Salads 19

3 Pasta, Pizza and Sandwiches 23
Pasta 24
Pizza 31
Sandwiches 33

4 Main Courses 35
Beef 36
Veal 42
Lamb 44
Pork 47
Poultry and Game 50
Fish and Shellfish 57
Eggs, Cheese and Vegetables 62

5 Vegetables, Grains and Breads 67

Vegetables   68
Grains   73
Breads   75

6 Desserts 81

Fruit Desserts   82
Custards, Puddings and Soufflés   84
Frozen Desserts   88
Pies, Tarts and Pastries   93
Cakes   103
Cookies   111

Index 115

Bon Appétit's News '89 119

❦ *Foreword*

Here in our fourth annual collection of recipes from *Bon Appétit* magazine, you'll find an exciting variety of fabulous dishes. Whether you're searching for the perfect menu for an elegant dinner party, a showstopper dessert or just a change-of-pace main course for a casual family supper, you'll find what you're looking for in these pages. Some of the country's most talented cooks and finest restaurants have contributed to the more than 200 recipes here, chosen by the editors to represent the year's best and to reflect important trends.

One of the first things you may notice as you leaf through the book is what an international selection of recipes it contains. A veritable United Nations of dishes, they run the gamut from Oriental Beef and Noodle Soup and Greek-style Pasta Salad to Moroccan-spiced Chicken with Lemon and Carrots and Shrimp Enchiladas. But you'll also find plenty of all-American food like Molasses- and Bourbon-glazed Pork with Yams and Turnips, Corn Fritters and Bread Pudding with Currants and Maple Syrup.

The recent trend toward bold flavors and assertive spicing is still going strong in everything from Tabasco-flavored Almonds and Cashews to Spicy Sesame Chinese Noodles. The popularity of southwestern cooking a couple of years back has left us with a new appreciation for chilies and peppers; they're used creatively along with fresh herbs and spices to enhance dishes such as Cowboy Steak with Red Chili Onion Rings and Lime Ginger Chicken with Tomato and Green Pepper Salsa.

Old favorites are well represented here, and many of them have been updated for today's tastes. Our version of bagels and lox starts with toasted mini bagels—they're dressed up with smoked salmon, sour cream and a sprinkling of caviar for a simple but sophisticated appetizer. The taco gets a new twist with a filling of sausage sautéed with vegetables and spices. And classic crème brûlée becomes a rich, creamy custard layered with fresh peaches and a crisp cinnamon topping.

The recipes in this collection come from all areas of the magazine, from departments like "The Weekday Cook," "Too Busy to Cook?" and "R.S.V.P." to cooking class, restaurant, entertaining and travel features.

The "Cooking Healthy" and "Shortcuts with Style" columns are among the most popular in the magazine, and you'll find some of their delicious, healthy and fast recipes here. Many of the instructions include do-ahead steps, so they can be easily incorporated into a busy schedule.

For all their variety, the recipes have a common theme—they taste great, and they all represent the kind of good eating that's never out of style—the kind of honest, unfussy cooking *Bon Appétit* is all about. So as we say good-bye to the eighties, we can look forward to a new decade filled with fun and terrific food.

At the back of the book we've included a section called "News '89— The Year of Food and Entertaining in Review." Consisting of brief notes on new food products and services, restaurants and people, cookbooks, travel tips and diet news, "News '89" tracks some of the most interesting developments of the year. All prices, addresses and other details have been updated as of this yearbook's publication date.

Here's to the best of 1989!

1 ❦ Appetizers

The zesty array of international appetizers presented here is sure to inspire you to throw a sensational cocktail party—it's a snap when so many of the recipes are quick, easy and often do-ahead. You might pair the rustic Tomato Croutons with Bacon and Basil with elegant Toasted Mini Bagels with Smoked Salmon and Caviar or Grilled Shrimp with Dilled Asparagus and Garlic Mayonnaise. If you're short on time, serve just three or four hearty, uncomplicated appetizers—choose from recipes like Ratatouille French Bread Pizzas, toasted bread slices rubbed with garlic and olive oil and topped with a classic combo of eggplant, zucchini, bell pepper and herbs; Marmalade-glazed Chicken Wings with the zip of lime and tequila; and California Nachos, a surprise version of the Mexican favorite, with pita bread wedges instead of tortillas, topped with goat cheese, avocado and sun-dried tomatoes. You might supplement the selection with a board of cheeses or a purchased country pâté.

Of course, you'll also find the perfect starter for any kind of meal, from simple to sophisticated. Iced Clams with Horseradish Salsa is a lively prelude to a casual seafood supper. Before an elegant entrée, serve Herbed Phyllo Purses with Camembert and Walnuts or Smoked Salmon Cream, a dressed-up dip topped with salmon caviar.

Tabasco-flavored Almonds and Cashews

Despite the prodigious quantity of Tabasco, these crisp nuts build slowly to a comfortable heat level.

Makes 3 pounds

6 tablespoons olive oil
1½ pounds roasted unsalted cashews
1½ pounds roasted unsalted almonds

¼ cup (or more) Tabasco or other hot pepper sauce
1 tablespoon (or more) coarse salt

Heat 3 tablespoons oil in each of 2 heavy large skillets over medium heat. Place cashews in 1 skillet and almonds in another. Cook nuts until crisp and brown, stirring frequently, about 5 minutes for cashews and 8 minutes for almonds. Transfer nuts to large rimmed baking sheet. Drizzle ¼ cup Tabasco over nuts, stirring constantly. Sprinkle 1 tablespoon salt over, tossing to coat evenly. Taste, adding more Tabasco and salt if desired. Cool completely. (*Can be prepared 2 days ahead. Store in airtight container. Rewarm nuts in 350°F oven before serving, if desired.*)

Black Olives with Cilantro, Garlic and Lemon

Makes about 4 cups

½ cup minced fresh cilantro
¼ cup olive oil
2 tablespoons fresh lemon juice
3 garlic cloves

1½ pounds brine-cured imported black olives, such as Kalamata,* rinsed and drained
1 tablespoon lemon peel julienne

Puree first 4 ingredients in blender. Pour into bowl. Add olives; toss to coat. (*Can be prepared 1 day ahead. Cover and refrigerate.*) Sprinkle lemon peel over. Serve at room temperature.

*Available at Greek and Italian markets and some specialty foods stores.

Avocado Pâté with Parsley and Pistachios

Here's a new guise for the ever-popular guacamole. Make it the day before.

8 to 10 servings

Oil
4 ripe avocados, peeled and pitted
2 8-ounce packages cream cheese, room temperature
2 tablespoons minced shallots or green onions
1 tablespoon fresh lemon juice
2 teaspoons minced garlic
1 teaspoon chili powder
½ teaspoon salt

¼ cup chopped fresh parsley
2 tablespoons chopped unsalted pistachios
4 butter lettuce or Boston lettuce leaves
½ cup pitted black olives
10 ripe cherry tomatoes
Tortilla chips

Line 6-cup rectangular glass loaf pan or ceramic dish with 3 layers of waxed paper, extending over long sides only. Brush top sheet of paper generously with oil. Puree avocados and cream cheese in processor. Add shallots, lemon juice, garlic, chili powder and salt and blend 30 seconds. Transfer mixture to prepared pan; smooth top. Press plastic wrap onto surface of pâté and refrigerate at least 6 hours or overnight.

Remove plastic from pâté. Unmold onto rectangular platter. Remove waxed paper. Mix parsley and pistachios in small bowl. Sprinkle over pâté. Arrange lettuce decoratively at corners of platter. Garnish with olives and tomatoes. Surround with tortilla chips.

White Bean Dip with Roasted Garlic Gremolata

Gremolata is the traditional minced garlic, parsley and lemon peel garnish for the Italian veal shank dish osso buco. Here a roasted garlic version flavors pureed white beans. Accompany the dip with endive and radicchio leaves, carrot and fennel sticks and snow peas.

Makes about 1½ cups

12 garlic cloves, unpeeled
Olive oil
⅓ cup packed Italian parsley, chopped
1 2 × ¾-inch lemon peel strip (yellow part only), chopped

1 16-ounce can cannellini beans (white kidney), rinsed and drained
3 tablespoons fresh lemon juice
1 tablespoon olive oil
¼ teaspoon salt
Freshly ground pepper

Preheat oven to 400°F. Place garlic in pie plate. Drizzle with olive oil. Roast until soft but not brown, about 15 minutes. Cool slightly, then trim ends and peel.

Mince parsley and lemon peel in processor. Add roasted garlic, beans, lemon juice, oil and salt. Season with pepper. Process until smooth. Transfer to serving bowl. (*Can be prepared 1 day ahead. Cover and refrigerate. Bring to room temperature before serving.*)

Smoked Salmon Cream with Crudités

10 servings

1 pound cream cheese, room temperature
½ cup whipping cream
2 green onions, chopped
¼ cup minced fresh parsley
2 tablespoons minced fresh dill or 2 teaspoons dried dillweed
2 teaspoons fresh lemon juice
1 garlic clove, minced
Dash of hot pepper sauce (such as Tabasco)
Salt and freshly ground pepper

8 ounces smoked salmon or lox trimmings, shredded

¼ cup salmon caviar or 1 small tomato, peeled, seeded and chopped
Assorted vegetables such as cucumber slices, carrot sticks, celery pieces
Cocktail rye or pumpernickel bread

Beat cream cheese and cream in large bowl until smooth. Stir in green onions, parsley, dill, lemon juice, garlic and hot pepper sauce. Season with salt and pepper. Fold in smoked salmon. (*Can be prepared 1 day ahead. Cover with plastic wrap and refrigerate. Bring to room temperature before using.*)

Garnish with caviar or tomato. Serve with vegetables and bread.

Warm Blue Cheese Dip with Garlic and Bacon

Makes about 1⅔ cups

7 bacon slices, diced
2 garlic cloves, minced

8 ounces cream cheese, room temperature
¼ cup half and half
4 ounces blue cheese, crumbled

2 tablespoons chopped fresh chives
3 tablespoons chopped smoked almonds (about 1 ounce)
Assorted crackers
Sliced French bread
Celery and/or carrot sticks

Cook bacon in heavy large skillet over medium-high heat until almost crisp, about 7 minutes. Drain excess fat from skillet. Add garlic and cook until bacon is crisp, about 3 minutes.

Preheat oven to 350°F. Using electric mixer, beat cream cheese until smooth. Add half and half and beat until combined. Stir in bacon mixture, blue cheese and chives. Transfer to 2-cup ovenproof baking dish. Cover with foil. (*Can be prepared 1 day ahead. Refrigerate. Bring to room temperature before continuing.*) Bake until heated through, about 30 minutes. Sprinkle with chopped almonds. Serve with crackers, bread and/or vegetables.

Cranberry-glazed Brie

A perfect appetizer—or surprising conclusion—to a festive holiday dinner, this is a sensational coupling of contrasting tastes, colors and textures. Spread it on apple or pear slices or on crisp crackers.

12 servings

Cranberry Marmalade
3 cups cranberries
¾ cup firmly packed golden brown sugar
⅓ cup dried currants
⅓ cup water
⅛ teaspoon dry mustard
⅛ teaspoon ground allspice
⅛ teaspoon ground cardamom
⅛ teaspoon ground cloves
⅛ teaspoon ground ginger

Cheese
1 2.2-pound Brie cheese wheel (8-inch diameter)

Crackers
Apple slices
Pear slices

For marmalade: Combine all ingredients in heavy nonaluminum saucepan. Cook over medium-high heat until most of berries pop, stirring frequently, about 5 minutes. Cool mixture to room temperature. (*Can be prepared 3 days ahead. Cover tightly and refrigerate.*)

For cheese: Using sharp knife, cut circle in top rind of cheese, leaving ½-inch border of rind. Carefully remove center circle of rind from cheese. Do not cut through side rind. Place cheese in 8-inch-diameter ceramic baking dish or on cookie sheet lined with foil. Spread cranberry marmalade over. (*Can be prepared 6 hours ahead. Cover and chill. Bring to room temperature before continuing.*)

Preheat oven to 300°F. Bake cheese until soft, about 12 minutes.

Set cheese on large platter. Surround with crackers and fruit slices. Let cool slightly. Serve warm or at room temperature.

Herbed Phyllo Purses with Camembert and Walnuts

These delicate cheese- and nut-filled pastries can be prepared the day before. Simply bake until crisp prior to serving.

Makes about 60

8 ounces Camembert cheese, cut into cubes with rind, room temperature
1 teaspoon dried rosemary, crumbled
¼ teaspoon cayenne pepper
1 egg, beaten to blend

3 tablespoons coarsely chopped walnuts
15 phyllo pastry sheets
1 cup (2 sticks) (about) unsalted butter, melted

Using electric mixer, beat cheese in small bowl until smooth. Beat in rosemary, cayenne and egg. Mix in nuts.

Butter large baking sheets. Place 1 phyllo sheet on work surface (keep remainder covered with slightly damp towel). Brush phyllo lightly with melted butter. Top with second phyllo sheet. Brush lightly with butter. Top with third phyllo sheet. Brush lightly with butter. Cut stacked, buttered phyllo lengthwise into 3½-inch-wide strips. Then cut crosswise into 3½-inch-wide squares. Place 1 teaspoon cheese filling in center of each square. Gather corners together over center and crimp firmly to form purses. Transfer to prepared sheets, spacing 1 inch apart. Brush tops lightly with butter. Repeat buttering, cutting, filling and crimping with remaining pastry, butter and filling. Refrigerate at least 1 hour. (*Can be prepared 1 day ahead.*)

Preheat oven to 350°F. Bake pastries until crisp and golden brown, about 22 minutes. Cool 5 minutes. Transfer to platter and serve.

Tomato Croutons with Bacon and Basil

Two perennial favorites—tomato and basil—are featured in this light, fresh-tasting hors d'oeuvre. Both the croutons and the topping can be prepared ahead. Just assemble and bake before serving.

8 servings

3 tablespoons unsalted butter
6 tablespoons olive oil
24 ½-inch-thick slices French bread baguette

⅓ cup chopped shallots or green onions
2 teaspoons finely chopped garlic

1½ cups chopped peeled seeded tomatoes (about 2 pounds)
¼ cup chicken stock or canned broth
¼ teaspoon dried red pepper flakes
Salt

6 cooked bacon strips, crumbled
3 tablespoons fresh basil julienne

Position rack in center of oven and preheat to 300°F. Melt butter with 3 tablespoons oil in heavy small saucepan over low heat, stirring occasionally. Arrange bread slices on heavy large baking sheet. Brush both sides of bread with butter mixture. Bake until crisp and golden brown, turning once, about 10 minutes. (*Can be prepared 1 day ahead. Cool; store in plastic bag at room temperature.*)

Heat remaining 3 tablespoons oil in heavy large skillet over medium-high heat. Add shallots and sauté 2 minutes. Add garlic and sauté 1 minute. Mix in tomatoes, stock and dried pepper flakes. Season with salt. Cook until almost all liquid evaporates, stirring frequently, about 10 minutes. (*Can be prepared 1 day ahead. Transfer mixture to bowl. Cover and refrigerate.*)

Preheat oven to 350°F. Spread tomato mixture over croutons. Top with bacon. Bake until heated through, about 8 minutes. Transfer croutons to platter. Sprinkle with basil julienne.

Toasted Mini Bagels with Smoked Salmon and Caviar

These miniature open-face sandwiches are simple to prepare. They look pretty on a bed of dark green spinach leaves.

8 servings

12 plain mini bagels*
¼ cup (½ stick) unsalted butter, melted

Fresh spinach leaves
Sour cream

4 ounces thinly sliced smoked salmon
Caviar
Freshly ground pepper

Preheat oven to 300°F. Halve bagels horizontally using serrated knife. Arrange cut side up on large baking sheet. Brush bagels generously with butter. Bake until light golden brown, about 8 minutes. Cool slightly. (*Can be prepared 3 hours ahead. Cool completely. Wrap tightly; store at room temperature.*)

Arrange spinach decoratively on large platter. Spread each bagel half with sour cream. Cover with salmon. Top with small dollop of sour cream and some caviar. Sprinkle with pepper. Transfer bagels to platter and serve.

*Available at some delicatessens, specialty foods stores and bagel shops.

Ratatouille French Bread Pizzas

These little "pizzas" are actually more like Italian bruschetta—toasted bread slices rubbed with garlic and olive oil.

Makes about 40

¼ cup olive oil
1 large onion, chopped
1 medium eggplant (unpeeled), cut into ½-inch cubes
2 small zucchini, diced
1 red bell pepper, chopped
3 garlic cloves, chopped
½ teaspoon salt

2 tomatoes, peeled, seeded and chopped

2 tablespoons drained capers
½ teaspoon freshly ground pepper
2 tablespoons chopped fresh basil

1 French bread baguette, cut into ½-inch-thick slices
1½ cups grated provolone or mozzarella cheese (about 6 ounces)

Heat oil in heavy large skillet over medium heat. Add onion and cook until beginning to soften, about 3 minutes. Add eggplant, zucchini, bell pepper, garlic and salt. Cook 5 minutes, stirring frequently. Reduce heat, cover and simmer until vegetables are tender, stirring occasionally, 30 minutes.

Add tomatoes, capers and pepper to vegetables. Simmer uncovered until most of liquid evaporates and mixture thickens, stirring frequently, about 15 minutes. Stir in basil. Adjust seasonings. (*Can be prepared 3 days ahead. Cover and refrigerate.*)

Arrange bread slices on baking sheets. Spoon about 1 tablespoon ratatouille on each. Top with cheese. (*Can be prepared 2 hours ahead. Cover and refrigerate.*)

Preheat broiler. Broil pizzas about 5 inches from heat until cheese melts and bubbles. Transfer to platter.

California Nachos

This version of nachos uses pita bread wedges instead of tortillas. They're topped with goat cheese, avocado and sun-dried tomatoes for a California twist.

4 servings

2 pita bread rounds, cut into 8 wedges each
2 tablespoons vegetable oil
6 ounces mild fresh goat cheese (such as Montrachet), room temperature
1 ripe avocado, peeled, pitted and sliced

8 oil-packed sun-dried tomatoes, drained and cut julienne
3 pickled jalapeño chilies, drained and thinly sliced
½ cup fresh cilantro leaves

Preheat oven to 500°F. Separate pita wedges at fold, forming 32 triangles. Arrange pita triangles insides up on large baking sheet. Brush with oil. Bake until edges are golden brown, about 5 minutes. Spread cheese over pita. Bake 3 more minutes. Transfer nachos to platter. Top with avocado slices, tomatoes, chilies and fresh cilantro leaves. Serve nachos immediately.

Coconut Chicken Bites

These tropical tidbits are blissfully simple to prepare and can be made the day before. Just bake at serving time.

4 servings

3½ cups sweetened shredded coconut
  2 teaspoons ground cumin
 ¾ teaspoon ground coriander
 ½ teaspoon cayenne pepper
    Salt and freshly ground pepper

2 pounds boneless skinless chicken breasts, cut into 1-inch pieces
2 eggs, beaten to blend

  Dijon mustard

Preheat oven to 325°F. Bake coconut on heavy large baking sheet until golden brown, stirring frequently, about 15 minutes. Transfer to bowl and cool. Coarsely grind in batches in processor using on/off turns.

Butter 2 heavy large baking sheets. Mix cumin, coriander, cayenne, salt and pepper in large bowl. Add chicken pieces, turning to coat. Add eggs and toss well. Dredge chicken pieces in coconut, coating completely. Transfer to prepared sheets. Cover and refrigerate 1 hour. (*Can be prepared 1 day ahead.*)

Preheat oven to 400°F. Bake chicken until crisp and golden brown, turning pieces over once, about 12 minutes. Arrange chicken on platter. Serve warm or at room temperature with Dijon mustard for dipping.

Marmalade-glazed Chicken Wings

Citrus marmalade adds a zesty sweet and sour taste to these succulent chicken wings. Begin marinating a day ahead. Chicken can be baked a couple of hours before your guests arrive and then quickly reheated. To "flatten" garlic, hit individual cloves with the flat side of a knife.

8 servings

3 pounds chicken wings, separated at joints, wing tips discarded
½ cup tequila
½ cup chopped fresh cilantro
7 tablespoons lime or lemon marmalade
¼ cup olive oil
4 tablespoons fresh lime juice
1 tablespoon coarsely ground pepper

3 medium garlic cloves, flattened
1 teaspoon hot pepper sauce (such as Tabasco)
1 teaspoon salt
1 teaspoon grated lime peel

2 limes, cut into wedges
  Fresh cilantro sprigs

Place chicken wings in large shallow glass baking dish. Mix tequila, chopped cilantro, 3 tablespoons marmalade, oil, 2 tablespoons lime juice, pepper, garlic, hot pepper sauce, salt and ½ teaspoon lime peel in small bowl. Pour over chicken. Cover and refrigerate overnight, turning chicken several times.

Preheat oven to 350°F. Remove chicken from marinade and arrange in large shallow baking pan; reserve marinade. Bake 30 minutes, turning occasionally.

Strain marinade into heavy medium saucepan. Boil until reduced by half, stirring occasionally, about 5 minutes. Add remaining 4 tablespoons marmalade, 2 tablespoons lime juice and ½ teaspoon lime peel and boil 1 minute. Brush marinade over chicken.

Preheat broiler. Broil chicken 6 inches from heat source until crisp and brown, turning several times. (*Can be prepared 2 hours ahead. Cover with foil. Uncover and rewarm in 300°F oven before continuing.*) Transfer chicken to platter. Garnish with lime wedges and cilantro sprigs and serve.

Iced Clams with Horseradish Salsa

The horseradish gives the salsa a nice, sharp bite. Although it isn't hard to open clams, many people prefer to call ahead and have the fishmonger do it.

12 servings

Salsa
1 large tomato, peeled, seeded and finely chopped
1 tablespoon prepared horseradish
2 teaspoons minced fresh cilantro
1 teaspoon minced shallot
¼ teaspoon salt

⅛ teaspoon freshly ground pepper
36 to 48 littleneck or cherrystone clams, well scrubbed
Crushed ice

For salsa: Combine tomato, horseradish, cilantro, shallot, salt and pepper in small bowl. Cover and refrigerate at least 30 minutes and up to 4 hours.

Open clams and discard top half of each shell. Cut clams loose from bottom shells using sharp knife; leave in bottom shells. Cover large platter with crushed ice. Set clams on top. Spoon 1 to 1½ teaspoons salsa on each clam.

Grilled Shrimp with Dilled Asparagus and Garlic Mayonnaise

The colorful combination of pink shrimp and bright green asparagus is paired with a creamy garlic mayonnaise. If you don't have metal skewers, use wooden ones that have been soaked in water one hour.

6 to 8 servings

1 large egg
4 medium garlic cloves
1 tablespoon fresh lemon juice
1 hard-cooked egg yolk
½ teaspoon Dijon mustard
¼ teaspoon freshly ground white pepper
¼ teaspoon (generous) salt
2 cups olive oil

2 pounds fresh asparagus, trimmed

2 pounds uncooked large shrimp, peeled and deveined
Olive oil

Fresh lemon leaves (optional)
1 tablespoon snipped fresh chives
2 tablespoons fresh lemon juice
1 tablespoon chopped fresh dill

Blend first 7 ingredients in processor. Gradually add 2 cups oil through feed tube and blend until thick and smooth. Transfer mayonnaise to bowl. (*Can be prepared 2 days ahead. Chill.*)

Blanch asparagus in large pot of boiling salted water until just tender, about 3 minutes. Drain. Refresh under cold water and drain again. (*Can be prepared 1 day ahead. Refrigerate.*)

Prepare barbecue (high heat). Thread shrimp on skewers. Brush generously with oil. Cook shrimp until just pink, about 2 minutes per side.

Arrange lemon leaves on platter. Place mayonnaise in center of platter and sprinkle chives over. Toss asparagus with 2 tablespoons lemon juice and dill. Remove shrimp from skewers. Arrange shrimp and asparagus around mayonnaise and serve.

2 ❦ Soups and Salads

Nothing beats soups and salads for their versatility—they're a perfect first course for any kind of dinner, from down-home casual to dressed-up elegant, and they also make great meals all by themselves. And although everyone knows that salads are easy to prepare, soups are also a snap, as you'll see from the recipes here—and they're ideal do-aheads. After some quick chopping, there's little to do but relax, sip a glass of wine and enjoy the heartwarming aroma of simmering homemade soup.

For cozy cold-weather entertaining, cheer your guests with steaming bowls of Oriental Beef and Noodle Soup, a quick vegetable and beef stir-fry combined with an oriental-flavored stock. Or warm them with Pasta and Mushroom Soup—just add a green salad, a crusty loaf of bread, fresh fruit and brownies for dessert, and you'll send them home happy. Soups are also wonderful warm-weather meals. Cold Zucchini Soup with Fresh Vegetable Salsa is accented with basil and topped with a chopped vegetable salsa for crunch—a refreshing starter for a sophisticated dinner, or serve it by itself for lunch or an easygoing supper.

Colorful, fresh-tasting salads are welcome at any time of year. For a zippy accompaniment to a creamy pasta dish, try Radicchio, Curly Endive, Fennel and Apple Salad. Or celebrate the season's best with Salad of Summer Greens and Herbs—serve this pretty collection of assorted greens in a glass bowl or arrange on a large platter to go with a barbecue or summer buffet.

You'll also find a selection of salads that make fast, fabulous main courses. Shrimp, Potato and Cucumber Salad with Dill Dressing is a hearty, fresh combination of boiled potatoes, bay shrimp and crunchy pickling cucumbers. Smoked Turkey and Artichoke Salad makes a delicious, easy entrée that can be prepared partially in advance—just add diced turkey and mayonnaise and toss before serving—the perfect dinner solution after a day at work.

 Soups

Cold Zucchini Soup with Fresh Vegetable Salsa

A beautiful, refreshing soup accented with basil and topped with a chopped vegetable salsa for crunch. Both the soup and the salsa can be made ahead.

6 servings

3 tablespoons butter
½ cup chopped yellow onion
2 pounds zucchini, coarsely chopped
1 cup chopped green onions
2 cups chicken stock or canned broth

2 cups buttermilk
½ cup sour cream
½ cup chopped fresh basil
1 teaspoon salt
Freshly ground pepper

Fresh Vegetable Salsa*

Melt butter in heavy large skillet over medium-high heat. Add ½ cup onion and sauté until translucent, about 3 minutes. Add zucchini and sauté until just tender, about 10 minutes. Mix in green onions. Puree vegetable mixture with stock, buttermilk, sour cream and basil in processor in batches. Transfer to bowl. Add salt. Season with pepper. Cover and refrigerate until well chilled. (*Can be prepared 1 day ahead.*)

Ladle soup into bowls. Top each with vegetable salsa and serve.

*Fresh Vegetable Salsa

Makes about 1¾ cups

½ cup peeled, seeded and chopped cucumber
½ cup finely chopped zucchini
1 medium tomato, peeled, seeded and chopped

2 tablespoons finely chopped red onion
1 tablespoon olive oil
1 teaspoon fresh lemon juice
½ teaspoon red wine vinegar

Mix all ingredients in small bowl. (*Can be prepared 8 hours ahead. Cover and refrigerate. Drain before serving.*)

Chilled Asparagus Soup

4 servings

2 pounds asparagus, trimmed

1 tablespoon butter
½ cup rice
1 small onion, chopped
5 cups (or more) chicken stock or canned low-salt broth

Freshly grated nutmeg
Salt and freshly ground white pepper

2 tablespoons fresh lemon juice

1 cup chilled whipping cream

Cook asparagus in large pot of boiling salted water until crisp-tender, about 1 minute. Drain. Refresh under cold water and drain again. Cut off asparagus tips and reserve. Cut stalks into 1-inch pieces; set aside.

Melt butter in heavy medium saucepan over medium-low heat. Add rice and onion and sauté until rice is opaque, about 5 minutes. Add 5 cups stock and bring to boil. Reduce heat and simmer until rice is very soft, stirring occasionally, about 30 minutes. Add asparagus stalks and bring to boil. Add nutmeg, salt and pepper. Cook until asparagus is soft, about 5 minutes.

Puree soup in batches in blender. Strain through sieve set over large bowl. Add lemon juice and refrigerate until well chilled. (*Can be prepared 1 day ahead. Cover and refrigerate reserved asparagus tips separately.*)

Stir cream into soup; thin with more stock if desired. Taste and adjust seasoning. Ladle soup into bowls. Top with reserved asparagus tips and serve.

Chestnut Soup

This rich and flavorful soup gets its creamy texture from roasted chestnuts.

6 servings

8 tablespoons (1 stick) unsalted butter
4 8-ounce jars whole roasted chestnuts*
1 carrot, peeled and sliced
1 parsnip, peeled and sliced
1 cup chopped, peeled celery root

7½ cups chicken stock or canned low-salt broth
½ cup Madeira wine
2 fresh parsley sprigs
Pinch of freshly grated nutmeg
Salt and freshly ground pepper
Sour cream
Cayenne pepper

Melt 4 tablespoons butter in heavy large skillet over medium heat. Add chestnuts and sauté until heated through, about 5 minutes. Set aside.

Melt remaining 4 tablespoons butter in heavy large pot over medium heat. Add carrot, parsnip and celery root and sauté until soft, about 7 minutes. Add stock and bring to boil. Reduce heat to low. Add chestnuts, Madeira, parsley, nutmeg, salt and pepper. Simmer 15 minutes. Puree soup in batches in processor. (*Can be prepared 2 days ahead. Cover and refrigerate.*) Transfer soup to heavy large saucepan. Bring to simmer, stirring frequently. Adjust seasoning. Ladle into bowls. Top each with dollop of sour cream. Sprinkle with cayenne.

*Available at specialty foods stores.

Summer Garden Soup

This quick main-course soup is good warm or at room temperature.

2 servings; can be doubled or tripled

1 tablespoon olive oil
1 medium onion, chopped
1 small zucchini
1 small yellow crookneck squash
Freshly ground pepper
1 15-ounce can cannellini beans (white kidney beans), undrained

1 14½-ounce can chicken broth
4 ounces ham steak, diced
1 medium tomato, seeded and chopped
1 tablespoon prepared pesto sauce
Additional pesto sauce

Heat oil in heavy medium saucepan over medium-low heat. Add onion and cook until translucent, stirring occasionally, about 8 minutes. Cut zucchini and squash lengthwise into fourths, then slice. Add to saucepan and season with pepper. Cook until crisp-tender, stirring occasionally, about 6 minutes. Remove from heat. Mix in beans with their juices, broth, ham and tomato. Mix in 1 tablespoon pesto. Cool to room temperature or bring to simmer. Ladle into bowls. Swirl additional pesto into each bowl and serve.

Pasta and Mushroom Soup

Simple and quick to make.

Makes about 16 cups

6 tablespoons (¾ stick) unsalted butter
2 medium onions, finely chopped
4 quarts chicken stock or canned low-salt broth

3 cups cavatelli or small shell pasta
3 cups frozen tiny peas
½ pound fresh shiitake or button mushrooms, cut julienne

4 teaspoons dried basil, crumbled
4 garlic cloves, minced
½ teaspoon crushed saffron
Salt and freshly ground pepper
1 cup chopped fresh Italian parsley
1 cup drained oil-packed sun-dried tomatoes, cut julienne
2 cups grated Fontina or Gruyère cheese (about 6 ounces)

Melt butter in heavy large saucepan over medium heat. Add onions and cook until translucent, stirring occasionally, about 12 minutes. Add stock and bring to boil. (*Can be prepared 1 day ahead. Cool, cover and refrigerate. Bring to boil before continuing.*)

Add pasta to stock and cook until just tender but still firm to bite, stirring occasionally, about 10 minutes. Add peas, mushrooms, basil, garlic and saffron. Season with salt and pepper. Simmer 2 minutes. Add parsley. Garnish with tomatoes. Pass cheese separately.

Santa Fe Cheese Soup

Full bodied and velvety smooth, soothing and rich—there's nothing like cheese soup. Double the recipe, if you want to: This soup keeps well.

Makes about 5 cups

2 large carrots, peeled, cut into 1-inch pieces
1 small onion, peeled, cut into 1-inch pieces
1 small apple, cored, cut into 1-inch pieces
3 small jalapeño or serrano chilies, seeded

3 tablespoons unsalted butter
2 cups chicken stock or canned broth
½ cup dry white wine

6 tablespoons unbleached all purpose flour
2 cups milk

6 ounces cheddar cheese
6 ounces chilled Monterey Jack cheese

Salt and freshly ground pepper

½ cup fresh cilantro, minced
2 small plum tomatoes, seeded and diced

Finely mince first four ingredients in processor.

Melt butter in heavy large saucepan over medium-low heat. Add contents of work bowl and cook until softened, stirring occasionally, about 8 minutes. Add stock and wine and bring to boil. Reduce heat, cover and simmer gently until vegetables are very soft, about 30 minutes. (**Or to microwave:** Melt butter in 4-cup microwave-safe dish. Add contents of work bowl and cook uncovered on High until slightly softened, about 4 minutes. Add stock and wine; cover and cook on High until very soft, about 12 minutes.)

Puree vegetable mixture in processor until very smooth, about 2 minutes. Press through fine strainer into bowl.

Place flour in large bowl. Gradually whisk in half of milk, making smooth paste. Mix in strained vegetable mixture and remaining milk. Return to same saucepan. Cook over medium heat until slightly thickened, stirring constantly, about 2 minutes. (**Or to microwave:** Return to 4-cup dish. Cook soup uncovered on High until thickened, about 1 minute.)

Shred cheddar and Monterey Jack in processor using light pressure.

Stir cheeses into soup. Cook over medium heat until smooth, stirring frequently. (**Or to microwave:** Add cheeses and cook uncovered on High, stirring every 60 seconds, until smooth.) Season with salt and pepper. (*Can be prepared 3 days ahead. Cover and refrigerate. Rewarm over low heat or on Medium in microwave, stirring soup occasionally; do not boil.*)

Mix cilantro and tomatoes. Ladle soup into bowls; spoon a dollop of tomato mixture into center of each.

Chicken, Corn and Escarole Soup

4 to 6 servings

1 pound chicken breasts with ribs, boned (bones reserved)
6 cups chicken stock or canned low-salt broth
1 medium onion, quartered
2 celery stalks, each cut crosswise into quarters
1 garlic clove
3 fresh parsley sprigs
1 bay leaf
12 whole black peppercorns
¼ teaspoon dried thyme, crumbled

1½ tablespoons vegetable oil
1 tablespoon chili powder
¼ teaspoon Hungarian hot paprika
Pinch of ground coriander
Pinch of salt

2 cups fresh corn kernels or frozen, thawed
2 cups shredded escarole or romaine lettuce

Place chicken bones in large pot. Add stock, onion, celery, garlic, parsley, bay leaf, peppercorns and thyme. Cover and bring to boil. Reduce heat and simmer soup 30 minutes.

Meanwhile, preheat broiler. Pound chicken breasts between sheets of waxed paper to thickness of ¼ inch using mallet. Mix oil, chili powder, paprika, coriander and salt in small bowl. Rub spice mixture over chicken. Let stand 5 minutes. Broil chicken on broiler rack or baking sheet until just cooked through, about 3 minutes per side. Transfer to plate and cool. Cut chicken crosswise into strips.

Strain soup into heavy large pot. (*Can be prepared 1 day ahead. Cover soup and chicken separately and refrigerate. Bring soup to simmer before continuing.*) Add chicken and corn to soup and cook 2 minutes. Add escarole and stir until just wilted. Ladle into bowls.

Oriental Beef and Noodle Soup

A quick vegetable and beef stir-fry combined with an oriental-flavored stock.

4 to 6 servings

3 ounces bean thread noodles*
5 cups chicken stock or canned low-salt broth
2 tablespoons vegetable oil
½ pound flank steak, cut across grain into 2-inch-long, ⅛-inch-thick slices
4 green onions, cut into 2-inch-long pieces and shredded
5 tablespoons shredded peeled fresh ginger

4 large bok choy (Chinese white cabbage) leaves, cut crosswise into 1-inch pieces
2 tablespoons soy sauce
1 tablespoon oriental sesame oil
Freshly ground pepper

Additional oriental sesame oil
Additional soy sauce

Place noodles in bowl. Cover with boiling water. Let stand 15 minutes.

Meanwhile, bring stock to boil in medium saucepan. Reduce heat and keep warm. Heat vegetable oil in heavy large skillet or wok over high heat. Add beef, half of green onions and 3 tablespoons ginger and stir-fry until beef is no longer pink, about 4 minutes. Add bok choy and stir-fry 1 minute. Add stock, remaining green onions, remaining 2 tablespoons ginger, 2 tablespoons soy sauce, 1 tablespoon sesame oil and pepper and bring to simmer.

Drain noodles and divide among bowls. Ladle soup over. Serve, passing additional sesame oil and soy sauce.

*Also known as transparent or cellophane noodles. Available at oriental markets and in specialty foods sections of many supermarkets.

Cream of Snow Pea Soup with Shrimp

This easy and elegant soup is the perfect starter. Delicious cold, too.

4 servings

½ cup (1 stick) butter
1 pound snow peas, strings removed
2 cups chicken stock or canned broth
1 cup whipping cream
¼ teaspoon minced fresh mint

Pinch of sugar
Pinch of freshly grated nutmeg
Salt and freshly ground white pepper
¼ pound bay shrimp

Melt ¼ cup butter in heavy medium saucepan over medium heat. Add snow peas and sauté until tender, about 5 minutes. Add stock and bring to boil. Reduce heat and simmer 20 minutes. Transfer to blender and purée. Return soup to saucepan and bring to boil. Reduce heat to low. Add cream and heat through. Add mint, sugar and nutmeg. Season with salt and pepper. (*Can be prepared 1 day ahead. Cover and refrigerate. Reheat before continuing.*) Stir in remaining ¼ cup butter. Divide shrimp among 4 warm bowls. Ladle soup into bowls.

Provençal Tomato Soup with Mussels and Vermicelli

6 servings

4 pounds mussels, scrubbed and debearded

¼ cup fresh parsley leaves
2 large garlic cloves
2 medium onions, quartered

2 tablespoons olive oil
3 large tomatoes (about 1¼ pounds), cored, halved, seeded and cut into ¼-inch dice
1 large leek, trimmed, green part discarded, white part cut into ⅛-inch-thick slices

3 cups (or more) bottled clam juice
1 cup canned chicken broth
2 tablespoons tomato paste
1 bay leaf
Pinch of saffron
2 ounces vermicelli pasta, broken into thirds

¼ teaspoon dried red pepper flakes
Salt

Place mussels in heavy large saucepan and cover with cold salted water. Soak 30 minutes. Drain well; rinse pan. Discard any open mussels; return remaining mussels to saucepan. Cover and cook over medium-high heat 5 minutes, stirring once. Remove opened mussels. Cover and continue cooking 5 minutes. Discard any unopened mussels. Let mussels cool; remove shells. Strain liquid exuded while cooking through double thickness of cheesecloth. Add enough water to liquid to measure 2 cups. Do not rinse pan.

Mince parsley in processor, about 30 seconds. Set aside. With machine running, drop garlic through feed tube and mince. Add onions and mince using several on/off turns.

Add oil to same saucepan used for cooking mussels and heat over medium heat. Add garlic and onion, tomatoes and leek and cook until soft but not brown, stirring frequently, about 10 minutes. Add strained mussel liquid, 3 cups clam juice, chicken broth, tomato paste, bay leaf and saffron. Bring to boil; reduce heat and simmer 10 minutes. Add vermicelli and simmer just until tender, about 7 minutes. (*Can be prepared 1 day ahead. Cover soup, mussels and parsley separately. Refrigerate.*)

Bring soup to simmer. Add mussels and cook just until hot. Add red pepper flakes. Season with salt. Garnish with reserved parsley and serve.

❧ *Side-Dish Salads*

Radicchio, Curly Endive, Fennel and Apple Salad

6 servings

1 tablespoon Dijon mustard
3 tablespoons Sherry wine vinegar
¾ cup olive oil
  Salt and freshly ground pepper
2 tart green apples, cored and thinly sliced

½ medium head curly endive, torn into bite-size pieces
1 large head radicchio, quartered, cored and thinly sliced
1 fennel bulb, trimmed, halved and cut into strips

Combine mustard and vinegar in small bowl. Gradually whisk in oil. Season with salt and pepper. Mix in apples. (*Can be prepared 3 hours ahead. Cover and chill.*)

Combine endive, radicchio and fennel in large bowl. Add apples and dressing and toss. Adjust seasoning.

Salad of Summer Greens and Herbs

Arrange this pretty collection of assorted greens on a large platter.

10 servings

¾ cup rice vinegar
¾ cup chopped fresh dill
4 large shallots, chopped
3 tablespoons coarse-grained mustard
1 cup vegetable oil
½ cup olive oil
  Salt and freshly ground pepper

36 snow peas

16 cups bite-size pieces mixed lettuce, such as oak leaf, Bibb, red romaine and romaine
4 large green onions, cut julienne
1½ cups mixed chopped fresh herbs, such as parsley, chive, thyme, marjoram and tarragon
½ cup shelled, roasted, salted sunflower seeds

Blend vinegar, dill, shallots and mustard in processor. With machine running, gradually add both oils through feed tube and blend until smooth. Season with salt and pepper. (*Dressing can be prepared 8 hours ahead. Cover and let stand at room temperature. Whisk before serving.*)

Blanch snow peas in medium saucepan of boiling water 1 minute. Drain and cool. Toss lettuce and green onions in large bowl with enough dressing to season to taste. Mound greens on large platter. Arrange snow peas in clusters around greens. Sprinkle herbs and sunflower seeds over and serve.

Spinach and Endive Salad with Stilton Vinaigrette

If you can't get Stilton, use another assertively flavored blue-veined cheese, such as Gorgonzola or Roquefort.

4 servings

Stilton Vinaigrette
 2 tablespoons white wine vinegar
 1 teaspoon Dijon mustard
 ¼ cup vegetable oil
 3 tablespoons olive oil
 2 ounces (½ cup) Stilton cheese, crumbled
 2 tablespoons minced shallots or green onions
 ¼ teaspoon freshly ground pepper

Salad
 1 bunch spinach leaves, torn into bite-size pieces
 1 large head curly endive, torn into bite-size pieces
 ½ cup thinly sliced celery

For vinaigrette: Mix vinegar and mustard in small bowl. Whisk in both oils in thin stream. Add cheese, shallots and pepper. Let stand at least 30 minutes to blend flavors. (*Can be prepared 1 day ahead. Refrigerate.*)

For salad: Combine spinach, endive and celery in large bowl. Toss salad with enough vinaigrette to coat to taste. Serve immediately.

Avocado, Chili and Bitter Greens Salad

8 servings

 3 tablespoons fresh lemon juice
 2 garlic cloves, minced
 ½ cup olive oil
 ½ cup fresh cilantro leaves, coarsely chopped
 Salt and freshly ground pepper

 4 firm but ripe avocados, halved, pitted and peeled

 1 head curly endive or escarole, torn into bite-size pieces
 1 small red chili or red bell pepper, seeded and slivered lengthwise
 Fresh cilantro sprigs

Combine lemon juice and garlic in small bowl. Gradually whisk in oil. Add chopped cilantro. Season with salt and pepper. (*Can be prepared 1 day ahead. Whisk to combine before using.*)

Cut avocados crosswise into ¼-inch-thick slices. Arrange in dish. Spoon dressing over. Let marinate at least 30 minutes or up to 2 hours.

Place endive in large bowl. Pour dressing from avocados over. Toss to coat. Arrange on platter. Top with avocados. Garnish with chili and cilantro.

Chick-Pea, Artichoke Heart and Romaine Salad

2 servings; can be doubled or tripled

2 teaspoons balsamic vinegar or red wine vinegar
½ teaspoon Dijon mustard
2 tablespoons olive oil

½ romaine lettuce head, torn into bite-size pieces

1 8¾-ounce can chick-peas (garbanzo beans), drained
1 6-ounce jar marinated artichoke hearts, drained
⅓ cup freshly grated Romano cheese (about 1½ ounces)
Salt and freshly ground pepper

Combine vinegar and mustard in small bowl. Gradually whisk in oil.

Combine lettuce, chick-peas and artichoke hearts in large bowl. Add dressing and toss to coat. Mix in cheese. Season with salt and pepper and serve.

Smoked Salmon and Endive Salad

Purchased salmon is made fancy with the addition of Belgian endive in this two-minute salad.

2 servings

4 ounces thinly sliced smoked salmon or lox
Olive oil (preferably extra-virgin)
Fresh lime juice
2 large Belgian endive heads, cut crosswise into 1-inch pieces and separated

1 tablespoon olive oil (preferably extra-virgin)
1½ tablespoons chopped fresh chives
Salt and freshly ground pepper
1 teaspoon fresh lime juice

Divide salmon between plates, arranging across center. Drizzle with oil and lime juice. Place endive in medium bowl. Add 1 tablespoon oil and toss to coat. Add chives; season with salt and pepper and toss. Add 1 teaspoon lime juice and toss. Mound atop salmon, allowing ends of salmon to show.

Greek-style Pasta Salad

2 servings; can be doubled or tripled

2 large tomatoes, seeded and diced
3 ounces feta cheese, cubed
1 large shallot or 2 green onions, minced
3 tablespoons olive oil
3 tablespoons chopped arugula or watercress
1 tablespoon fresh lemon juice

1 cup fusilli pasta or large elbow macaroni

Salt and freshly ground pepper

Green and/or red bell pepper strips
Tomato wedges
Greek olives
Lemon wedges
Arugula or watercress sprigs

Combine first 6 ingredients in bowl.

Cook pasta in large pot of boiling salted water until just tender but still firm to bite, stirring occasionally. Drain. Rinse with cold water until cool and drain well. Add to tomato mixture. Season with salt and pepper. (*Can be prepared 4 hours ahead. Refrigerate.*)

Spoon salad into centers of 2 large plates. Garnish with bell peppers, tomato wedges, olives, lemon wedges and arugula sprigs and serve.

Green Bean, Potato, Tomato and Onion Salad

8 servings

1 pound green beans, trimmed
1 pound new potatoes
  Creamy Vinaigrette*

1 1-pint basket yellow cherry
  tomatoes, halved

1 1-pint basket red cherry
  tomatoes, halved
1 medium red onion, thinly sliced

Cook beans in large pot of boiling salted water until crisp-tender, about 3 minutes. Transfer to bowl using slotted spoon. Refresh under cold water and drain again. Add potatoes to same pot and cook until knife pierces centers easily, about 10 minutes. Drain and cool slightly. Quarter potatoes. Transfer to large bowl. Pour ⅓ of vinaigrette over warm potatoes; toss gently. Cool completely. (*Can be prepared 1 day ahead. Refrigerate potatoes, beans and remaining vinaigrette separately. Let stand 1 hour at room temperature before using.*)

Add beans, tomatoes, onion and ½ of remaining vinaigrette to potatoes and toss. Divide salad among plates. Serve with remaining vinaigrette.

*Creamy Vinaigrette

Makes about 2¼ cups

½ cup red wine vinegar
2 tablespoons Dijon mustard
2 tablespoons dry vermouth
2 egg yolks

½ teaspoon salt
  Freshly ground pepper
1⅓ cups olive oil

Blend first 6 ingredients in blender or processor. With machine running, gradually add oil and blend until thick. (*Can be prepared 1 day ahead. Cover and refrigerate. Let stand 1 hour at room temperature and rewhisk before using.*)

Spicy Sesame Chinese Noodles

10 servings

½ cup oriental sesame seed paste*
  (surface oil discarded) or old-
  fashioned style or freshly ground
  peanut butter
1 1-inch piece fresh ginger, peeled
  and chopped
1 garlic clove
½ cup warm brewed black tea
½ cup red wine vinegar
⅓ cup low-sodium soy sauce
1½ tablespoons sugar

½ cup corn oil or peanut oil
4 tablespoons oriental sesame oil
1½ teaspoons chili oil*

1½ pounds penne, ziti, rigatoni or
  other short, tubular pasta

1 English hothouse cucumber,
  halved and sliced
7 green onions, thinly sliced
  Pickled ginger* (optional)

Combine sesame paste, fresh ginger and garlic in processor and blend until smooth, about 1 minute, stopping once to scrape down sides of bowl. With machine running, pour tea through feed tube in slow steady stream and process until smooth. Add vinegar, soy sauce and sugar to work bowl and blend until smooth, about 1 minute, stopping once to scrape down sides of work bowl. With machine running, pour corn oil, 2 tablespoons sesame oil and chili oil through feed tube in slow steady stream. (*Can be prepared 3 days ahead. Refrigerate.*)

Cook penne in large pot of boiling salted water until just tender but still firm to bite, stirring occasionally. Drain. Rinse under cold water and drain well. Place penne in large bowl. Toss with remaining 2 tablespoons sesame oil. Cover and refrigerate until chilled. (*Can be prepared 1 day ahead.*)

Add half of cucumber and half of green onions to pasta and toss well. Add dressing and toss gently. Transfer to serving platter. Top with remaining cucumber and green onions. Garnish with pickled ginger if desired.

*Ingredients are available at oriental markets and some supermarkets.

❦ Main-Dish Salads

Chicken, Endive and Roquefort Salad

Accompany this distinctively flavored main-course salad with crusty rolls and a dry white wine. If you have any leftover roast chicken on hand, use six cups bite-size pieces and skip the first step.

6 servings

6 chicken breast halves
Soy sauce
Olive oil
Dried thyme, crumbled
Freshly ground pepper

1 large bunch curly endive, torn into bite-size pieces
4 Belgian endive heads, cut into 1-inch pieces

8 ounces Roquefort cheese, crumbled
1½ bunches radishes, trimmed, thinly sliced
1½ cups walnuts, broken into large pieces
Mustard Vinaigrette*

Preheat oven to 450°F. Place chicken breasts in baking pan. Brush both sides with soy sauce and olive oil. Sprinkle both sides with thyme and pepper. Arrange skin side up. Roast until just cooked through, about 20 minutes. Cool slightly. Skin and bone chicken; reserve drippings in pan. Cut chicken into bite-size pieces. Return to roasting pan and turn to coat with drippings. Cool completely. (*Can be prepared 1 day ahead. Cover and chill. Bring to room temperature before using.*)

Combine curly endive, Belgian endive, Roquefort and radishes in large bowl. (*Can be prepared 3 hours ahead. Cover and refrigerate.*) Just before serving, add chicken, walnuts and vinaigrette and toss to coat.

*Mustard Vinaigrette

Makes about 1 cup

4 teaspoons Dijon mustard
1 2-ounce can anchovies, drained and minced
¼ cup red wine vinegar

⅔ cup olive oil
2 green onions, minced
1½ teaspoons dried thyme, crumbled
Freshly ground pepper

Combine mustard and anchovies in medium bowl. Whisk in vinegar, then gradually whisk in oil. Add onions, thyme and generous amount of pepper. (*Can be prepared 3 days ahead. Cover and refrigerate. Bring vinaigrette to room temperature before using.*)

Marinated Mongolian Steak Salad

4 servings

Marinade
1 cup fresh orange juice
¼ cup grated orange peel
¼ cup honey
2 tablespoons soy sauce
2 teaspoons chopped peeled fresh ginger
2 teaspoons minced garlic
¼ teaspoon dried red pepper flakes
4 ¾-pound New York (top loin) steaks, fat trimmed

Dressing
2 tablespoons red wine vinegar
1 tablespoon Dijon mustard
1 tablespoon chopped fresh tarragon or 1 teaspoon dried, crumbled
1 tablespoon chopped shallots or green onions
½ teaspoon minced garlic
½ cup olive oil
Salt and freshly ground pepper

Assorted mixed greens such as Boston lettuce, oak leaf lettuce and mustard greens, torn into bite-size pieces

For marinade: Mix first 7 ingredients in large shallow glass baking dish just large enough to accommodate steaks. Add steaks, turning to coat. Cover and let stand 1 hour at room temperature.

For dressing: Whisk vinegar, mustard, tarragon, shallots and garlic in small bowl. Whisk in oil in slow steady stream. Season with salt and pepper.

Prepare barbecue (high heat). Remove steaks from marinade; reserve marinade. Grill steaks about 5 minutes per side for medium-rare, basting occasionally with marinade. Toss greens with enough dressing to season to taste. Divide among plates. Cut steaks into thin slices. Arrange atop greens.

Tuscan-style Rice Salad with Ham

4 servings

2½ cups water
1 cup brown rice (preferably short-grain*)
Pinch of salt

1 large carrot, peeled and diced
½ cup shelled fresh or thawed frozen baby lima beans
½ cup shelled fresh or thawed frozen peas

⅓ cup fresh lemon juice
¼ cup finely chopped fresh Italian parsley
2 tablespoons chopped fresh basil
½ teaspoon salt
Freshly ground pepper
⅓ cup olive oil

¼ cup diced red onion
4 ounces baked ham, slivered (optional)

Romaine lettuce leaves
2 ripe tomatoes, cored and cut into wedges
Fresh basil sprigs

Combine water, rice and salt in heavy medium saucepan and bring to boil. Stir once, cover, reduce heat and simmer until water is absorbed and rice is tender but not mushy, 45 to 50 minutes. Drain and cool.

Pour 1 inch of water into saucepan or steamer fitted with rack. Bring water to boil. Place carrot on rack, cover and steam 3 minutes. Add lima beans and peas. Cover and steam 3 minutes. Remove rack; rinse vegetables under cold water until completely cool.

Blend lemon juice, parsley, 2 tablespoons basil, salt and pepper in processor. With machine running, gradually add oil through feed tube. Season dressing with pepper.

Combine rice, steamed vegetables and red onion in large bowl. Drizzle dressing over and toss gently. Mix in ham if desired. (*Can be prepared 1 day ahead. Cover and refrigerate. Bring to room temperature before serving.*)

Line plates with lettuce. Spoon rice mixture into center of each. Garnish with tomatoes and basil and serve.

*Available at natural foods stores and also at some supermarkets.

Smoked Turkey and Artichoke Salad

4 servings

½ cup olive oil
5 medium garlic cloves, pressed
1 teaspoon dried thyme, crumbled
1 teaspoon dried basil, crumbled
½ teaspoon (scant) dried red pepper flakes
2 pounds mushrooms, quartered
¼ cup white wine vinegar
¾ teaspoon salt
½ teaspoon freshly ground pepper
2 14¾-ounce jars marinated artichoke hearts, drained (6 tablespoons marinade reserved), halved

2 14-ounce cans hearts of palm, drained, tough fibers removed, cut into ½-inch-thick slices
1 pound smoked turkey, cut into ½-inch dice
Chive Mayonnaise**
1 small head radicchio,* cut julienne
2 heads Belgian endive, cut julienne
¾ pound smoked turkey, cut into thin slices
Belgian endive leaves
4-inch-long chive tops

Heat oil in heavy Dutch oven over medium-high heat. Add garlic, thyme, basil and pepper flakes and sauté 2 minutes. Add mushrooms, vinegar, salt and pepper. Pour reserved artichoke marinade over and toss well. Reduce heat to medium. Cover and cook until mushrooms are almost tender, about 4 minutes. Transfer mixture to medium bowl. Add artichokes and hearts of palm and toss gently. Let stand 1 hour at room temperature. (*Can be prepared 2 days ahead. Cover and refrigerate. Bring to room temperature before continuing.*)

Drain salad thoroughly in colander or sieve. Return to bowl. Add diced turkey and all but ¼ cup mayonnaise. Toss well. Adjust seasoning.

Arrange radicchio around edge on half of each plate. Arrange endive julienne around edge on other half of each plate. Mound salad in center. Drape turkey slices over salads. Top each with dollop of remaining mayonnaise. Garnish with endive leaves and chives.

*A bright red and white Italian chicory that grows in small, round and long, tapered heads. Available at specialty foods stores and some supermarkets.

**Chive Mayonnaise

Makes about 1 cup

1 cup mayonnaise
⅔ cup snipped fresh chives

3 medium garlic cloves, pressed
Freshly ground white pepper

Mix all ingredients in small bowl. (*Can be prepared 1 day ahead. Cover with plastic wrap and refrigerate.*)

Shrimp, Potato and Cucumber Salad with Dill Dressing

A quick and easy meal.

2 servings; can be doubled

4 medium-size red potatoes, cut into ¾-inch pieces
1 tablespoon plus 2 teaspoons Dijon mustard
1 tablespoon white wine vinegar
⅓ cup olive oil
3 green onions, chopped

1 tablespoon minced fresh dill
  Salt and freshly ground pepper
4 pickling cucumbers, halved lengthwise and sliced crosswise (about 1½ cups)
½ pound bay shrimp

Cook potatoes in medium pot of boiling water until just tender, about 15 minutes. Drain well. Place in large bowl. Combine mustard and vinegar in small bowl. Gradually whisk in oil. Add half of dressing to warm potatoes. Mix in green onions and dill; season with salt and pepper. Cool completely. Add cucumbers, shrimp and remaining dressing and toss to coat. Adjust seasoning to taste.

Mediterranean Tuna Salad

This is a variation of the popular Niçoise salad. It can be marinated up to two days. If you're in a hurry, the cooked fish can be cut into pieces and tossed together with the other salad ingredients. This would take a little less time than doing individual composed plates.

2 servings

¼ pound green beans, trimmed

¾ cup olive oil
1 tablespoon plus 1 teaspoon drained capers, very coarsely chopped
1 teaspoon salt
1 teaspoon coarsely ground white pepper
2 tablespoons fresh lime juice
1 tablespoon white wine vinegar
1½ cups drained canned cannellini beans or Great Northern beans
1 red bell pepper, cut julienne

1 large head butter lettuce
4 ounces feta cheese, crumbled

½ small red onion, thinly sliced
2 small plum tomatoes, quartered
2 hard-cooked eggs, peeled and cut into quarters

2 1-inch-thick 4-ounce yellowfin tuna or mahimahi fillets
1 teaspoon cracked white peppercorns
16 Niçoise olives or other black imported olives
1 tablespoon chopped fresh parsley (preferably Italian)
2 fresh parsley sprigs (preferably Italian)

Blanch green beans in saucepan of boiling water until just tender, about 3 minutes. Drain. Refresh under cold water and drain again. Halve beans lengthwise. Transfer to small bowl.

Mix oil, capers, salt and pepper in another small bowl. Pour 3 tablespoons over green beans; toss to coat. Mix lime juice and vinegar into remaining oil mixture. Toss cannellini with 3 tablespoons dressing in medium bowl. Toss red bell pepper with 3 tablespoons dressing in another medium bowl. Cover salads and let stand 1 hour. (*Can be prepared 2 days ahead. Refrigerate salads. Cover remaining dressing and let stand at room temperature.*)

Arrange 1 lettuce leaf at each end of each oval plate. Tear remaining lettuce into bite-size pieces. Mound lettuce in centers of plates. Arrange green beans, cannellini, red bell pepper, feta and onion in rows across lettuce, leaving center portion of lettuce uncovered. Place tomatoes and eggs at ends of plates.

Preheat broiler. Dredge fish in 2 tablespoons dressing. Rub cracked peppercorns into one side of fish. Broil pepper side up 2 minutes. Turn fish over and cook about 2 more minutes for medium. Arrange fish atop lettuce in centers of plates. Garnish with olives. Mix chopped parsley into remaining dressing. Drizzle over salads. Garnish fish with parsley sprigs and serve.

3 🍎 Pasta, Pizza and Sandwiches

Pasta, pizza and sandwiches rank high on many a list of all-time favorites. It's easy to understand why when you consider their versatility, ease of preparation and great taste.

Here you'll find pastas that make super starters or irresistible entrées. Bow Ties with Shrimp and Scallops is a stylish first course with a light sauce of chopped tomatoes. A hearty main course like Lasagne with Roasted Red and Green Bell Peppers or Pasta with Gorgonzola and Walnut Sauce needs only a loaf of crusty Italian bread and a crisp green salad for a delicious, satisfying meal.

Pizza is made as easy as pie with the shortcuts presented here—the food processor makes quick work of the do-ahead dough in Grilled Tomato Pizza with Herbs and Thin-crusted Pizza with Bacon, Brie and Muenster Cheese.

The humble sandwich takes on exciting new dimensions in recipes like Chicken Sandwich with Three-Onion Relish, sliced chicken breast topped with a quick onion relish made with marinated red, yellow and green onions, then stacked on sourdough bread with roasted red peppers and watercress. There's also a savory Italian version of the classic ham and cheese—Grilled Prosciutto and Fontina Sandwiches.

 Pasta

Pasta with Gorgonzola and Walnut Sauce

You can make the sauce one day ahead. Reheat and toss with the pasta just before serving. Enjoy an antipasto platter and Campari and soda while the pasta cooks.

6 servings

2 tablespoons (¼ stick) butter
5 shallots or green onions, finely chopped
1 tablespoon plus 2 teaspoons chopped fresh thyme or 1½ teaspoons dried, crumbled
2 cups whipping cream
½ pound Gorgonzola cheese, crumbled

Freshly ground pepper

1½ pounds fusilli, penne or ziti pasta
1 cup walnuts, coarsely chopped
½ cup freshly grated Romano or Parmesan cheese (about 2 ounces)

Melt butter in heavy medium skillet over medium heat. Add shallots and sauté until translucent, about 5 minutes. Stir in thyme. Add cream and Gorgonzola and stir until cheese melts and sauce thickens slightly. Season with pepper. (*Can be prepared 1 day ahead. Cover and refrigerate. Rewarm over low heat before using.*)

Cook pasta in large pot of rapidly boiling salted water until tender but still firm to bite, stirring occasionally. Drain well. Return to pot. Add sauce and stir over low heat until pasta is coated. Mix in walnuts. Transfer to serving dish. Sprinkle with Romano cheese and serve immediately.

Fettuccine with Cream, Basil and Romano Cheese

This sauce is so quick to make, it can be stirred up while the pasta cooks. A salad of sliced tomatoes and a loaf of Italian bread would round out the main course nicely.

2 servings; can be doubled

4 thick-cut bacon slices, chopped
4 green onions, chopped
½ cup whipping cream
½ cup freshly grated Romano or Parmesan cheese
⅓ cup chopped fresh basil

½ pound fettuccine
Salt and freshly ground pepper
Additional freshly grated Romano or Parmesan cheese

Cook bacon in heavy medium skillet over medium heat until beginning to brown. Add green onions and stir until softened, about 1 minute. Add cream and simmer until beginning to thicken, about 1 minute. Mix in ½ cup Romano cheese and chopped fresh basil.

Meanwhile, cook fettuccine in large pot of boiling salted water until just tender but still firm to bite, stirring occasionally. Drain well. Return to hot pot. Add sauce and stir to coat. Season with salt and pepper. Serve immediately, passing additional cheese separately.

Red Peppers Stuffed with Spicy Linguine

An ingenious way to serve a robust pasta. Works well as an appetizer or entrée.

8 servings

8 large, evenly shaped red bell peppers
¼ cup olive oil
1 garlic head, cloves separated but not peeled, flattened with side of knife
5 jalapeño chilies, halved lengthwise
6 medium tomatoes, peeled and finely chopped (about 2½ cups)
20 oil-cured black olives, pitted and slivered
24 fresh basil leaves, chopped
3 tablespoons drained capers
1 tablespoon mashed anchovy fillets (about 6 small)
1 teaspoon salt

1 pound linguine

Freshly grated Parmesan cheese

Broil peppers until light brown on all sides, turning frequently, about 10 minutes. (Do not overcook or peppers will lose shape.) Place peppers in paper bag. Seal tightly and let stand 1 hour.

Carefully remove skin from peppers. Cut off tops and reserve. Using spoon, scoop out seeds from peppers.

Heat oil in heavy large skillet over medium-high heat. Add garlic and chilies and cook until beginning to brown around edges, stirring constantly, about 5 minutes. Strain oil, discarding garlic and chilies. Return oil to skillet and heat over medium heat. Add tomatoes and next 5 ingredients and cook until sauce begins to thicken, stirring occasionally, about 10 minutes.

Meanwhile, cook linguine in boiling salted water until just tender but still firm to bite. Drain. Add to skillet and stir to coat with sauce.

Fill peppers with some of linguine. Set each pepper on side on plate. Spoon some of remaining linguine at opening of each pepper. Garnish with reserved pepper tops. Serve immediately, passing Parmesan cheese separately.

Bow Ties with Shrimp and Scallops

Chopped tomatoes, both cooked and uncooked, make a delicious sauce.

4 first-course or 2 main-course servings

2 large shallots or green onions, cut into 1-inch pieces
1 small serrano chili,* stemmed

4 tablespoons olive oil
1 tablespoon tomato paste
¾ teaspoon sugar
1 pound plum tomatoes, peeled, seeded and diced
½ cup bottled clam juice
1 tablespoon fresh lemon juice
1 tablespoon dry vermouth
4 ounces uncooked large shrimp, peeled and deveined
5 ounces bay scallops

5 ounces (about 3 cups) pasta bows

4 tablespoons (½ stick) unsalted butter, cut into 4 pieces, room temperature
10 small oil-cured black olives, such as Niçoise or Kalamata
Salt and freshly ground pepper
3 tablespoons fresh basil, cut julienne

Insert steel knife in processor. With processor running, drop shallots and chili through feed tube. Process until minced.

Heat 3 tablespoons olive oil in heavy large skillet over medium heat. Add shallot mixture and sauté until soft, about 5 minutes. Stir in tomato paste and sugar. Reserve ⅓ cup tomatoes for garnish; add remainder to skillet. Mix in clam juice, lemon juice and vermouth. Simmer until tomatoes soften slightly, about 5 minutes. Add shrimp and cook until bottoms are pink, about 1 minute.

Turn shrimp over and add scallops. Cook until shrimp and scallops are just opaque, approximately 1 minute.

(**Or to microwave:** Heat 3 tablespoons oil in shallow, 10-inch round microwave-safe dish. Add shallot mixture and cook uncovered on High until soft, about 2 minutes. Blend in tomato paste and sugar and cook 1 minute. Set aside ⅓ cup tomatoes for garnish; add remainder and cook 1 minute. Add clam juice, lemon juice and vermouth and cook on High until tomatoes soften slightly, about 3 minutes. Add shrimp in a ring around edge of dish; place scallops in center. Cover tightly with plastic wrap; pierce plastic wrap once with sharp knife. Cook on Medium 3 minutes. Stir scallops and cook covered until shrimp and scallops are just opaque, about 1½ minutes.)

Meanwhile, cook pasta in large pot of boiling salted water until just tender but still firm to bite, stirring occasionally. Drain well; return to pot and toss with remaining 1 tablespoon olive oil.

Whisk butter into sauce 1 piece at a time. Add olives and pasta and toss gently. Season with salt and pepper. Mix in basil and reserved tomatoes.

*A *serrano* is a very hot, small, fresh green chili available at Latin American markets and in specialty produce sections of some supermarkets.

Farfalle with Bitter Greens and Sausage

2 servings; can be doubled or tripled

1 tablespoon olive oil
1 large onion, chopped
3 Italian hot sausages, casings removed
2 garlic cloves, minced
1 large bunch mustard greens, stems trimmed and cut crosswise into 2-inch pieces (about 4 cups cut)

⅓ cup whipping cream

8 ounces farfalle (bow tie) pasta
½ cup freshly grated Romano cheese
Salt and freshly ground pepper
Additional freshly grated Romano cheese

Heat oil in heavy large skillet over medium heat. Add onion and cook until soft, stirring occasionally, about 8 minutes. Add sausages and garlic. Cook until sausages are no longer pink, crumbling with fork. Add greens and stir until just wilted, about 3 minutes. Add ⅓ cup whipping cream and boil until slightly thickened, about 2 minutes.

Meanwhile, cook pasta in large pot of rapidly boiling salted water, stirring occasionally. Drain well; return pasta to pot. Mix in sauce and ½ cup Romano. Season with salt and pepper. Serve, passing additional Romano separately.

Rigatoni with Lamb, White Beans and Tomatoes

4 servings

1 tablespoon olive oil (preferably extra-virgin)
6 garlic cloves, sliced
1½ pounds trimmed lamb shoulder, cut into ½-inch pieces
¾ cup dry white wine
1 28-ounce can Italian plum tomatoes (undrained)

10 ounces rigatoni pasta
1½ cups drained canned cannellini beans or Great Northern beans
2 bunches arugula, torn into pieces
Salt and freshly ground pepper
Freshly grated Parmesan cheese

Heat oil in heavy large saucepan over medium-high heat. Add garlic and sauté 2 minutes. Transfer garlic to small bowl using slotted spoon. Add lamb to pan in batches and brown well, about 10 minutes. Return garlic to pan. Add wine and bring to boil, scraping up any browned bits. Add tomatoes with juices and bring to boil. Reduce heat and simmer until lamb is tender, breaking up tomatoes with spoon, about 30 minutes. (*Can be prepared 1 day ahead. Cover and refrigerate. Bring sauce to simmer before continuing.*)

Cook pasta in large pot of boiling salted water until just tender but still firm to bite, stirring occasionally to prevent sticking. Drain well. Mix pasta, beans, arugula, salt and pepper into sauce and stir to heat through. Transfer to large bowl. Serve with cheese.

Rigatoni with Sliced Steak and Spicy Tomato-Vegetable Sauce

4 servings

1 tablespoon vegetable oil
8 ounces boneless trimmed top sirloin steak, about ¾ inch thick

½ cup chopped onion
½ cup diced carrot
½ cup diced celery
½ cup canned low-salt beef broth

1 garlic clove, crushed
1 28-ounce can Italian plum tomatoes with basil, chopped, liquid reserved

¼ teaspoon dried red pepper flakes
1 bay leaf

½ cup diced fresh green beans
  Salt and freshly ground pepper

8 ounces dried rigatoni, ziti or penne pasta

1 tablespoon minced fresh parsley
  Freshly grated Parmesan cheese

Heat oil in heavy medium skillet over medium-high heat. Add steak and brown quickly on both sides, then continue cooking 2 to 3 minutes per side for medium-rare. Transfer to plate.

Stir onion, carrot, celery and broth into skillet. Reduce heat to low. Cover and cook until vegetables are tender, approximately 10 minutes.

Add garlic to skillet and stir 1 minute. Add tomatoes and their liquid, dried red pepper flakes and bay leaf. Increase heat to medium-high and cook until sauce thickens, stirring occasionally, about 10 minutes.

Reduce heat to medium-low. Add green beans, cover and simmer until tender, about 10 minutes. Season sauce generously with salt and pepper.

Cook pasta in large pot of boiling salted water until just tender but still firm to bite. Drain. Transfer to bowl.

Using sharp knife, cut steak crosswise into thin slivers. Reheat sauce. Add steak and exuded juices and cook to heat through. Pour over pasta. Toss well. Garnish with parsley. Serve immediately, passing cheese separately.

Spinach-stuffed Shells with Tomato Concassé

For this recipe, large pasta shells are filled with a garlicky spinach mixture and topped with diced tomatoes. Because the shells tear easily, cook extra.

6 first-course or 4 main-course servings

Filling

1½ bread slices
 4 large garlic cloves

 1 bunch fresh spinach, stemmed, or
 1 10-ounce package frozen leaf spinach, thawed and squeezed dry

 3 tablespoons olive oil
¼ cup pine nuts
 6 large green onions, trimmed and coarsely chopped
1¼ teaspoons balsamic vinegar* or red wine vinegar
¼ teaspoon (or more) salt

Freshly ground pepper
Freshly grated nutmeg

 6 ounces Fontina cheese, chilled

2½ ounces diced ham (about ¾ cup)
12 large pasta shells (or more), freshly cooked

Tomato Concassé

 2 large tomatoes (about 1 pound)
 4 tablespoons olive oil
 1 teaspoon dried basil, crumbled
½ teaspoon sugar
¼ teaspoon salt

For filling: Insert steel knife in processor. Break bread into pieces and process to fine crumbs, about 40 seconds. Set aside. With machine running, drop garlic through feed tube and mince.

Blanch fresh spinach in large pot of boiling salted water until wilted, about 2 minutes. Drain well. Squeeze out excess moisture and pat dry.

Heat olive oil in heavy medium skillet over medium heat. Add pine nuts and cook until golden, stirring frequently, about 4 minutes. Transfer to small dish using slotted spoon. Reduce heat to medium-low. Add garlic and green onions to skillet and cook until soft, stirring occasionally, about 5 minutes. Mix in fresh or thawed frozen spinach, vinegar, ¼ teaspoon salt, pepper and nutmeg and cook until hot, about 2 minutes. Remove from heat. (**Or to microwave:** Heat olive oil in 2-quart microwave-safe casserole on High 1 minute. Add pine nuts and cook uncovered on High until golden, about 3 minutes. Transfer to small dish using slotted spoon. Add garlic and green onions to casserole and cook uncovered on High until soft, stirring once to coat with oil, about 2½ minutes. Stir in spinach, vinegar, ¼ teaspoon salt, freshly ground pepper and nutmeg and cook until hot, approximately 1½ minutes.)

Insert shredding disk in processor. Shred Fontina using light pressure.

Add cheese, ham, pine nuts and breadcrumbs to spinach mixture and mix well. Season to taste with salt. Fill each shell with spinach mixture.

For tomato concassé: Core tomatoes, cut in half crosswise and squeeze to seed. Cut into ⅜-inch dice. Place in 9-inch square glass baking dish. Mix in 2 tablespoons oil, basil, sugar and salt. (**Or to microwave:** Combine in 9-inch square microwave-safe dish.)

Spread tomato concassé over bottom of dish; arrange shells over. Brush outsides of shells with remaining 2 tablespoons oil. (*Can be prepared 1 day ahead; chill. Bring to room temperature.*)

Position rack in center of oven and preheat to 350°F. Cover dish tightly with foil and bake 30 minutes. Uncover and spoon tomatoes over shells. Bake uncovered 10 minutes. (**Or to microwave:** Cover with plastic wrap; pierce plastic once with sharp knife. Cook on Medium-High 8 minutes. Spoon tomatoes over shells. Cook uncovered on Medium-High until hot, about 5 minutes.) Serve hot.

* Available at specialty foods stores, Italian markets, some supermarkets.

Lasagne with Roasted Red and Green Bell Peppers

Layers of red and green peppers and lasagne noodles are slathered with a creamy Parmesan-flavored white sauce and an herbed tomato sauce.

4 servings

1 pound red bell peppers
1 pound green bell peppers

1 teaspoon olive oil
1 medium onion, chopped
1 garlic clove, minced
1 16-ounce can Italian plum tomatoes, chopped (juices reserved)
⅓ cup dry white wine
2 tablespoons tomato paste
1 teaspoon dried basil, crumbled
1 teaspoon dried oregano, crumbled

½ teaspoon fennel seeds
½ teaspoon dried rosemary, crumbled
½ teaspoon salt
¼ teaspoon freshly ground pepper

6 ruffled lasagne noodles

Parmesan Béchamel Sauce*
¼ cup freshly grated Parmesan cheese

Fresh herb sprigs

Char peppers over gas flame or in broiler until blackened on all sides. Wrap in paper bag and let stand 10 minutes to steam. Peel and seed peppers. Cut into 2-inch pieces, separating red peppers from green peppers.

Heat oil in heavy medium saucepan over medium heat. Add onion and sauté until softened, about 5 minutes. Add garlic and stir 30 seconds. Add tomatoes with reserved juices, wine, tomato paste, basil, oregano, fennel, rosemary, salt and pepper and bring to boil. Reduce heat and simmer sauce until reduced to 1½ cups, stirring occasionally, about 30 minutes. (*Can be prepared 1 day ahead. Cover and refrigerate bell peppers and sauce separately.*)

Cook pasta in large pot of boiling salted water until just tender but still firm to bite, stirring occasionally to prevent sticking. Drain well. Arrange on kitchen towels; pat dry. Trim noodles to 8-inch lengths; reserve trimmings.

Position rack in top third of oven and preheat to 400°F. Spread ¼ cup tomato sauce in 8-inch square baking dish with 2-inch-high sides. Arrange two 8-inch noodles and 2 trimmed ends in pan, covering sauce completely. Spread ¼ cup tomato sauce over. Spoon 3 tablespoons béchamel sauce over. Top with red bell peppers. Spread ¼ cup tomato sauce over. Spoon 3 tablespoons béchamel sauce over. Top with two 8-inch noodles and 2 trimmed ends, covering completely. Spread ¼ cup tomato sauce over. Spread 3 tablespoons béchamel sauce over. Top with green bell peppers. Spread ¼ cup tomato sauce over. Top with remaining two 8-inch noodles and 2 trimmed ends, covering completely. Spoon remaining béchamel and tomato sauces over. Sprinkle with cheese. (*Lasagne can be prepared up to 8 hours ahead. Cover and refrigerate.*)

Bake lasagne until bubbling, about 30 minutes. Cool 15 minutes. Cut into squares. Transfer to plates. Garnish with herb sprigs and serve.

*Parmesan Béchamel Sauce

This variation on a classic white sauce is made without any butter.

Makes about 1¼ cups

3 tablespoons all purpose flour
1¼ cups whole milk
1 garlic clove, minced
½ teaspoon salt

¼ teaspoon freshly grated nutmeg
¼ teaspoon freshly ground pepper
½ cup freshly grated Parmesan cheese

Mix flour and 2 tablespoons milk in heavy medium saucepan until paste forms. Gradually add remaining milk and whisk until smooth. Add garlic, salt, nutmeg and pepper and boil 2 minutes, whisking constantly. Reduce heat and simmer 3 minutes, stirring constantly. Mix in Parmesan.

Pasta Rolls Stuffed with Ricotta, Spinach and Prosciutto

This festive dish is prepared a day ahead and refrigerated. The pasta rolls are sliced to show beautiful spirals of spinach filling. Top this and some sliced tomatoes with the Sun-dried Tomato Vinaigrette.

6 to 8 servings

Pasta
  3 cups all purpose flour
  3 eggs
  ½ cup plus 1 tablespoon water
  1½ teaspoons olive oil

Filling
  3 pounds fresh spinach, rinsed and stemmed
  3 cups ricotta cheese
  3 eggs

  1½ teaspoons freshly grated nutmeg
  1½ cups grated Parmesan cheese
     Salt and freshly ground pepper

  24 paper-thin slices prosciutto
  18 ounces mozzarella cheese, thinly sliced

     Olive oil
     Sun-dried Tomato Vinaigrette*

For pasta: Place flour in large bowl. Mix eggs, water and oil; add to flour and blend well. Knead on floured surface until smooth and elastic, about 10 minutes. Cover and let rest 15 minutes.

For filling: Place spinach in heavy large skillet over medium heat. Cover and cook until wilted, stirring occasionally. Drain. Squeeze dry. Chop spinach. Mix ricotta, eggs and nutmeg in large bowl. Stir in spinach and Parmesan. Season with salt and pepper.

Cut off ⅓ of dough. Roll out on lightly floured surface as thinly as possible. Trim to 18 × 11-inch rectangle. Spread with ⅓ of spinach mixture, leaving ½-inch border on all sides. Cover filling with 8 prosciutto slices, then ⅓ of mozzarella. Fold 1 inch of each long side over filling. Brush edges of short ends with water. Starting at 1 short end, roll pasta up jelly roll fashion. Wrap in cheesecloth and tie with string to hold shape. Repeat with remaining dough and filling.

Bring 2 inches of water to boil in large roasting pan on top of stove. Add pasta rolls. Reduce heat, cover and simmer 35 minutes. Using 2 spatulas, remove rolls and cool. Gently remove string and cheesecloth. Wrap pasta rolls tightly and refrigerate overnight.

Cut pasta rolls into ½-inch-thick slices. Arrange on platter. Brush with olive oil. Serve at room temperature with Sun-dried Tomato Vinaigrette.

*Sun-dried Tomato Vinaigrette

Makes about 2½ cups

  40 oil-packed sun-dried tomato halves, drained (⅓ cup oil reserved)
  ½ cup minced shallots
  2 tablespoons minced garlic

  2 cups chopped fresh basil
  1 cup plus 3 tablespoons olive oil
  ½ cup red wine vinegar
     Salt and freshly ground pepper

Mince tomatoes in processor. Mix in shallots and garlic. Add ⅓ cup reserved tomato oil, basil, olive oil and vinegar and blend until creamy. Season with salt and pepper. (*Can be prepared 3 days ahead. Cover and refrigerate. Bring to room temperature before using.*)

 Pizza

Thin-crusted Pizza with Bacon, Brie and Muenster Cheese

The addition of rolled oats creates an all-new, unconventional crust. Serve as a snack or team up with a crisp salad for a well-rounded light meal.

Makes one 14-inch pizza

Oatmeal Crust
- 1 teaspoon dry yeast
- ½ cup plus 1 tablespoon (or more) warm water (105°F to 115°F)
- ½ teaspoon honey

- 1⅓ cups (or more) bread flour
- ¼ cup rolled oats
- 1½ teaspoons safflower oil
- ½ teaspoon salt

Topping
- 1 large red bell pepper
- 1 medium onion

- 1½ tablespoons unsalted butter
  Salt
- 4 slices bacon

- 1 3-ounce piece Muenster cheese, chilled

  Rolled oats
- 4 ounces chilled Brie cheese, rind discarded, cut into small pieces
  Dried red pepper flakes

- 3 tablespoons julienne of fresh basil leaves or 2 teaspoons dried, crumbled

For crust: Sprinkle yeast over ½ cup plus 1 tablespoon warm water in small bowl. Add honey; stir to dissolve. Let stand until foamy, about 10 minutes.

Combine 1⅓ cups flour, oats, oil and salt in processor. With machine running, pour yeast mixture through feed tube and process until dough forms. If dough sticks to bowl, add more flour through feed tube 1 tablespoon at a time, incorporating each addition before adding next. If dough is dry, add water through feed tube 1 teaspoon at a time, incorporating each addition before adding next. Process until smooth and elastic, about 50 seconds. Transfer dough to lightly floured surface and knead 1 minute.

Transfer dough to large plastic bag. Seal tightly, leaving space for dough to rise. Let dough rise in warm draft-free area until doubled in volume, about 50 minutes. (*Can be prepared 1 day ahead. Punch dough down and refrigerate.*)

For topping: Char bell pepper over gas flame or in broiler until blackened on all sides. Transfer to paper bag and let stand 10 minutes to steam. Peel and seed; rinse under cold water and pat dry. Cut into ½-inch squares.

Insert medium slicer in processor. Stand onion in feed tube and slice using firm pressure.

Melt butter in heavy small skillet over medium heat. Add onion and cook until soft, stirring occasionally, about 8 minutes. Increase heat to high and cook until golden, stirring frequently, about 2 minutes. Season with salt. Transfer to plate. Cook bacon in same skillet until crisp. (**Or to microwave:** Place bacon on paper plate and cook uncovered on High about 4 minutes.) Drain bacon on paper towels. Crumble bacon coarsely.

Insert shredding disk in processor. Shred Muenster cheese using light pressure. Set aside.

Position rack in center of oven and preheat to 425°F. Grease large baking sheet (preferably black steel) and sprinkle with rolled oats. Roll dough out on lightly floured surface to 14-inch square. Transfer to prepared baking sheet. Spread onions over crust. Sprinkle Brie and Muenster over crust. Top with red bell pepper, crumbled bacon and dried red pepper flakes.

Bake pizza until bottom of crust is golden, about 15 minutes. Transfer to rack; sprinkle with basil. Cut into squares and serve hot.

Grilled Tomato Pizza with Herbs

Makes four 8-inch pizzas

Herb Oil
- 10 large fresh basil leaves
- 6 large fresh sage leaves
- ¼ cup fresh oregano leaves
- 2 large garlic cloves
- ⅔ cup olive oil
- ½ teaspoon salt

Topping
- 2 small onions (about ½ pound), peeled

- 1 2-ounce piece Parmesan cheese, room temperature
- 8 ounces mozzarella cheese

- 3 large tomatoes (about 1 pound), cored, halved, seeded, cut into ¼-inch dice

Pizza Dough Rounds*
Dried red pepper flakes
- ⅓ cup fresh basil leaves, cut julienne

For herb oil: Place herbs in processor. With machine running, drop garlic through feed tube and mince. Add oil and salt and mix. Transfer to small bowl.

For topping: Insert thin slicer in processor. Slice onions.

Insert shredding disk in processor. Stand Parmesan cheese in feed tube and shred using light pressure. Transfer to bowl. Stand mozzarella in feed tube and shred using firm pressure. Transfer to another bowl.

Toss tomatoes with 1½ tablespoons herb oil. (*Can be prepared 6 hours ahead. Cover tomatoes, oil, onions and cheeses separately and refrigerate.*)

Prepare barbecue (medium heat). Preheat oven to 250°F. Place 2 Pizza Dough Rounds on barbecue. Cover and cook until undersides are brown, 1 to 2 minutes. Transfer to sheet of foil, grilled side up. Stir herb oil and spoon 1 tablespoon atop each pizza round and brush evenly over. Top each with ¼ of onions, mozzarella, tomatoes and Parmesan. Sprinkle with red pepper flakes. Return to barbecue, removing foil, cover and cook just until bottoms are brown and cheese melts, about 3 minutes. Dab with herb oil. Keep warm in oven. Repeat with remaining dough and topping. Garnish pizzas with basil julienne and serve hot.

*Pizza Dough Rounds

Makes four 8-inch pizza crusts

- 1 envelope dry yeast
- 1 teaspoon sugar
- ¾ cup plus 1 tablespoon (or more) warm water (105°F to 115°F)

- 2⅓ cups (or more) unbleached all purpose flour
- 1½ tablespoons olive oil
- ¾ teaspoon salt

Sprinkle yeast and sugar over ¾ cup plus 1 tablespoon warm water in medium bowl; stir to dissolve. Let stand until foamy, about 5 minutes.

Combine 2⅓ cups flour, oil and salt in processor. With machine running, pour yeast mixture through feed tube and process until dough cleans sides of work bowl, about 15 seconds. If dough sticks to bowl, add more flour through feed tube 1 tablespoon at a time, incorporating each before adding next. If dough is too dry, add more water through feed tube 1 teaspoon at a time, incorporating each before adding next. Process until smooth and elastic.

Transfer dough to large plastic bag. Twist bag to release air and seal at top, leaving space for dough to expand. Let dough rise in warm draft-free area until doubled in volume, about 1 hour. (*Can be prepared 1 day ahead. Punch down and refrigerate in bag.*)

Divide dough into 4 equal portions; form each into ball. Roll each out on lightly floured surface to 8-inch round. (*Can be prepared 6 hours ahead. Place between oiled foil sheets and chill.*)

❦ Sandwiches

Chicken Sandwiches with Three-Onion Relish

2 servings

½ cup thinly sliced red onion
½ cup thinly sliced yellow onion
4 large green onions (white and light green parts only), sliced diagonally
1 teaspoon salt
2 tablespoons white wine vinegar
2 teaspoons sugar or honey
½ teaspoon grated orange peel
Pinch of dried thyme, crumbled

2½ cups canned chicken broth or water

1 leafy celery top
1 onion slice
1 bay leaf
½ teaspoon salt
1 1-pound chicken breast

4 slices sourdough bread
½ cup roasted red peppers from jar, rinsed and dried
8 large watercress sprigs
Freshly ground pepper

Toss onions with 1 teaspoon salt in bowl. Transfer to colander set in sink and let stand 30 minutes. Rinse onions in cold water; squeeze dry. Transfer to non-aluminum bowl. Add vinegar, sugar, orange peel and thyme. Cover and refrigerate onion relish at least 1 hour. (*Can be prepared 1 day ahead.*)

Pour broth into 8-inch skillet. Add next 4 ingredients. Cover and bring to boil. Add chicken. Reduce heat, cover and simmer until chicken is firm to touch and no pink remains, about 10 minutes. Let cool uncovered in liquid. Drain, reserving liquid for another use. Skin, bone and trim chicken. Cut breast in half. Cut halves crosswise into ¼-inch-thick slices. (*Can be prepared 1 day ahead. Wrap and refrigerate.*)

Drain onion relish. Place 2 bread slices on plates. Layer each with half of peppers, watercress and chicken. Sprinkle with pepper. Cover with relish. Top each with bread slice, pressing gently. Cut each in half crosswise.

Aram Sandwiches

Pinwheels of Armenian cracker bread wrapped around smoked turkey, cucumber, lettuce and tomatoes. Large flour tortillas can replace the lavash; do not rinse them in water before using.

Makes about 24

2 15-inch rounds lavash*
1 8-ounce package cream cheese, room temperature
¼ cup mango chutney
¾ teaspoon curry powder
Salt and freshly ground pepper
1 head red leaf lettuce, leaves separated

⅔ pound smoked turkey, sliced ⅛ inch thick
1 small English hothouse cucumber, thinly sliced
1 medium tomato, thinly sliced
Fresh parsley sprigs

Hold 1 lavash under cold running water until thoroughly moistened, about 1 minute. Place on damp towel. Cover with another damp towel. Repeat with second bread. Let stand until soft enough to roll, about 45 minutes.

Combine cream cheese, chutney and curry in processor and blend until smooth. Season with salt and pepper. Place 1 lavash on flat surface. Spread ½ of cream cheese mixture over bread. Arrange 3 or 4 lettuce leaves over cream cheese at one end of cracker bread. Top lettuce with ½ of smoked turkey, ½ of cucumber and ½ of tomato slices. Roll bread up tightly jelly roll fashion, starting at end with turkey. Repeat with second bread and remaining filling. (*Can be prepared 1 day ahead. Cover tightly with plastic and refrigerate.*) Cut rolls diagonally into 1-inch-thick slices. Arrange on platter. Garnish with parsley and serve.

*Thin cracker breads available at Armenian markets and some supermarkets.

Grilled Prosciutto and Fontina Sandwiches

An Italian ham and cheese sandwich. Serve with sliced tomatoes on the side.

2 servings; can be doubled or tripled

4 ounces Fontina or Havarti cheese
4 large slices sourdough bread
6 thin slices prosciutto or fried bacon

Fresh basil leaves

Olive oil
Freshly ground pepper

Thinly slice cheese, using cheese plane. Divide half of cheese between 2 bread slices, covering completely. Cover cheese with prosciutto. Cover prosciutto with basil leaves, then remaining cheese. Top each sandwich with second sourdough bread slice.

Heat heavy large skillet over medium heat. Brush one side of each sandwich with oil and sprinkle generously with pepper. Arrange oiled side down in skillet. Brush top side with oil and sprinkle with pepper. Grill until golden brown and cheese melts, pressing down occasionally with spatula, about 3 minutes per side. Cut each sandwich in half and serve immediately.

Skirt Steak, Onion and Bell Pepper Sandwiches

Add a tossed salad of escarole and tomato wedges and you've got a great dinner.

2 servings; can be doubled or tripled

2½ tablespoons olive oil
1 red onion, halved and sliced
1 medium red bell pepper, cut into thin strips
Salt and freshly ground pepper
½ pound skirt steak, cut crosswise into ¼-inch-thick strips

¼ teaspoon ground cumin
¼ teaspoon dried thyme, crumbled
1 2.5-ounce can sliced black olives, drained
2 pita bread rounds, halved

Heat 2 tablespoons oil in heavy medium skillet over medium-low heat. Add onion and bell pepper. Season with salt and pepper. Cook until onion and bell pepper are very tender, stirring occasionally, about 15 minutes. Transfer onion and pepper to plate.

Heat remaining ½ tablespoon oil in same skillet over high heat. Add steak and season with salt and pepper. Stir until no longer pink, about 1 minute. Return vegetables to skillet. Add cumin and thyme and stir 30 seconds. Remove from heat and mix in black olives. Spoon into pita breads and serve.

4 ❧ Main Courses

With the exciting variety of recipes here, there's a main course to fit any occasion, from a simple get-together or family supper to a fabulous pull-out-the-stops dinner party. For a hearty, down-home meal, you might serve Spiced Baby Back Ribs with Barbecue Sauce, Chicken Breasts with Mushroom-Sherry Sauce or a lively version of an old favorite—Meat Loaf with Sun-dried Tomatoes. More sophisticated entrées include Flank Steak Stuffed with Sausage, Basil and Cheese, Red Snapper with Chili-Corn Sauce and Chicken Sauté in Tomato-Vinegar Sauce.

If you're among the growing ranks of people who are cutting back on red meat—and even if you're not—you'll find some delectable vegetarian entrées here. These imaginative egg, cheese and vegetable combinations are nutritious, economical, a snap to prepare—and they taste great. Serve Baked Eggs with Peppers and Mushrooms as a special family breakfast or festive brunch, with bacon, fruit compote and fragrant cinnamon-raisin bread. Corn Bread and Goat Cheese Soufflé is topped with a zippy salsa—perfect with a green salad for a light lunch or supper. For a change-of-pace dinner party, try Spicy Squash and Black Bean Stew with Cilantro Pesto—both the stew and the pesto can be prepared ahead, leaving little more than a quick rewarming and garnish before serving.

 Beef

Filet Mignon with Mustard Cream Sauce

This is so easy, no advance preparation is necessary.

2 servings

Freshly ground pepper
2 1¼-inch-thick beef filet mignon
   steaks
1 tablespoon butter
½ tablespoon vegetable oil
   Salt

1 shallot or green onion, minced
1 tablespoon brandy
⅓ cup whipping cream
½ teaspoon country-style or regular
   Dijon mustard
   Fresh parsley sprigs

Grind pepper generously over both sides of steaks and press in. Melt ½ tablespoon butter with oil in heavy medium skillet over high heat. Salt steaks on one side and add to skillet salted side down. Cook until brown, about 2 minutes. Salt tops, turn and cook until second sides are brown. Reduce heat to medium and cook to desired degree of doneness, turning occasionally, about 6 minutes for rare. Transfer steaks to heated plates and set aside.

Discard drippings from skillet. Add remaining ½ tablespoon butter to same skillet and melt over medium heat. Add shallot and stir 1 minute. Remove from heat and add brandy. Return to heat and bring to boil, scraping up any browned bits. Boil until reduced to glaze. Add cream and boil until mixture begins to thicken, about 1 minute. Stir in mustard and any juices exuded from steaks. Remove from heat. Season with salt and pepper. Spoon sauce over steaks. Garnish with parsley.

Grilled Flank Steak with Spicy Garlic Sauce

Marinating the steak overnight intensifies its flavor.

6 servings

Steak
2½ pounds flank steak, trimmed
  2 tablespoons minced peeled fresh
     ginger
  2 tablespoons soy sauce
  1 tablespoon oriental sesame oil
  1 tablespoon sake or Chinese
     rice wine
  1 teaspoon freshly ground pepper

Sauce
  ¼ cup soy sauce

3 tablespoons minced fresh parsley
2 tablespoons water
1 tablespoon sake or Chinese
   rice wine
2 teaspoons sugar
2 teaspoons minced garlic
1 teaspoon oriental sesame oil
1 teaspoon chili paste*

For steak: Make ¼-inch-deep lengthwise cuts in steak, spacing 1 inch apart, then cut crosswise, forming crosshatch design. Place steak in large shallow glass dish. Mix next 5 ingredients in small bowl. Pour over steak, rubbing ginger into cuts. Cover and refrigerate overnight, turning steak once.

For sauce: Mix all ingredients in medium bowl. Cover and refrigerate until cold. (*Can be prepared 1 day ahead.*)

Prepare barbecue (high heat). Grill steak to desired degree of doneness, about 7 minutes per side for medium-rare. Transfer to platter. Let stand 10 minutes. Thinly slice steak across grain. Cool steak to room temperature. (*Can be prepared 1 day ahead. Cover and refrigerate.*) Pour sauce over steak. Serve cold or at room temperature.

*Available at oriental markets and some specialty foods stores.

Cowboy Steak with Red Chili Onion Rings

Ask your butcher to cut these large steaks for you. If you prefer smaller portions, buy standard-size steaks and grill them for a shorter time. They are equally delicious panfried.

2 servings

1 small red onion, diced
3 cups water
1 pound tomatoes, cut into ¼-inch pieces
3 tablespoons fresh lime juice
3 tablespoons finely chopped fresh cilantro
1 tablespoon finely chopped seeded jalapeño chilies

1 tablespoon olive oil
Salt

2 1½-inch-thick T-bone or porterhouse steaks, room temperature
Freshly ground pepper
Red Chili Onion Rings*

Soak red onion in water in large bowl 1 hour. Drain thoroughly. Transfer to medium bowl. Add tomatoes, lime juice, cilantro, chilies, oil and salt and toss well. Cover salsa with plastic wrap and refrigerate until ready to serve. (*Can be prepared 6 hours ahead.*)

Prepare barbecue (medium-high heat). Season steaks with salt and pepper. Grill steaks to desired doneness, about 7 minutes per side for medium-rare. Transfer to plates. Drain salsa and spoon onto plates. Serve steaks immediately with onion rings.

*Red Chili Onion Rings

2 servings

2 white onions, cut into ¹⁄₁₆- to ⅛ inch-wide rings
1½ cups milk
1½ cups sifted all purpose flour
¼ cup chili powder
1 tablespoon plus 1 teaspoon cornstarch

1½ teaspoons salt
1½ teaspoons ground cumin
1 teaspoon (generous) sugar
1 teaspoon (generous) Hungarian hot paprika
Vegetable oil (for deep frying)

Soak onions in milk in large bowl 1 hour. Drain thoroughly. Mix all remaining ingredients except oil in another large bowl. Dredge onions in flour mixture; shake off excess. Heat oil in heavy large saucepan to 360°F. Add onions in batches and cook until golden brown, about 45 seconds. Transfer to paper towels using slotted spoon; drain well. Serve immediately.

Flank Steak Stuffed with Sausage, Basil and Cheese

Some buttered steamed greens, such as spinach, chard or beet greens, and oven-roasted potatoes would round out this meal. To accompany the steak, pour an earthy, full-flavored red wine, such as a Barolo, a Rhône or a California Merlot.

4 servings

16 (about) fresh large basil leaves or spinach leaves
1 1½-pound flank steak
4 thin slices Swiss cheese
2 sweet Italian sausages
   Salt and freshly ground pepper

3 tablespoons olive oil
1 large onion, thinly sliced
8 garlic cloves

1 cup dry red wine, such as Burgundy
½ cup beef stock or canned low-salt broth
¼ cup red wine vinegar
2 bay leaves
2 fresh basil leaves, chopped

Preheat oven to 350°F. Arrange enough basil leaves atop steak to cover, leaving ½-inch border on each short side. Top basil with cheese slices. Place sausages end to end lengthwise down center. Starting at one long side, roll steak over sausage, then roll into cylinder. Tie with string to secure. Season with salt and pepper.

Heat oil in 6-quart Dutch oven. Add steak and brown on all sides, about 5 minutes. Transfer steak to platter. Reduce heat to medium. Add onion to Dutch oven. Cover and cook until golden brown, stirring occasionally, about 15 minutes. Add garlic and sauté 1 minute. Add wine, stock, vinegar, bay leaves and chopped basil and bring to boil, scraping up any browned bits. Add steak seam side up. Cover and bake until meat is tender, about 1 hour.

Transfer steak to platter. Boil juices until reduced to 1 cup, about 3 minutes. Cut steak into ¾-inch-thick slices. Serve, passing juices separately.

Deviled Short Ribs of Beef

Have the butcher cut the rib bones for you. When this is done crosswise, it's called "flanken style."

4 servings

4½ cups (or more) beer
1 teaspoon salt
5 to 5½ pounds meaty beef short ribs, cut crosswise or into individual ribs

¾ cup Dijon mustard
¾ cup coarse-grained mustard
1 tablespoon plus 1 teaspoon Worcestershire sauce

2 teaspoons hot pepper sauce (such as Tabasco)
4 cups fresh white breadcrumbs

¼ cup (½ stick) unsalted butter
¼ cup olive oil

Bring 4½ cups beer to boil in large Dutch oven or heavy large deep skillet. Add salt. Arrange ribs in beer in single layer. Add additional beer if necessary to cover ribs. Cover and simmer until ribs are tender, turning ribs over once and skimming off any foam from surface, about 80 minutes.

Line large baking sheet with paper towels. Transfer ribs to prepared sheet using tongs. Cool ribs. Cover and refrigerate until well chilled. (*Can be prepared 1 day ahead to this point.*)

Line large baking sheet with aluminum foil. Lightly oil foil. Mix both mustards, Worcestershire and hot pepper sauce in small bowl. Brush ribs with mustard mixture, coating all sides. Dredge ribs in breadcrumbs; shake off excess. Place on prepared sheet. Chill uncovered at least 30 minutes and up to 2 hours.

Preheat oven to 400°F. Melt butter in heavy small skillet over medium heat. Mix in oil. Drizzle half of butter mixture over one side of ribs. Bake 15 minutes. Carefully turn ribs over. Drizzle remaining butter mixture over. Bake 20 more minutes. Turn ribs over again. Bake until golden brown, about 15 minutes.

Beef Brisket with Aromatic Vegetables

4 to 6 servings

1 2½- to 3-pound lean beef brisket
3⅓ cups beef stock or canned low-
    salt broth
3⅓ cups (about) water
1 onion, halved and stuck with
    3 whole cloves
2 medium carrots
1 celery stalk with leafy tops,
    halved
3 garlic cloves, crushed
8 fresh parsley sprigs
2 fresh thyme sprigs
1 bay leaf

1 teaspoon coarse salt

6 small leeks
2 medium celery roots, peeled and
    quartered
4 carrots, peeled, halved crosswise,
    then halved lengthwise
    Salt and freshly ground pepper

Fresh thyme sprigs
Vegetable Herb Sauce*
Prepared horseradish
Coarse-grained mustard

Place meat in large pot. Add stock and enough cold water to cover by 2 inches. Transfer meat to plate. Bring liquid to boil. Return meat to pot and return liquid to boil, skimming foam from surface. Add onion, 2 carrots, celery stalk, garlic, parsley, 2 thyme sprigs, bay leaf and coarse salt. Reduce heat, cover and simmer until meat is almost tender, skimming foam from surface, about 2 hours.

Using slotted spoon, remove onion, carrots, celery stalk, garlic, parsley, thyme sprigs and bay leaf from broth and discard. Add leeks, celery roots and 4 carrots to meat and broth. Season with salt and ground pepper. Cover and simmer until meat and vegetables are very tender, about 45 minutes.

Transfer meat to work surface. Cut across grain into slices. Arrange on platter; surround with leeks, celery roots and carrots. Ladle generous amounts of broth over. Garnish with thyme sprigs. (Strain remaining broth through fine sieve and reserve for another use.) Serve, passing herb sauce, horseradish and coarse-grained mustard separately.

*Vegetable Herb Sauce

Makes about 2¼ cups

¾ cup olive oil (preferably extra-
    virgin)
1 small red onion, finely chopped
½ cup chopped fresh Italian parsley
⅓ cup drained diced pimientos
    (packed in jars)
1 celery stalk, finely chopped
1 hard-cooked egg, finely chopped

3 tablespoons balsamic or red wine
    vinegar
2 tablespoons red wine vinegar
2 garlic cloves, minced
    Salt and freshly ground pepper
¼ cup snipped fresh chives
2 tablespoons chopped fresh sage
    (optional)

Mix first 9 ingredients in medium bowl. Season with salt and pepper. (*Can be prepared 1 day ahead. Cover and refrigerate.*) Add chives and sage and let stand 30 minutes at room temperature before serving.

Southwest Beef Stew

It's a good idea to make this stew in advance so the flavors have a chance to marry. Serve it over buttered egg noodles or layer with your favorite taco garnishes in tortillas.

6 to 8 servings

4 large garlic cloves
2 medium onions, quartered
1 cup prepared chili sauce
1 tablespoon tomato paste
1 small chipotle chili (from can of chipotle chilies in adobo sauce)*

2 pounds lean beef stew meat, cut into ¾-inch cubes

1 tablespoon ground cumin
1 teaspoon salt

3 tablespoons (about) safflower oil

1 cup (about) canned beef broth

Position rack in center of oven and then preheat to 350°F.

Insert steel knife in processor. With machine running, drop garlic through feed tube and mince. Add onions and mince. Transfer to sheet of waxed paper. Process chili sauce, tomato paste and canned chipotle chili until smooth.

Combine beef with cumin and salt in large plastic bag. Seal bag with twist-tie and then toss well until meat cubes are uniformly seasoned.

Heat ½ tablespoon oil in heavy 3-quart stove-to-oven casserole over medium-high heat. Brown meat in batches, adding more oil as necessary. Transfer to plate. Add 1 tablespoon oil to casserole; add garlic and onions. Cover with sheet of waxed paper. Cook over medium heat until soft, stirring occasionally to loosen any browned bits, approximately 6 minutes.

Return meat to casserole. Add chili sauce mixture and ¾ cup beef broth. Stir to combine. Cover and bake until tender, stirring occasionally and adding more broth as necessary to keep meat covered, about 1½ hours. (*Can be prepared 3 days ahead. Cover and refrigerate. Bring to room temperature. Reheat in 350°F oven for 30 minutes, adding more broth to thin sauce if desired. Or reheat in microwave in microwave-safe casserole on High until hot, about 10 minutes.*) Serve stew hot.

*Canned chipotle chilies are available at Latin American markets and some supermarkets.

Meat Loaf with Sun-dried Tomatoes

Italian sausage keeps the meat loaf moist, while plenty of garlic, herbs and onions provide seasoning. Leftovers taste great cold, in a sandwich.

20 servings

1 8-ounce jar sun-dried tomatoes packed in oil, drained (¼ cup oil reserved) and chopped
1 pound onions, finely diced
3 celery stalks, finely diced
6 garlic cloves, minced
2 teaspoons dried basil, crumbled
2 teaspoons dried oregano, crumbled
2 teaspoons dried thyme, crumbled

3 pounds ground beef (not lean)

2 pounds sweet Italian sausages, casings removed
1 cup minced fresh Italian parsley
4 eggs, beaten to blend
½ cup fine dry breadcrumbs
1 tablespoon freshly ground pepper

16 1-inch-long onion strips
Fresh Italian parsley sprigs
French bread baguette slices
Garlic Mayonnaise*

Position rack in center of oven and preheat to 350°F. Heat reserved oil in heavy medium skillet over medium heat. Mix in onions, celery, garlic, basil, oregano and thyme. Cover and cook until vegetables are very tender, stirring occasionally, about 12 minutes. Transfer to large bowl. Cool slightly.

Mix beef and sausage into vegetable mixture. Add tomatoes, parsley, eggs, breadcrumbs and pepper and mix well. Press mixture into two oval-shaped loaves in large shallow baking dish. Bake until meat thermometer inserted in centers of loaves registers 160°F, pouring off accumulated fat as necessary, about 1½ hours. Cool slightly in dish. (*Can be prepared 1 day ahead. Cool. Wrap tightly and refrigerate.*)

Set loaves on platter. Place onion on top. Garnish with parsley. Serve warm or at room temperature with bread and mayonnaise.

*Garlic Mayonnaise

Makes about 2 cups

3 egg yolks, room temperature
3 tablespoons (or more) fresh lemon juice
3 garlic cloves
1 tablespoon Dijon mustard
¾ teaspoon salt
1 cup corn oil or other vegetable oil

⅔ cup olive oil
Freshly ground pepper
2 tablespoons chopped drained sun-dried tomatoes packed in oil (optional)

Blend yolks, 3 tablespoons lemon juice, garlic, mustard and salt in processor. With machine running, gradually add oils through feed tube in very slow steady stream and process until thickened. Season generously with pepper. Transfer to bowl. Mix in tomatoes if desired. Taste, adding more lemon juice if desired. (*Can be prepared 2 days ahead. Cover and refrigerate.*)

Cottage Pie

Here, meat and potatoes combine in a perfect one-dish supper. The English original was usually made with leftover roast mutton and leftover mashed potatoes. This version can be prepared with leg of lamb or roast beef. Accompany the pie with a mixed green salad and a crusty loaf of bread. Pour a light-bodied Cabernet Sauvignon. For dessert, offer scoops of ice cream with fresh berries.

4 to 6 servings

2½ pounds potatoes, peeled and sliced

1½ tablespoons vegetable oil
2 large onions, chopped
8 mushrooms, sliced
3 green onions, thinly sliced
3½ cups ½-inch dice cooked leg of lamb or roast beef
7 tablespoons unsalted butter
1 10-ounce package frozen peas

3 carrots, peeled and cut into ½-inch pieces

¼ cup chopped fresh Italian parsley
1 teaspoon chopped fresh thyme or ¼ teaspoon dried, crumbled
Salt and freshly ground pepper

1 cup (about) beef stock or canned low-salt broth
1 tablespoon tomato paste
3 tablespoons all purpose flour

¼ cup whipping cream
Freshly grated nutmeg

Place potatoes in large pot with enough cold water to cover. Cover and bring to boil. Reduce heat and simmer until potatoes are tender, about 25 minutes. Drain potatoes; reserve cooking liquid and set aside.

Heat oil in heavy large skillet over medium-high heat. Add 2 chopped onions and cook until softened, stirring frequently, about 10 minutes. Add mushrooms and green onions and sauté until mushrooms soften, about 3 minutes. Transfer to large bowl. Mix in lamb. Melt 1 tablespoon butter in same skillet over medium-high heat. Add peas and sauté until just tender, about 3 minutes. Mix with lamb.

Cook carrots in large pot of boiling salted water until just tender, about 5 minutes. Drain thoroughly. Mix carrots, parsley and thyme into lamb. Season with salt and pepper.

Butter 12½ × 8 × 3-inch oval baking dish. Bring stock and tomato paste to boil in heavy small saucepan. Melt 2 tablespoons butter in another heavy small saucepan over low heat. Add flour and stir until light golden brown, about 4 minutes. Whisk in broth mixture. Increase heat and boil until slightly thickened, whisking constantly, about 5 minutes. Pour over lamb mixture. Season with salt and pepper. Transfer mixture to prepared dish.

Press potatoes through food mill or coarse sieve into large bowl. Cut 3 tablespoons butter into small pieces. Mix into potatoes with ¼ cup reserved potato cooking liquid and cream. Season with salt, pepper and nutmeg. Spread potato mixture over lamb; smooth top. Run fork tines diagonally across surface to form crosshatch pattern. Dot surface with remaining 1 tablespoon butter. (*Can be prepared 1 day ahead. Refrigerate. Let stand 30 minutes at room temperature before baking.*)

Position rack in center of oven and preheat to 400°F. Place dish on baking sheet. Bake until top is golden brown, about 1 hour. Serve hot.

Veal

Pan-seared Veal Chops with Apple Bourbon Sauce

For the sauce, have your butcher cut the veal shank bone into sections.

4 servings

3 cups chicken stock or unsalted canned broth
1 cup veal stock or unsalted canned beef broth

2 tablespoons peanut oil
1 1-pound veal shank bone, cut into 2-inch sections
1 medium onion, sliced
3 large mushrooms, sliced
6 tablespoons bourbon
2 tart green apples, sliced

2 shallots, chopped
1 small bunch fresh thyme
2 teaspoons cracked black peppercorns

¼ cup (½ stick) butter, cut into 4 pieces
1 tablespoon fresh lemon juice
Salt

4 9-ounce center-cut veal chops with rib bone attached
3 tablespoons peanut oil

Combine 1 cup chicken stock and veal stock; boil until reduced to 1 cup.

Heat 2 tablespoons oil in heavy large saucepan over medium heat. Add veal shank bone and onion and cook until browned, stirring frequently, about 15 minutes; do not burn. Add mushrooms and stir 1 minute. Stir in 4 tablespoons bourbon, scraping up browned bits. Add reduced chicken-veal stock mixture, remaining 2 cups chicken stock, apples, shallots, thyme and peppercorns and bring to boil, skimming foam from surface. Reduce heat and simmer gently for 1 hour to blend flavors.

Strain sauce through fine sieve into clean saucepan, pressing on solids to extract as much liquid as possible. Degrease. If necessary, simmer until reduced to ¾ cup. Stir in remaining 2 tablespoons bourbon. (*Can be prepared 1 day ahead. Cool, cover and refrigerate. Reheat before continuing.*) Whisk in butter 1 piece at a time. Add lemon juice. Season with salt. Keep warm in double boiler over gently simmering water or in vacuum bottle.

Preheat oven to 375°F. Pat veal dry. Season with salt. Heat 3 tablespoons oil in heavy large ovenproof skillet over medium heat. Add chops and cook until golden-brown crust forms, about 5 minutes. Turn chops over. Transfer skillet to oven and cook chops until meat thermometer registers 140°F for medium-rare, about 10 minutes.

Ladle sauce onto plates. Top with chops.

Veal "Dino"

A signature dish of Dino's restaurant on St. Croix. The luscious sauce combines shallots, pine nuts and sun-dried tomatoes.

4 servings

16 shallots
3 tablespoons olive oil
  Salt and freshly ground pepper

1 cup chicken stock or canned low-salt broth
1 cup beef stock or canned low-salt broth
1 tablespoon unsalted butter
⅔ cup pine nuts (about 6 ounces)

1 pound veal scaloppine

¼ cup (½ stick) unsalted butter
  All purpose flour

¼ cup dry white wine
16 oil-packed sun-dried tomatoes, drained and cut into thin julienne
½ cup (1 stick) unsalted butter, cut into tablespoon-size pieces
1 tablespoon chopped fresh basil or 1 teaspoon dried, crumbled

Preheat oven to 325°F. Place shallots in small baking pan. Coat with oil. Season with salt and pepper. Roast shallots until brown and soft, about 30 minutes. Set shallots aside.

Combine chicken and beef stocks in small saucepan. Boil until reduced to ½ cup, about 15 minutes. Melt 1 tablespoon butter in heavy small skillet over low heat. Add pine nuts to skillet and cook until golden brown, shaking skillet frequently, about 1 minute. (*Can be prepared 1 day ahead. Cover pine nuts and store at room temperature. Cover shallots and stock separately. Chill.*)

Place veal between sheets of waxed paper and pound with mallet to thickness of ⅛ inch. Melt ¼ cup butter in heavy large skillet over medium-high heat. Dredge veal in flour, shaking off excess. Add to skillet in batches (do not crowd). Cook until light brown, 1 to 2 minutes per side. Transfer to plates; keep warm.

Pour off butter from skillet. Add shallots, pine nuts, wine and sun-dried tomatoes to skillet and cook until wine is nearly evaporated, scraping up any browned bits, about 2 minutes. Add reduced stock and simmer until reduced to sauce consistency, about 8 minutes. Whisk in ½ cup butter 2 tablespoons at a time. Add basil. Spoon over veal.

Veal with Roquefort Cream and Oven-fried Potatoes

4 servings

2 tablespoons olive oil
6 medium-size red potatoes, cut into 8 wedges each

  Olive oil
1½ to 2 pounds veal tenderloin, trimmed and cut into 4 pieces

½ cup (1 stick) butter

¼ cup chopped shallots
2 cups veal or beef stock or canned unsalted beef broth
1 cup whipping cream
2 ounces Roquefort cheese, crumbled (about ⅔ cup)

  Minced fresh thyme

Preheat oven to 375°F. Heat 2 tablespoons oil in heavy large skillet over medium-high heat. Add potatoes and brown well on all sides, turning frequently, about

10 minutes. Transfer to baking sheet. Bake potatoes until crisp and cooked through, 10 to 15 minutes. Reduce oven temperature to 250°F and keep warm.

Meanwhile, heat thin layer of oil in heavy large skillet over medium-high heat. Add veal and brown well on all sides. Reduce heat and cook about 15 minutes for medium-rare, turning frequently. Transfer veal to heated plate.

Pour off drippings from skillet. Melt ¼ cup butter in same skillet over medium heat. Add shallots and stir until softened, about 2 minutes. Add stock and boil until reduced to 1 cup. Add cream and boil until mixture is reduced to 1 cup. Pour in any exuded meat juices. Reduce heat to low. Add cheese and remaining butter; do not boil.

Slice veal. Cover plates with sauce. Top with veal. Spoon potatoes to side and sprinkle with thyme.

 Lamb

Grilled Lamb and Melon Kebabs

A delicious combination. The kebabs can be made four hours ahead.

4 servings

3 tablespoons olive oil
2 tablespoons balsamic vinegar* or red wine vinegar
1½ teaspoons chopped fresh rosemary or ½ teaspoon dried, crumbled
1 garlic clove, finely chopped
½ teaspoon ground cumin
½ teaspoon salt
½ teaspoon freshly ground pepper
¼ teaspoon cayenne pepper

¼ teaspoon ground coriander
1 pound lean lamb (leg or well-trimmed shoulder), cut into 1-inch cubes

30 (about) 1-inch cubes cantaloupe
16 (about) 12-inch-long bamboo skewers, soaked in water 1 hour and drained

Combine first 9 ingredients in small bowl. (*Can be prepared 2 days ahead. Cover and refrigerate.*) Place lamb in glass baking dish. Pour marinade over lamb, turning to coat well. Cover and marinate 2 hours at room temperature, or up to 8 hours in refrigerator.

Drain lamb, reserving marinade. Alternate lamb and melon on skewers. Return to baking dish. Spoon reserved marinade over meat. (*Kebabs can be prepared 4 hours ahead. Cover and refrigerate.*)

Prepare barbecue grill (medium heat). Arrange skewers around edges of grill. Cook until lamb is slightly charred on outside and pink on inside, turning occasionally, about 5 minutes.

Arrange skewers on platter.

*Available at specialty foods stores, Italian markets and some supermarkets.

Garlic-studded Racks of Lamb

Ask your butcher to remove the backbones from the racks and trim two inches of fat starting from the tips of the rib bones (this is called frenching the racks). You will need to save the backbones to make the lamb stock for the sauce.

6 servings

Lamb
- ¾ **cup olive oil**
- ¼ **cup red wine vinegar**
- ¼ **cup chopped fresh parsley**
- 1 **teaspoon Dijon mustard**
- 1 **teaspoon salt**
- 1 **teaspoon dried thyme, crumbled**
- 2 **bay leaves, crumbled**
- 3 **racks of lamb with 6 ribs each, frenched, backbones reserved for Lamb Stock***
- 4 **garlic cloves, slivered**

Sauce
- ½ **cup dry red wine**
- ⅓ **cup finely chopped shallots**
- 1 **cup Lamb Stock***

   Cracked pepper
- ⅓ **cup olive oil**

- 8 **tablespoons (1 stick) chilled unsalted butter, cut into 8 pieces**
   Salt and freshly ground pepper
- 2 **tablespoons finely chopped fresh parsley**

For lamb: Mix ¾ cup oil, vinegar, parsley, mustard, salt, thyme and bay leaves in medium bowl. Cut small slits in lamb. Press garlic slivers into slits. Place lamb in large glass baking dish. Pour marinade over. Cover and refrigerate overnight, turning occasionally.

For sauce: Boil wine and shallots in heavy medium saucepan until liquid is reduced to 2 tablespoons. Add Lamb Stock and boil until liquid is reduced to ⅔ cup, about 5 minutes. Set aside.

Preheat oven to 450°F. Remove lamb from marinade and pat dry. Rub with cracked pepper. Heat ⅓ cup oil in heavy large roasting pan over medium heat. Add lamb and cook until brown, about 3 minutes per side. Transfer lamb in pan to oven and roast until meat thermometer inserted in center of meat registers 130°F for rare, about 25 minutes. Transfer to platter. Tent with foil to keep warm.

Pour off any fat from roasting pan. Place roasting pan over medium-high heat. Add reduced stock and bring to boil, scraping up any browned bits. Return mixture to same saucepan. Whisk in 2 pieces butter. Set pan over low heat and whisk in remaining butter 1 piece at a time, removing pan from heat briefly if drops of melted butter appear. (If sauce breaks down at any time, remove from heat and whisk in 2 tablespoons butter.) Season with salt and pepper. Mix in finely chopped parsley.

Cut racks into individual chops. Place 3 on each plate. Spoon sauce over lamb chops and serve.

*Lamb Stock

Make the stock one day ahead.

Makes 1 cup

- 2 **tablespoons olive oil**
   Backbones reserved from Garlic-studded Racks of Lamb (see recipe)

- 2 **cups chicken stock or canned low-salt broth**
- 2 **cups water**

Heat oil in heavy large saucepan over medium-high heat. Add bones and brown well, stirring frequently, about 15 minutes. Pour off oil. Add stock and water to pan and bring to boil, scraping up any browned bits. Cook over medium-high heat until liquid is reduced to 1 cup. Strain into bowl. (*Can be prepared 1 day ahead; refrigerate.*)

Lamb Shanks in Cilantro Sauce

4 to 6 servings

6 ¾-pound lamb shanks
  Salt and freshly ground pepper
¼ cup olive oil
1 large onion, thinly sliced
1 carrot, peeled and cut into ½-inch pieces
4 medium leeks (white parts only), thinly sliced

2 bunches fresh cilantro, stems chopped, leaves reserved
2 garlic cloves, minced
1 teaspoon ground fenugreek*
2 cups water

3 to 4 tablespoons fresh lemon juice
  Freshly cooked basmati rice*

Preheat oven to 350°F. Season lamb with salt and pepper. Heat oil in 6- to 7-quart Dutch oven over high heat. Add lamb in batches and brown well, about 7 minutes per side. Transfer lamb to platter. Add onion, carrot and ⅔ of leeks to Dutch oven. Reduce heat to medium. Cover and cook until vegetables soften, stirring occasionally, about 10 minutes. Add cilantro stems, garlic and fenugreek and sauté 1 minute. Add water and bring to boil. Return lamb, cover and bake until meat is very tender and begins to pull away from bone, about 70 minutes. (*Can be prepared 1 day ahead. Cool. Refrigerate. Rewarm before continuing.*)

Transfer lamb to platter using slotted spoon. Tent with foil to keep warm. Add remaining leeks to Dutch oven and cook over medium heat 5 minutes, stirring occasionally. Mince all but ⅓ cup cilantro leaves. Add to Dutch oven and cook 3 minutes. If sauce is thin, increase heat and boil until thickened. Add 3 tablespoons lemon juice. Taste, adding remaining 1 tablespoon lemon juice if desired. Pour juices over lamb. Garnish with remaining cilantro leaves. Serve with basmati rice.

*Available at Indian markets.

Spring Lamb Ragout

This stew, which is ladled over noodles, is also good served on couscous or rice.

10 servings

6 tablespoons vegetable oil
4 large onions, chopped
6 garlic cloves, chopped
1½ teaspoons sugar

5 pounds lamb stew meat, cut into 1-inch pieces
  Salt and freshly ground pepper
½ cup all purpose flour
4 medium tomatoes, peeled, seeded and chopped
1½ cups chicken stock or canned broth
1 cup beef stock or canned broth
¾ cup dry white wine
2 tablespoons chopped fresh rosemary or 2 teaspoons dried, crumbled

1 tablespoon tomato paste
1 teaspoon dried thyme, crumbled
2 bay leaves

5 tablespoons butter
12 ounces mushrooms, sliced
1 9-ounce package frozen artichoke hearts, thawed, quartered
3 small zucchini (about 8 ounces), cut into ½-inch cubes
¾ cup Kalamata* or black olives, pitted
3 tablespoons minced fresh parsley
  Buttered freshly cooked egg noodles

Position rack in lowest third of oven and preheat to 350°F. Heat 2 tablespoons oil in heavy large Dutch oven over medium heat. Add onions and garlic and cook until soft and translucent, stirring occasionally, about 12 minutes. Sprinkle with sugar and cook until lightly browned, about 5 minutes. Transfer to bowl.

Add remaining 4 tablespoons oil to same pan over medium heat. Season lamb with salt and pepper; dredge in flour. Add lamb to Dutch oven in batches if necessary and cook until brown, about 6 minutes. Add any remaining flour to pan and stir 1 minute. Add onion mixture, tomatoes, both stocks, wine, rosemary, tomato paste, thyme and bay leaves. Stir to combine. Cover, transfer to oven and bake until lamb is tender, about 65 minutes.

Melt butter in heavy medium skillet over medium heat. Add mushrooms and sauté until golden, about 8 minutes. Add artichokes and zucchini and sauté until tender, about 5 minutes. Stir vegetables into stew. (*Can be prepared 1 day ahead. Cover with plastic wrap and refrigerate. Rewarm over medium heat.*) Mix in olives. Garnish with parsley. Serve over noodles.

*Black brine-cured Kalamata olives are available at Greek and Italian markets and in specialty foods sections of some supermarkets.

 Pork

Pork Chops with Garlic and Mushrooms

4 servings

4 4-ounce boneless pork chops
½ cup all purpose flour
¼ teaspoon ground ginger
    Salt and pepper

½ cup (1 stick) butter

8 garlic cloves, sliced

1 pound mushrooms, sliced
3 tablespoons sweet Sherry

Flatten pork to thickness of ¼ inch, using meat mallet, rolling pin or skillet. Combine flour and ginger. Season with salt and pepper. Dredge pork in flour.

Melt butter in heavy large skillet over medium heat. Add garlic and stir until softened, about 2 minutes. Remove with slotted spoon; set aside. Add pork and sauté until cooked through, about 2 minutes per side. Transfer to heated plates; keep warm.

Add mushrooms to skillet and stir until just soft, about 4 minutes. Mix in Sherry. Increase heat and boil until thickened to sauce consistency, about 3 minutes. Stir in garlic. Pour over pork and serve.

Molasses- and Bourbon-glazed Pork with Yams and Turnips

A green salad goes well with this.

2 servings; can be doubled or tripled

2 small turnips, peeled, halved and cut into ¼-inch-thick slices
2 small yams, cut into ⅓-inch-thick rounds
3 tablespoons butter
1 teaspoon dried thyme, crumbled
    Salt and freshly ground pepper

1 tablespoon butter
¾ to 1 pound pork tenderloins, patted dry
2 tablespoons light molasses
1 tablespoon bourbon

Preheat oven to 425°F. Mix turnips and yams in large baking dish. Top with 3 tablespoons butter and ½ teaspoon thyme. Season with salt and pepper. Bake until vegetables are tender, stirring occasionally to coat with butter, about 30 minutes.

Melt 1 tablespoon butter in heavy medium skillet over medium-high heat. Season pork with salt and pepper. Add to skillet and brown on all sides. Remove skillet from heat. Transfer pork to vegetable baking dish, pushing vegetables aside. Mix molasses and remaining ½ teaspoon thyme into drippings in skillet, then mix in bourbon. Spoon over pork and vegetables. Roast about 15 minutes for medium, turning vegetables occasionally. Transfer vegetables to plates. Slice pork. Arrange on plates and serve immediately.

Spiced Baby Back Ribs with Barbecue Sauce

4 servings

Ribs
- 16 cups canned beef broth or 8 cups beef broth and 8 cups water
- 1½ cups ground cumin
- 1 cup tomato paste
- 1 cup hot paprika
- ¾ cup red wine vinegar
- ¼ cup honey
- 3 tablespoons ground ginger
- 1½ tablespoons garlic powder
- 1 tablespoon cayenne pepper
- 1 tablespoon salt

- 4 1¼-pound trimmed pork baby back rib slabs

Spice Paste
- 1 cup hot paprika
- ½ cup (or more) beer
- ½ cup Worcestershire sauce
- ¼ cup red wine vinegar
- ¼ cup dry mustard
- 2 tablespoons garlic salt

Rattlesnake Club Barbecue Sauce*

For ribs: Combine all ingredients except ribs in heavy large pot and bring to simmer over medium heat. Add ribs and simmer until tender but not falling apart, turning occasionally, about 1¾ hours. Drain ribs; place on baking sheet.

For paste: Stir paprika, ½ cup beer, Worcestershire sauce, vinegar, mustard and salt in bowl, adding more beer if necessary to form paste. Rub over ribs. Wrap in foil. (*Can be prepared 4 days ahead. Refrigerate.*)

Position rack in center of oven and preheat to 400°F. Bake ribs 10 minutes. Turn on broiler. Remove ribs from foil and broil until blackened. Serve immediately with sauce.

*Rattlesnake Club Barbecue Sauce

Perfect with chicken, pork, lamb or beef.

Makes about 3 cups

- 1½ cups catsup
- ½ cup prepared chili sauce
- ¼ cup prepared steak sauce
- 3 tablespoons dry mustard
- 2 tablespoons grated fresh horseradish or prepared horseradish
- 1 tablespoon molasses
- 1 tablespoon red wine vinegar
- 1 tablespoon minced jalapeño chili
- 1 tablespoon garlic juice
- 1 tablespoon seedless tamarind paste,* dissolved in hot water (optional)
- 1 tablespoon (or more) hot pepper sauce (such as Tabasco)

Whisk first 10 ingredients in bowl. Add hot pepper sauce to taste. (*Can be prepared 1 week ahead. Cover and chill. Bring to room temperature.*)

*Seedless tamarind paste is available at Indian and Southeast Asian markets.

Crown Roast of Pork with Spiced Fruit Chutney

Molasses and soy sauce give this impressive main course a shiny glaze. Offer steamed broccoli as a side dish, and serve a chilled Alsatian Gewürztraminer.

8 servings

1 8-pound crown roast of pork
Salt and freshly ground pepper
1 teaspoon dried thyme, crumbled
½ cup dark unsulfured molasses

½ cup light soy sauce

Red and green grapes
Spiced Fruit Chutney*

Position rack in center of oven and preheat to 350°F. Season pork inside and out with salt and pepper. Rub with thyme. Place roast on rack set in large roasting pan. Mix molasses and soy sauce in small bowl. Brush some of mixture over roast. Roast about 2 hours for medium, basting occasionally with molasses mixture. Transfer pork to platter. Tent with foil and let stand 20 minutes.

Pour any juices accumulated on platter into sauceboat. Remove any string from roast. Fill center with grapes. Cut roast into chops at table. Spoon juices over. Serve with chutney.

*Spiced Fruit Chutney

The sweet-tart chutney is a natural with the delicious roast pork.

Makes about 6 cups

2 cups cider vinegar
1 medium onion, finely chopped
½ cup water
1 tablespoon ground ginger
2 teaspoons grated orange peel
1½ teaspoons salt
½ teaspoon cinnamon
1 garlic clove, minced
¼ teaspoon dried red pepper flakes

3 cups firmly packed golden brown sugar
2 small Bartlett pears, cored and diced
1 large Granny Smith apple, cored and diced
2 cups cranberries
½ cup dried currants

Combine first 9 ingredients in heavy medium saucepan over medium-high heat. Bring to boil, stirring frequently. Reduce heat to low and cook 15 minutes, stirring occasionally.

Add sugar, pears, apple, cranberries and currants and stir until sugar dissolves. Cook until fruits are soft and liquid thickens slightly, stirring occasionally, about 1 hour. Cool to room temperature (chutney will thicken more as it cools). (*Can be prepared 4 days ahead. Cover and refrigerate. Bring to room temperature before serving.*)

Spicy Sausage-filled Soft Tacos

2 servings; can be doubled or tripled

6-inch corn or flour tortillas
1½ tablespoons olive oil
1 onion, chopped
1 green bell pepper, diced
1 pound bulk sausage
2 teaspoons chili powder
1 teaspoon ground cumin

2 tablespoons catsup
Salt and freshly ground pepper

Shredded iceberg lettuce
Grated sharp cheddar cheese
Sour cream

Preheat oven to 350°F. Wrap tortillas in foil. Heat oil in heavy large skillet over medium heat. Add onion and cook 5 minutes, stirring occasionally. Add bell pepper and cook 3 minutes. Add sausage and cook until no longer pink, breaking up with fork. Add chili powder and cumin and cook 5 minutes. Mix in catsup. Season with salt and pepper. Cook 3 minutes, stirring. Heat tortillas in oven 10 minutes.

Serve warmed tortillas, sausage filling, lettuce, cheese and sour cream, allowing diners to assemble tacos.

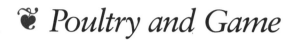 Poultry and Game

Chicken Breasts with Mushroom-Sherry Sauce

Round out the meal with broccoli.

2 servings; can be doubled

2½ tablespoons butter
3 boneless chicken breast halves, skinned

8 ounces mushrooms, quartered
3 green onions, chopped

Salt and freshly ground pepper
¼ cup dry Sherry
¼ cup canned chicken broth
⅓ cup whipping cream
Freshly cooked rice

Melt 1 tablespoon butter in heavy large skillet over medium heat. Add chicken and sauté until cooked through, turning occasionally, about 12 minutes. Transfer to plate. Pour off fat.

Melt remaining 1½ tablespoons butter in same skillet over medium-high heat. Add mushrooms and ⅔ of green onions. Season with salt and pepper. Sauté until mushrooms begin to color, about 2 minutes. Add Sherry and broth and boil until syrupy, scraping up any browned bits, about 1 minute. Add cream and boil until sauce begins to thicken, about 2 minutes. Return chicken and exuded juices on plate to skillet. Simmer until chicken is heated through and sauce thickens, about 1 minute. Adjust seasoning. Top with remaining green onions. Serve over freshly cooked rice.

Chicken Sauté in Tomato-Vinegar Sauce

Steamed broccoli is a colorful side dish.

4 servings

3 tablespoons olive oil
4 garlic cloves, chopped
1 16-ounce can Italian plum tomatoes, drained (½ cup juices reserved) and finely chopped
2 cups chicken stock or canned low-salt broth
⅓ cup (or more) red wine vinegar
1 bay leaf, broken in half

4 boneless chicken breast halves

1 teaspoon chopped fresh rosemary or ¼ teaspoon dried, crumbled
Salt and freshly ground pepper

2 tablespoons (¼ stick) unsalted butter, cut into 8 pieces
2 tablespoons chopped fresh parsley
Fresh rosemary sprigs (optional)

Heat 1 tablespoon oil in heavy large saucepan over low heat. Add garlic and sauté 2 minutes. Add tomatoes with ½ cup reserved juices, stock, ⅓ cup vinegar and bay leaf. Bring to boil. Reduce heat and simmer gently until reduced to sauce consistency, about 25 minutes. (*Can be prepared 1 day ahead. Cover and refrigerate.*)

Cut each chicken breast in half crosswise. Season both sides with rosemary, salt and pepper. Heat remaining 2 tablespoons oil in heavy large skillet over medium heat. Add chicken skin side down. Sauté until cooked through, about 5 minutes per side. Transfer chicken to platter; keep warm.

Add sauce to same skillet and bring to simmer, scraping up any browned bits. Reduce heat to low. Mix in butter 1 piece at a time. Stir in parsley. Taste sauce and adjust seasoning, adding more vinegar if sharper flavor is desired. Discard bay leaf. Spoon sauce over chicken. Garnish with rosemary sprigs if desired and serve.

Lime Ginger Chicken with Tomato and Green Pepper Salsa

4 servings

Chicken
4 boneless chicken breast halves, skinned

⅓ cup fresh lime juice
2 teaspoons grated peeled fresh ginger
3 garlic cloves, flattened
½ teaspoon dried red pepper flakes

Salsa
8 ounces ripe plum tomatoes, diced
1 medium green bell pepper, diced

¼ cup diced red onion
1 tablespoon chopped fresh cilantro
1 tablespoon olive oil
1 tablespoon fresh lime juice
1 small garlic clove, minced
Salt and freshly ground pepper

1 teaspoon olive oil
4 thick lime slices
Fresh cilantro sprigs

For chicken: Halve breasts; trim edges and fat. Pull out fillet from underside of each breast half. Cut each breast half lengthwise into three 1-inch-wide strips.

Mix lime juice, ginger, garlic and pepper flakes in nonaluminum bowl. Stir in chicken fillets and strips. Cover. Chill at least 2 hours or overnight.

For salsa: Combine first 7 ingredients in nonaluminum bowl. Season with salt and freshly ground pepper.

Heat 1 teaspoon oil in heavy large skillet (preferably nonstick) over high heat. Add chicken (in batches if necessary) and cook until brown, 1 to 2 minutes per side. Transfer to plates. Add lime slices to skillet and brown on both sides. Set 1 on each plate. Garnish with cilantro. Serve immediately with salsa.

Stir-fried Chicken with Onion and Hoisin Sauce

Nuts add crunch to a quick and tasty dish.

4 servings

1 egg white
1 tablespoon dry Sherry
½ teaspoon salt
1 pound skinned and boned chicken breasts, trimmed of all fat and sinew, cut into 1 × 2-inch pieces
1 tablespoon cornstarch
1 tablespoon vegetable oil

1 tablespoon minced peeled fresh ginger
1 large garlic clove, minced
¼ teaspoon dried red pepper flakes

6 tablespoons hoisin sauce*
1 tablespoon soy sauce
2 teaspoons dry Sherry

6 cups water
4 tablespoons vegetable oil

1 large onion, cut into 1-inch pieces
1 large red bell pepper, cut into 1-inch pieces
Salt
¾ cup unsalted toasted cashews
Freshly cooked rice

Beat egg white, 1 tablespoon Sherry and ½ teaspoon salt in medium bowl to blend. Add chicken and stir to coat. Mix in cornstarch, then 1 tablespoon oil. Refrigerate at least 30 minutes. (*Can be prepared 1 day ahead.*)

Combine ginger, garlic and pepper flakes in small bowl. Combine hoisin, soy and 2 teaspoons Sherry in another small bowl.

Bring 6 cups water to boil in large saucepan. Add 1 tablespoon oil, then chicken and stir gently to separate. Cook until coating is white, about 45 seconds. Drain in colander.

Heat 1 tablespoon oil in wok or heavy large skillet over medium-high heat. Add onion and stir-fry 2 minutes. Add bell pepper. Sprinkle with salt. Stir-fry until vegetables begin to soften, about 2 minutes. Transfer to plate. Add remaining 2 tablespoons oil to wok and heat over medium-high heat. Add ginger mixture and stir until aromatic, about 20 seconds. Add liquid mixture and bring to simmer. Add chicken and return vegetables to wok. Stir until chicken is cooked through, about 2 minutes. Mix in cashews. Serve immediately with rice.

*Available at oriental markets and in oriental sections of some supermarkets.

Coq au Vin Kebabs

The classic dish gets reinterpreted as quick and easy kebabs that you broil. The cooking time is less than 20 minutes.

8 servings

1½ cups light fruity red wine
¾ cup olive oil (preferably extra-virgin)
2 garlic cloves, pressed
2 teaspoons dried thyme, crumbled
¼ teaspoon freshly ground pepper
Pinch of salt
Pinch of freshly grated nutmeg
16 chicken thighs, meat cut in 4 pieces off each bone (skin intact)

8 small white boiling onions, peeled and halved through root end
32 medium mushrooms, stemmed

16 12-inch wooden skewers, soaked in water 1 hour, drained
Salt and freshly ground pepper

Combine first 7 ingredients in large bowl. Add chicken and onions. Toss to coat. Cover and refrigerate at least 6 hours or overnight, turning occasionally. Add mushroom caps to marinade and toss to coat. Let mixture stand 30 minutes at room temperature.

Preheat broiler. Drain chicken and vegetables; discard marinade. Thread chicken and vegetables on each skewer in following order: chicken, mushroom, chicken, onion half, chicken, mushroom and chicken. Season with salt and pepper. Broil 5 inches from heat source until chicken is cooked through, turning occasionally, about 15 minutes. Transfer to platter.

Moroccan-spiced Chicken with Lemon and Carrots

A light and exotic entrée subtly flavored with lemon.

4 servings

3 tablespoons olive oil
4 large chicken leg-thigh pieces, separated at joints
Salt and freshly ground pepper

1 large onion, chopped
1 pound carrots, peeled, cut on diagonal into ½-inch-thick slices
2 teaspoons paprika

1 teaspoon ground ginger
¼ teaspoon turmeric
⅛ teaspoon cinnamon
1 lemon, cut into 8 wedges and seeded
1 cup chicken stock or canned broth

Heat oil in heavy large skillet over medium-high heat. Season chicken with salt and pepper. Add to skillet and cook until brown on both sides. Transfer to plate.

Add onion to skillet. Reduce heat to medium-low and cook until tender, stirring occasionally, about 8 minutes. Add carrots and stir 2 minutes. Add paprika, ginger, turmeric and cinnamon and stir 1 minute. Return chicken to skillet. Add lemon and stock. Bring to boil. Reduce heat, cover and simmer until chicken is cooked through, turning chicken occasionally, about 30 minutes. (*Can be prepared 1 day ahead. Cover and refrigerate. Rewarm, covered, over medium heat, stirring occasionally.*) Garnish with cooked lemon wedges.

Sesame-coated Fried Chicken

In this version of fried chicken, boneless cubes of breast meat are marinated, threaded on skewers, coated with sesame seeds and fried. It's delicious with the soy-ginger dipping sauce.

6 servings

3 tablespoons soy sauce
2 tablespoons sake or Chinese rice wine
1½ tablespoons minced peeled fresh ginger
1 teaspoon oriental sesame oil
1 teaspoon five-spice powder*
1 teaspoon minced garlic
½ teaspoon sugar
½ teaspoon freshly ground white pepper
2 pounds boneless chicken breasts, skinned, cut into 1½-inch pieces

Cornstarch
1 large egg, beaten to blend
6 9-inch bamboo skewers, soaked 1 hour in water
1 cup cornstarch
6 tablespoons sesame seeds

4 cups safflower or corn oil (for deep frying)
Oriental Dipping Sauce*

Mix first 8 ingredients in large bowl. Add chicken and toss to coat. Cover and refrigerate overnight.

Lightly coat large baking sheet with cornstarch. Add egg to chicken mixture and toss to coat. Thread chicken on skewers, leaving small space between each piece. Mix 1 cup cornstarch with sesame seeds on large plate. Dredge skewers in mixture, pressing to adhere. Place on prepared sheet. Cover and refrigerate 1 hour, turning once.

Heat 4 cups oil in wok or heavy large deep skillet to 350°F. Add 3 chicken skewers and fry until deep golden brown and cooked through, turning constantly with tongs, about 6 minutes. Transfer to paper towels and drain. Repeat with remaining chicken skewers. Cool chicken completely. (*Can be prepared 2 hours ahead.*) Place dipping sauce in center of platter. Surround with chicken skewers and serve.

*Five-spice powder is available in the oriental sections of many supermarkets.

*Oriental Dipping Sauce

Makes about 1 cup

½ cup low-sodium soy sauce
¼ cup water
1½ tablespoons Worcestershire sauce

1 tablespoon finely shredded peeled fresh ginger

Mix all ingredients in small bowl. (*Can be prepared 1 day ahead. Chill.*) Serve at room temperature.

Parsley, Sage, Rosemary and Thyme Chicken

That classic, lyrical herb combination flavors the chicken. It's cooked and served with potatoes and shallots, making it a terrific one-dish supper. All you need is a salad. Pour a fruity Beaujolais.

4 servings

1 4½-pound chicken
    Salt
2 teaspoons dried rosemary, crumbled
1½ teaspoons ground or rubbed sage
1½ teaspoons dried thyme, crumbled
    Freshly ground pepper
2 bay leaves
5 tablespoons olive oil
4 small russet potatoes (unpeeled), quartered lengthwise, cut crosswise into ½-inch pieces

8 large shallots, peeled
1¾ cups (about) chicken stock or canned low-salt broth
¼ cup balsamic vinegar* or 3 tablespoons red wine vinegar and ¼ teaspoon sugar
6 tablespoons (¾ stick) unsalted butter, cut into 6 pieces
    Minced fresh parsley

Preheat oven to 425°F. Rub chicken inside and out with salt. Combine rosemary, sage, thyme and generous amount of pepper in small bowl. Rub some of mixture inside chicken. Place 1 bay leaf in cavity. Tie legs together to hold shape. Brush chicken with some of olive oil. Sprinkle with half of remaining herb mixture. Place in large baking pan. Surround with potatoes and shallots. Sprinkle vegetables with remaining herb mixture and remaining olive oil. Add remaining bay leaf to vegetables and mix well.

Bake chicken until juices run clear when pierced in thickest part of thigh and legs can be moved easily, basting chicken with pan juices and turning vegetables occasionally, about 1 hour 15 minutes. Transfer chicken to platter. Surround with vegetables, using slotted spoon. Tent with foil to keep warm.

Pour pan juices into large glass measuring cup and degrease. Add enough stock to measure 2 cups. Add vinegar to baking pan and bring to boil over medium heat, scraping up any browned bits. Boil until reduced to glaze, about 4 minutes. Add stock mixture and boil until reduced to ½ cup, about 10 minutes. Reduce heat to low and whisk in butter 1 piece at a time. Adjust seasoning to taste. Stir in parsley.

Surround chicken with vegetables. Pour sauce over and serve.

*Available at specialty foods stores, Italian markets and some supermarkets.

Prairie Grilled Chicken

A robust mix of catsup, honey and mustard is used to marinate chicken and then, after it is cooked, to sauce it.

6 servings

Marinade
4 large shallots
4 large garlic cloves
1½ cups catsup
¾ cup water
6 tablespoons walnut oil
6 tablespoons safflower oil
6 tablespoons honey
3 tablespoons Dijon mustard

1½ tablespoons dried tarragon, crumbled

3 3½-pound chickens, halved

Sauce
½ cup whipping cream
½ cup (1 stick) chilled unsalted butter, cut into pieces

For marinade: Insert steel knife in processor. With machine running, drop shallots and garlic through feed tube and mince. Add all remaining ingredients except chicken and mix 10 seconds.

Refrigerate 1 cup marinade for sauce. Divide remaining marinade between 2 large plastic bags. Add chicken to bags and seal tightly. Place each bag in another bag and seal. Refrigerate 24 hours, turning occasionally.

Preheat oven to 400°F. Line large baking pan with foil. Drain chicken, reserving marinade. Arrange skin side up in prepared pan. Bake until juices run clear when thigh is pierced, basting with marinade, about 40 minutes.

Meanwhile, prepare sauce: Boil reserved 1 cup marinade with cream in heavy medium saucepan until reduced by half, about 12 minutes. Remove from heat and whisk in butter.

Blend sauce in processor until completely smooth, about 2 minutes.

Preheat broiler. Broil chicken until skin browns. Return sauce to saucepan and whisk over low heat until warmed through. Transfer chicken to plates. Spoon some of sauce over. Serve, passing remaining sauce separately.

Roast Goose with Apricot and Rice Stuffing

Round out the meal with roasted potatoes and steamed broccoli. Pour either a Rhône-style red or a California Syrah.

6 servings

Stuffing
- 1 cup dried apricots, coarsely chopped
- ½ cup dried currants
- 2 cups ruby Port

- 4 cups chicken stock or canned broth
- 2 tablespoons butter
- 2 tablespoons vegetable oil
- 2 small onions, minced
- 2 celery stalks, chopped
- 2 cups long grain rice

- ½ cup chopped fresh parsley
- 2 tablespoons minced fresh thyme or 2 teaspoons dried, crumbled
- 1 teaspoon salt
- ½ teaspoon freshly ground pepper

Sauce
- 2 cups apple cider
- 4 cups Goose Stock*

Goose
- 1 11- to 13-pound goose, fat removed from cavity; neck, gizzard and heart reserved for Goose Stock*
- 1 lemon, halved
- 1 tablespoon salt
- 1 tablespoon freshly ground pepper

- 2 cups Goose Stock*

- ½ cup currant jelly

For stuffing: Place apricots and currants in separate bowls. Pour 1 cup Port over each. Let stand 6 hours.

Bring stock to boil in medium saucepan. Melt butter with oil in heavy large saucepan over medium heat. Add onions and celery and sauté 5 minutes. Add rice and stir until translucent, about 3 minutes. Add hot stock and mix well. Reduce heat to low. Cover and cook until rice is tender and all liquid is absorbed, about 20 minutes. Transfer to large bowl.

Drain apricots and currants; reserve 1 cup Port. Mix apricots, currants, parsley, thyme, salt and pepper into rice. Set rice mixture aside.

For sauce: Boil cider in heavy medium saucepan until reduced to 1 cup, about 15 minutes. Add stock and 1 cup reserved Port. Reduce heat and simmer until reduced to 1½ cups, stirring occasionally, about 30 minutes. (*Can be prepared 1 day ahead. Cover and refrigerate stuffing and Port sauce separately. Let stuffing stand 1 hour at room temperature before continuing with recipe.*)

For goose: Preheat oven to 350°F. Pierce goose skin (not meat) all over with fork. Cut off wing tips at joint. Rub goose inside and out with lemon. Sprinkle goose inside and out with salt and pepper. Fill main cavity and neck cavity loosely with stuffing. Skewer neck cavity closed. Leave main cavity open. Tie legs together. Place any remaining stuffing in a small buttered baking dish; cover with aluminum foil.

Place goose breast side up on rack set in large roasting pan. Roast goose 1¾ hours, basting every 30 minutes with stock and pan drippings.

Pour off fat accumulated in pan. Continue roasting goose until meat thermometer inserted in thickest part of thigh registers 180°F, basting goose with stock and drippings in pan every 30 minutes and covering goose with foil if browning too quickly, about 1 hour. (Place stuffing in baking dish in oven during last hour and baste with stock every 30 minutes.)

Transfer goose to heated platter. Strain pan juices into bowl and degrease. Set roasting pan over medium heat. Return juices and bring to boil, scraping up any browned bits. Transfer juices to heavy medium saucepan. Add Port sauce and simmer until reduced to 1½ cups, about 10 minutes. Add jelly and stir over medium heat until melted. Serve goose and stuffing, passing sauce separately.

*Goose Stock

Makes 6 cups

9 cups chicken stock or canned low-salt broth
Neck, gizzard and heart from 1 goose
2 celery stalks, chopped

1 carrot, peeled and chopped
1 bouquet garni (1 celery stalk, 1 bay leaf, 2 thyme sprigs, 6 peppercorns)

Simmer all ingredients in heavy large pot until liquid is reduced to 6 cups, skimming surface occasionally, about 50 minutes. Strain. (*Can be prepared 2 days ahead. Cover and refrigerate.*)

Turkey Scaloppine with Red Pepper Cream Sauce

If you can't purchase sliced breast of fresh turkey, semifreeze a whole breast and slice it on the diagonal.

4 servings

Sauce
2 large red bell peppers (about 14 ounces total)

2 oil-packed sun-dried tomatoes, drained
⅓ cup whipping cream
2 tablespoons olive oil
½ teaspoon salt

Turkey
¼ cup all purpose flour
½ teaspoon salt

¼ teaspoon Hungarian hot paprika
Cayenne pepper
4 ½-inch-thick turkey breast slices (about 2 ounces each)

2 tablespoons (¼ stick) unsalted butter
2 tablespoons olive oil

Minced fresh thyme or chives

For sauce: Preheat broiler. Line baking pan with foil. Cut bell peppers lengthwise into 4 pieces, discarding cores and seeds. Arrange skin side up on prepared baking pan. Broil 6 inches from heat source until skin is blackened. Transfer to paper bag and seal tightly. When cool, remove skin and cut into ½-inch dice.

Insert steel knife in processor. Place roasted bell peppers and sun-dried tomatoes in work bowl. Puree until smooth, about 2 minutes. Add remaining sauce ingredients and process until smooth, about 20 seconds. Strain through fine sieve. (*Sauce can be prepared 2 days ahead. Cover and refrigerate.*)

For turkey: Combine first 3 ingredients on large sheet of waxed paper. Season with cayenne pepper. Place each turkey slice between two sheets of

Cowboy Steak with Red Chili Onion Rings

Michael Lamotte

Clockwise from center: Herbed Phyllo Purses with Camembert and Walnuts; Marmalade-glazed Chicken Wings; Tomato Croutons with Bacon and Basil and Toasted Mini Bagels with Smoked Salmon and Caviar; Avocado Pâté with Parsley and Pistachios; Grilled Shrimp with Dilled Asparagus and Garlic Mayonnaise

Aaron Rezny

Antipasto of Italian Cured Meats, Olives and Breadsticks (recipe not included); Pasta with Gorgonzola and Walnut Sauce; Radicchio, Curly Endive, Fennel and Apple Salad; Flash-in-the-Pan Birthday Cake

Clockwise from upper right: Maple Crème Caramel; Apple Cider Tartlet; Bittersweet Chocolate Terrine with Vanilla Custard Sauce; Sweet Plum Cream; Walnut Lace Cookies

Grilled Prosciutto and
Fontina Sandwiches;
Fig, Melon and Mint Salad

Kathryn Russell

plastic wrap. Flatten with meat pounder until ⅛ inch thick. Remove from plastic. Pat dry. Dip into flour mixture.

Melt butter with oil in heavy large skillet over high heat. Add turkey and cook until brown, about 1 minute per side. Transfer to warm platter.

Heat sauce in heavy small saucepan over low heat or in microwave on Medium. Spoon over turkey. Garnish with thyme or chives and serve.

Turkey Cutlets Piccata

2 servings; can be doubled or tripled

All purpose flour
Salt and freshly ground pepper
¾ **pound turkey cutlets or breast slices cut ⅜ inch thick**

4 **tablespoons (½ stick) butter**

1 **tablespoon vegetable oil**
2 **tablespoons fresh lemon juice**
1½ **tablespoons dry white wine**
1½ **tablespoons minced fresh parsley**
1 **tablespoon drained capers**

Place flour on plate; season with salt and pepper. Dredge turkey in flour.

Melt 1 tablespoon butter with oil in heavy medium skillet over medium-high heat. Add turkey and sauté until just cooked through, about 2 minutes per side. Divide turkey between heated plates. Add remaining 3 tablespoons butter to same skillet and melt over medium heat. Add lemon juice, wine and turkey juice from plates and bring to boil, scraping up any browned bits. Add parsley and capers. Season with salt and pepper. Spoon over turkey.

❦ Fish and Shellfish

Sea Bass with Garlic Herb Oil

Keep this recipe for herb oil in your files for cooking any white-fleshed fish or even chicken.

2 servings; can be doubled or tripled

6 **tablespoons olive oil (preferably extra-virgin)**
3 **large garlic cloves, flattened and peeled**
⅛ **teaspoon (generous) dried red pepper flakes**
4 **teaspoons fresh lemon juice**

1 **teaspoon dried marjoram, crumbled**

2 **¾-inch-thick sea bass fillets**

Salt and freshly ground pepper
Minced fresh Italian parsley

Cook oil and garlic in heavy small saucepan over low heat until garlic begins to brown, about 1 minute. Discard garlic. Add pepper flakes to oil and stir 30 seconds. Remove from heat. Add lemon juice and marjoram.

Place fish on large plate. Spoon oil over, turning to coat both sides. Let stand 30 minutes.

Preheat broiler. Season fish with salt and pepper. Broil until just cooked through, about 7 minutes, turning once. Sprinkle fish with parsley and serve.

Bluefish with Fried Capers and Spinach

4 servings

2 12-ounce bluefish, mahimahi or yellowtail fillets (about ½ inch thick), each cut on diagonal into 4 pieces
2 tablespoons olive oil
2 tablespoons minced fresh chives
2 tablespoons minced fresh tarragon or 1 teaspoon dried, crumbled
1 tablespoon minced garlic
   Salt and freshly ground pepper

4 thin tomato slices, halved
4 thin red onion slices, halved
¼ cup fine dry breadcrumbs

¾ cup olive oil
¼ cup capers, drained and patted dry

½ pound fresh spinach, stemmed
   Fresh lemon juice

   Lemon wedges

Preheat oven to 375°F. Set 4 pieces of fish in baking pan. Drizzle with 2 tablespoons olive oil. Sprinkle with chives, tarragon, garlic and salt and pepper. Top each piece of fish with 1 tomato slice half and 1 red onion slice half. Cover each with another piece of fish. Top each with another tomato slice half and red onion slice half. Sprinkle with ¼ cup dry breadcrumbs. Bake until fish is cooked through, about 12 minutes.

Heat ¾ cup olive oil in heavy medium skillet to 325°F. Add capers and fry until crisp, about 4 minutes. Remove capers using slotted spoon and drain thoroughly on paper towels.

Transfer 2 tablespoons olive oil to heavy large skillet (reserve remaining oil for another use) and heat over medium-high heat. Add spinach and cook until wilted. Season to taste with salt, pepper and lemon juice.

Set 1 layered fish on each plate. Sprinkle with capers. Surround with spinach. Serve with lemon wedges.

Salmon with Garlic Mayonnaise

2 servings

½ cup mayonnaise
¼ cup chopped fresh parsley
1 teaspoon lemon juice
1 teaspoon Dijon mustard

1 garlic clove, minced
   Salt and freshly ground pepper
2 7-ounce salmon fillets
   Olive oil

Preheat broiler. Combine first 5 ingredients in bowl. Season with salt and pepper. Brush salmon with oil. Broil to desired degree of doneness, about 3 minutes per side for medium. Transfer to plates. Spoon garlic mayonnaise on side.

Salmon in Vodka Cream Sauce with Green Peppercorns

6 servings

8 tablespoons (1 stick) unsalted butter
1 onion, thinly sliced

1 pound spinach

6 6-ounce salmon fillets
   Salt and freshly ground pepper

3 tablespoons olive oil
1½ cups whipping cream
½ cup vodka
2 tablespoons green peppercorns in water, drained and crushed
3 tablespoons fresh lime juice

¼ cup snipped fresh chives

Preheat oven to 350°F. Combine 4 tablespoons butter and onion in large Dutch oven. Cover and bake until onion is golden brown, stirring occasionally, approximately 45 minutes.

Stir spinach into onion and bake until just wilted, about 3 minutes. Remove from oven; keep warm.

Season salmon with salt and pepper. Heat oil in heavy large skillet over high heat. Add salmon in batches and cook about 3 minutes per side for medium. Transfer to platter. Tent with foil to keep warm. Pour off excess oil from skillet. Add cream and vodka and boil until slightly thickened, about 4 minutes. Add green peppercorns and remaining 4 tablespoons butter and stir until butter is just melted. Mix in lime juice; season with salt and pepper.

Divide spinach and onion mixture among plates. Top each with salmon fillet. Spoon sauce over. Sprinkle with snipped fresh chives and serve.

Red Snapper with Chili-Corn Sauce

4 servings

4 ears corn
2 tablespoons olive oil
2 jalapeño chilies, seeded and minced
1 teaspoon chopped shallot
1 teaspoon chopped garlic

1 tablespoon chili powder
1 cup whipping cream
  Salt and freshly ground pepper
  Fresh lemon juice

4 6-ounce red snapper fillets

Cut kernels from corn. Heat 1 tablespoon oil in heavy medium saucepan over medium heat. Add chilies, shallot and garlic and sauté 2 minutes. Mix in chili powder, then cream and corn. Cook until sauce thickens, stirring occasionally, about 5 minutes. Season with salt, pepper and lemon juice.

Heat remaining 1 tablespoon oil in heavy large skillet over medium-high heat. Add fish and cook until golden brown, about 4 minutes per side.

Meanwhile, rewarm sauce over medium heat. Spoon onto plates. Top with fish fillets and serve.

Broiled Swordfish with Olives and Thyme

2 servings; can be doubled or tripled

⅓ cup meat from pitted Kalamata (Greek) olives (about 8 large)
1½ tablespoons olive oil
½ teaspoon dried thyme, crumbled

2 swordfish steaks (about 1 inch thick)
  Olive oil
  Freshly ground pepper

Finely mince olives in processor. Add 1½ tablespoons oil and thyme and blend until well combined. (*Can be prepared 1 day ahead. Refrigerate.*)

Preheat broiler. Brush one side of fish with oil; sprinkle with pepper. Broil 3½ minutes. Turn. Brush second side with oil and sprinkle with pepper. Broil until almost cooked through, about 3½ minutes. Spread olive mixture over fish. Broil 30 seconds. Serve hot.

Grilled Tuna with Salade Niçoise

This is a one-dish dinner.

2 servings; can be doubled

2 ⅓- to ½-pound tuna or swordfish
  steaks or salmon or sea bass fillets
  (½ inch thick)
  Olive oil
  Fresh lemon juice

4 small White Rose potatoes,
  halved lengthwise
½ pound green beans, trimmed and
  cut into thirds

1½ tablespoons white wine vinegar
1½ tablespoons Dijon mustard
2 small shallots, minced
6 tablespoons olive oil
2 teaspoons minced fresh thyme or
  ½ teaspoon dried, crumbled
  Salt and freshly ground pepper
⅓ cup Niçoise olives

1 tomato, sliced

Rub fish with oil and lemon juice. Let stand while preparing salad.

Add potatoes and beans to large pot of boiling salted water. Cook beans until just crisp-tender. Remove with slotted spoon. Refresh under cold water; drain well. Continue cooking potatoes until tender. Drain. Cut crosswise into ½-inch-thick slices. Transfer potato slices to medium bowl.

Combine vinegar, mustard and shallots in small bowl. Gradually whisk in 6 tablespoons olive oil. Mix in thyme. Season with salt and pepper. Mix ⅓ of dressing into potatoes. Cool. Add beans, olives and half of remaining dressing to potatoes and toss to blend. Adjust seasoning with salt and pepper.

Preheat broiler. Season fish with salt and pepper. Broil until just cooked through, about 4 minutes per side. Divide fish and salad between plates. Garnish with tomato. Serve, passing remaining dressing separately.

Grilled Whitefish with Marinated Peppers, Tomatillos and Cilantro

4 servings

2 medium red bell peppers, cut into
  1-inch-long julienne strips
2 medium yellow bell peppers, cut
  into 1-inch-long julienne strips
2 medium green bell peppers, cut
  into 1-inch-long julienne strips
4 tomatillos,* husked and cut into
  ⅛-inch-thick wedges
3 jalapeño chilies, seeded and
  minced

¾ cup olive oil (preferably extra-
  virgin)
½ cup fresh lime juice

2 bunches fresh cilantro, stemmed
  and minced
4 8-ounce whitefish fillets with
  skin, patted dry
  Salt and freshly ground pepper

Toss bell peppers, tomatillos and chilies with ½ cup oil and lime juice in large bowl. Let stand 2 hours.

Add cilantro to bell pepper mixture. Prepare barbecue (high heat). Brush both sides of fish with remaining ¼ cup oil. Season with salt and pepper. Place fish on rack skin side down and grill until just opaque, 2 to 3 minutes per side. Transfer to plates. Spoon pepper mixture over and serve.

*A tomatillo resembles a green tomato with a paper-thin husk. Available at Latin American markets, specialty foods stores and many supermarkets.

Margarita Shrimp

This is a great do-ahead taco or tostado filling.

4 servings

5 tablespoons corn oil
1 pound uncooked medium shrimp, peeled, deveined and halved lengthwise
½ cup minced green onions
2 large garlic cloves, minced

¼ cup tequila

2 tablespoons fresh lime juice
½ teaspoon Margarita salt or coarse salt
Lime wedges

Heat oil in heavy large skillet over medium-high heat. Add shrimp, green onions and garlic and sauté until shrimp turn pink, about 1 minute. Remove from heat and add tequila. Return to heat and bring to boil, scraping up any browned bits. Transfer to medium bowl; cool. (*Can be prepared 6 hours ahead. Refrigerate.*)

Toss shrimp with lime juice and salt. Garnish with lime wedges and serve.

Shrimp Enchiladas con Queso

6 servings

½ cup (1 stick) butter
½ cup chopped red bell pepper
½ cup minced onion
1 medium jalapeño chili, minced
1 fresh Anaheim (California) chili,* diced
1 garlic clove, minced
1 teaspoon minced fresh oregano or ½ teaspoon dried, crumbled
½ teaspoon salt
Pinch of freshly ground white pepper
Pinch of cayenne pepper
1 cup whipping cream

3 cups grated Monterey Jack cheese (about 12 ounces)
½ cup sour cream

1 pound uncooked medium shrimp, peeled and deveined
1 cup chopped green onions
2 medium tomatoes, peeled, seeded and chopped

12 9-inch flour tortillas

Hot pepper sauce
Worcestershire sauce

Melt ¼ cup butter in heavy large saucepan over medium heat. Add bell pepper, onion, both chilies, garlic and oregano and cook until vegetables are tender, stirring occasionally, about 5 minutes. Add salt. Season with white pepper and cayenne. Add cream and bring to boil, scraping up any browned bits. Reduce heat and simmer 3 minutes. Slowly mix in 1 cup cheese and stir until melted. Remove sauce from heat. Stir in sour cream.

Preheat oven to 350°F. Melt remaining ¼ cup butter in heavy large skillet over high heat. Add shrimp and ½ cup green onions and cook until shrimp are just pink, stirring frequently, about 2 minutes. Stir in half of tomatoes and half of cream sauce. Spoon about ⅓ cup shrimp mixture into each tortilla. Roll up tightly. Arrange seam side down in 9 × 16-inch baking dish. (*Can be prepared 2 hours ahead. Cover tortillas and remaining sauce separately and refrigerate.*) Spoon remaining sauce over tortillas. Cover with foil. Bake until warmed through, about 30 minutes.

Sprinkle enchiladas with remaining 2 cups cheese, ½ cup green onions and tomatoes. Serve enchiladas immediately, passing hot pepper sauce and Worcestershire sauce separately.

*Anaheim chilies are available at Latin American markets and some supermarkets.

❧ *Eggs, Cheese and Vegetables*

Corn Bread and Goat Cheese Soufflé

Assemble this a day ahead and pop it in the oven about one hour before you're ready to eat. The salsa adds color and zip.

6 servings

Corn Bread
- 1½ cups yellow cornmeal
- 1 cup unbleached all purpose flour
- 2 tablespoons sugar
- 2 teaspoons baking powder
- ½ teaspoon baking soda
- ⅛ teaspoon salt
- 1 cup buttermilk
- 3 tablespoons unsalted butter, melted
- 1 egg, beaten to blend

Soufflé
- 12 eggs
- 2½ cups milk
- 1½ cups buttermilk
- 2 teaspoons Dijon mustard
- ½ teaspoon freshly grated nutmeg
- ⅛ teaspoon cayenne pepper
- Salt and freshly ground pepper
- 12 ounces fresh goat cheese (such as Montrachet), crumbled (about 3 cups)
- 4 ounces sharp cheddar cheese, grated (about 1½ cups)

Fresh cilantro sprigs
Salsa Cruda*

For corn bread: Preheat oven to 400°F. Grease 9 × 13-inch glass baking dish. Mix cornmeal, flour, sugar, baking powder, baking soda and salt in medium bowl. Make well in center. Add buttermilk, butter and egg to well. Mix until just blended. Spread batter into prepared dish. Bake until tester inserted in center comes out clean and top is golden brown, about 18 minutes. Invert bread onto rack and cool (bread may break into pieces).

For soufflé: Grease clean 9 × 13-inch glass baking dish. Whisk eggs, milk, buttermilk and mustard in medium bowl. Add nutmeg and cayenne. Season with salt and pepper. Cut corn bread in half horizontally into 2 layers, using serrated knife. Place bottom half of corn bread in prepared dish. Sprinkle half of goat cheese and half of cheddar cheese over. Top with second half of corn bread. Cover with remaining cheeses. Pour egg and milk mixture over. Cover and refrigerate overnight.

Preheat oven to 350°F. Bake soufflé until custard is set, about 45 minutes. Let stand 15 minutes before serving. Garnish with cilantro. Serve with salsa.

*Salsa Cruda

Makes about 3 cups

- 4 medium tomatoes
- 1 cup finely chopped red onion
- 2 tablespoons (about) minced seeded jalapeño chilies
- 2 tablespoons finely chopped fresh cilantro
- 1 tablespoon red wine vinegar
- 1 tablespoon fresh lime juice
- 1 garlic clove, minced
- ½ teaspoon salt

Peel, seed and chop tomatoes. Transfer tomatoes and their juice to medium bowl. Mix in onion, 1 tablespoon chilies, cilantro, vinegar, lime juice, garlic and salt. Taste and add remaining chilies if desired. (*Can be prepared 4 hours ahead. Cover and refrigerate.*) Serve at room temperature.

Baked Eggs with Peppers and Mushrooms

So much easier than last-minute omelets, this delicious dish can be baked without any attention from the cook.

6 servings

1 small onion, quartered
1 red bell pepper
1 green bell pepper
5 large mushrooms
2 tablespoons (¼ stick) unsalted butter
   Freshly ground pepper

4 ounces chilled mild Colby cheese

6 large eggs
1 cup whipping cream
¼ cup milk
1¼ teaspoons salt
¼ teaspoon ground cumin
¼ teaspoon dried thyme, crumbled
2 dashes of hot pepper sauce (such as Tabasco)

Insert steel knife in processor. Using on/off turns, process onion until minced.

Cut bell peppers and mushrooms into ¼-inch dice. Melt butter in heavy medium skillet over medium heat. Add onion, bell peppers and mushrooms. Cook until tender, stirring occasionally, about 7 minutes. Season to taste with pepper. (**Or to microwave:** Melt butter in shallow 10-inch round microwave dish. Add vegetables. Cook uncovered on High until soft, stirring every 2 minutes, about 7 minutes. Season to taste with pepper.) (*Can be prepared 1 day ahead. Cover and refrigerate.*)

Position rack in center of oven and preheat to 325°F. Generously butter shallow 8-cup round baking dish.

Insert shredding disk in processor. Using light pressure, shred cheese. Sprinkle evenly over bottom and sides of dish, pressing lightly.

Insert steel knife. Process eggs, cream, milk, salt, cumin, thyme and hot pepper sauce 5 seconds. Set aside ⅓ cup of vegetable mixture; add remainder to processor and mix until combined, using 1 or 2 on/off turns.

Pour egg mixture into prepared dish. Bake until eggs are almost set in center, about 30 minutes. Sprinkle reserved vegetables over top. Bake until eggs are just set, about 10 minutes longer. Serve hot, cutting into wedges.

Green Onion and Red Pepper Tart

Sweet and sour vegetables, goat cheese and a light custard make this tart as distinctive as it is delicious. Try it as an hors d'oeuvre, a first course or light entrée.

Makes 1 tart

3½ tablespoons unsalted butter
¼ cup pine nuts
1 large red bell pepper, diced
2 teaspoons sugar
2 teaspoons red wine vinegar
2 bunches green onions, trimmed and coarsely chopped
1½ tablespoons unbleached all purpose flour

⅔ cup half and half
2 egg whites

3 egg yolks
1 tablespoon snipped fresh dill or 1 teaspoon dried dillweed
½ teaspoon salt
   Freshly ground pepper

1½ teaspoons Dijon mustard
1 9-inch baked Butter-Flake Pastry Crust*
3 ounces fresh goat cheese (such as Montrachet)

Position rack in center of oven and preheat to 375°F. Melt ½ tablespoon butter in heavy large skillet over medium heat. Add pine nuts and cook until light brown, stirring frequently, about 4 minutes. Remove using slotted spoon. Add remaining 3 tablespoons butter to skillet and melt. Add bell pepper and cook until slightly softened, stirring occasionally, about 4 minutes. Add sugar and vinegar and stir until syrupy, about 1½ minutes. Add green onions and flour and stir until onions are hot, about 1 minute. (**Or to microwave:** Melt ½ tablespoon butter in shallow microwave-safe dish. Add pine nuts; cook uncovered on High until light brown, watching carefully and stirring often, about 3½ minutes. Remove using slotted spoon. Add remaining butter to dish and melt. Add bell pepper and cook on High until slightly softened, about 3 minutes. Add vinegar and sugar and cook until syrupy, about 4 minutes. Mix in green onions and flour and cook until thickened, stirring once, about 1 minute.)

Mix half and half, whites, yolks, dill, salt and pepper in processor.

Spread mustard over bottom of crust. Spoon in vegetables; spread custard evenly over. Break cheese into small pieces and dot evenly atop, pressing lightly to adhere. Place tart in pan on baking sheet and bake 35 minutes. Sprinkle pine nuts over; continue baking until puffed and lightly browned, about 10 minutes.

*Butter-Flake Pastry Crust

Makes one 9-inch pastry shell

½ cup (1 stick) chilled unsalted butter, cut into 8 pieces
5 tablespoons ice water
1 large egg yolk

½ teaspoon salt
1½ cups unbleached all purpose flour

Coarsely chop butter in processor using on/off turns. Add water, egg yolk and salt and process until just combined. Add flour and process until dough just starts to gather together, about 4 seconds. Do not overprocess; do not allow dough to form ball.

Transfer dough to large plastic bag. Working through bag, form into ball; flatten into disk. Refrigerate dough at least 25 minutes.

Let dough stand at room temperature until soft enough to roll without cracking. Roll dough out on well-floured surface to ⅛-inch-thick round. Transfer to 9-inch-diameter tart pan with removable bottom. Fit dough into pan loosely, easing into corners with fingers. Trim edges, leaving ½-inch overhang. Fold in overhang and press lightly. Pinch edge to form decorative border. Refrigerate pastry 30 minutes.

Position rack in center of oven and preheat to 425°F. Pierce pastry with fork. Line shell with parchment or foil. Fill with pie weights or dried beans. Place on baking sheet and bake until pastry is set, about 12 minutes. Remove beans and foil. Bake until pastry is golden brown, about 10 minutes. Cool on rack.

Vegetarian Chili

A colorful assortment of vegetables and beans makes this dish a hearty winner.

Makes 6 cups

1 cup dried pinto beans

2 tablespoons olive oil
2 cups diced peeled eggplant
1 cup chopped onion
1 large garlic clove, chopped
1 tablespoon chili powder
1 teaspoon ground cumin
1½ cups diced unpeeled zucchini
1 cup diced peeled carrots
1 cup diced red bell pepper
1 cup diced green bell pepper
2 cups chopped ripe tomatoes or one 28-ounce can Italian plum tomatoes with juice

1 tablespoon (or more) minced seeded fresh jalapeño chili or pickled jalapeño chili
2 cups (or more) cold water

Freshly ground pepper
Salt (optional)
1 cup diced trimmed green beans
1 cup diced yellow crookneck squash

½ cup plain nonfat yogurt
1 tablespoon chopped fresh cilantro

Soak pinto beans in enough water to cover in bowl overnight. Or, combine beans with enough water to cover in heavy medium saucepan and boil 2 minutes. Remove from heat, cover and let stand 1 hour. Drain beans.

Heat oil in heavy large saucepan over medium heat. Add eggplant, onion and garlic and cook until onion is translucent, stirring frequently, about 10 minutes. Add chili powder and cumin and stir 1 minute. Reduce heat to low. Add 1 cup zucchini, carrots and ½ cup each red and green bell pepper. Cover and cook until tender, stirring occasionally, about 10 minutes. Add tomatoes and 1 tablespoon jalapeño chili and bring to simmer. Add pinto beans and 2 cups water and bring to boil, stirring occasionally. Reduce heat, cover and simmer until beans are almost tender, stirring occasionally, 1¾ hours.

Uncover chili and simmer until pinto beans are very tender, stirring occasionally and adding up to 1 cup additional water as necessary, about 45 minutes. Season to taste with additional jalapeño chili, pepper and salt, if desired. Stir in remaining ½ cup zucchini, ½ cup each red and green bell peppers, green beans and squash and simmer until crisp-tender, stirring occasionally, about 10 minutes. (*Can be prepared 2 days ahead. Refrigerate. Rewarm before serving.*)

Ladle chili into bowls. Spoon yogurt onto each. Garnish with cilantro.

Spicy Squash and Black Bean Stew with Cilantro Pesto

Round out this satisfying main course with a tossed green salad and some steamed flour tortillas.

8 servings

1 cup dried black beans, rinsed
8 cups water
4 dried ancho chilies,* stemmed and seeded
1 1-inch piece cinnamon stick

⅓ cup plus 3 tablespoons olive oil
2 medium onions, diced
4 garlic cloves, minced
1 tablespoon coriander seeds, ground
2 teaspoons cumin seeds, ground
1 teaspoon dried oregano, crumbled
1 teaspoon dried sage, crumbled
1 teaspoon dried marjoram, crumbled
1 teaspoon ground mace
1 teaspoon freshly ground pepper

½ cup dry white wine
1¼ pounds butternut squash, peeled, seeded, cut into 1-inch cubes
2 yams, peeled, cut into 1-inch cubes
1 28-ounce can Italian plum tomatoes, chopped, juices reserved

¾ pound mushrooms, sliced
3 tablespoons mushroom soy sauce** or regular soy sauce

2 zucchini, halved lengthwise and cut crosswise into ½-inch-thick slices
Salt and freshly ground pepper
1 yellow bell pepper, cut julienne
1 red bell pepper, cut julienne
Cilantro Pesto***
Fresh cilantro sprigs

Combine beans with 5 cups water in heavy large saucepan. Combine chilies with 3 cups water in heavy medium saucepan. Let chilies soak for 3 hours and beans soak for 8 hours.

Drain chilies, reserving ¼ cup soaking liquid. Puree chilies with reserved soaking liquid in blender.

Bring beans to boil in their soaking liquid. Add cinnamon. Reduce heat and simmer until tender, about 1¼ hours.

Heat ⅓ cup oil in another heavy large saucepan over high heat. Add onions, garlic, coriander, cumin, oregano, sage, marjoram, mace and pepper and sauté 2 minutes. Add wine and boil until almost all liquid evaporates, stirring constantly, about 4 minutes. Add squash and yams and sauté 1 minute. Add chili puree and tomatoes with ½ cup reserved juices. Reduce heat to low, cover and cook until vegetables are almost tender, stirring occasionally and adding more reserved tomato juices if necessary, about 35 minutes. Add to beans.

Heat remaining 3 tablespoons oil in heavy large skillet over high heat. Add mushrooms and sauté until golden, about 4 minutes. Add soy sauce and sauté 1 minute. Add to beans. (*Stew can be prepared 1 day ahead. Cover and refrigerate. Rewarm before continuing.*)

Add zucchini to stew. Increase heat to high and cook 2 minutes, stirring constantly. Season with salt and pepper. Ladle stew into bowls. Sprinkle bell peppers over. Top with dollop of pesto. Garnish with cilantro sprigs.

*Available at Latin American markets and specialty foods stores.

**Mushroom soy sauce is available at oriental markets and natural foods stores.

***Cilantro Pesto

A takeoff on the traditional Italian pesto sauce, this southwestern version is made with pumpkin seeds instead of pine nuts and cilantro instead of basil.

Makes about 2 cups

2 cups loosely packed fresh cilantro leaves
1 cup loosely packed fresh parsley leaves
¾ cup roasted salted pumpkin seeds*
½ cup freshly grated Parmesan cheese (about 1½ ounces)
½ cup fresh lime juice
1 large jalapeño chili, seeded
1 garlic clove
¾ cup olive oil
Salt and freshly ground pepper

Puree first 7 ingredients in blender, stopping occasionally to scrape down sides of container. With machine running, gradually add oil and blend until smooth. Season with salt and pepper. (*Can be prepared 3 days ahead. Press plastic wrap onto surface of pesto. Cover tightly and refrigerate. Bring to room temperature before serving.*)

*Also known as *pepitas*. Available at Latin American markets and many supermarkets.

5 ❦ Vegetables, Grains and Breads

Side dishes often make the difference between a good meal and a truly memorable one. The recipes here offer a delightful change from ordinary boiled carrots or potatoes, and although they're short on preparation time, they're long on flavor and character. Add pizzazz to a broiled steak with Roasted New Potatoes and Shallots with Caraway or Green Beans with Browned Butter and Balsamic Vinegar. Or pair grilled tuna with zesty Broccoli and Carrots in Garlic Oil; an ideal do-ahead dish, the vegetables are marinated in a chili-and-garlic oil and then tossed with lemon juice just before serving. Butternut Squash with Apples and Cranberries is a natural with the holiday turkey. Liven up roast chicken with Jalapeño Cheese Grits or Spiced Couscous—the nutty grain is studded with currants and scented with allspice.

Fragrant breads, rolls and muffins fresh from the oven are everybody's favorite. And they're easier to make than you might think—as you'll see in the recipes here. Many of the steps are do-ahead, and breads also freeze beautifully, so you can make them when you have some extra time, then pop them into the freezer. Serve a basket of Corn Sticks with Bacon with some hearty soups for an easygoing supper. Add a festive note to a breakfast or brunch with Cinnamon Raisin Bread, made simple with the processor, or a selection of muffins and quick breads including Apricot Pecan Bread and Power Pear-Oat Muffins, packed with whole grains, fruits and high-fiber yams.

❧ *Vegetables*

Green Beans with Browned Butter and Balsamic Vinegar

6 servings

3 tablespoons butter
1 tablespoon balsamic vinegar*
Salt and freshly ground pepper

1½ pounds string beans, trimmed

Combine butter, vinegar, salt and pepper in heavy medium skillet over medium heat. Cook until mixture begins to brown, stirring constantly, about 4 minutes.

Blanch beans in large pot of boiling water until crisp-tender, about 5 minutes. Drain in colander. Transfer to serving dish. Spoon browned butter mixture over beans and serve.

*Available at specialty foods stores, Italian markets and some supermarkets.

White Beans with Sage, Garlic and Olive Oil

For best flavor, you should begin to prepare this side dish two days ahead.

16 servings

2 pounds dried navy beans

1⅓ cups olive oil
18 fresh sage leaves

5 garlic cloves, pressed

6 tablespoons olive oil
Salt and freshly ground pepper

Rinse beans and place in large bowl. Cover generously with cold water. Let soak overnight at room temperature.

Position rack in center of oven and preheat to 300°F. Drain beans and transfer to large Dutch oven or covered casserole. Add 1⅓ cups oil, 12 sage leaves and garlic. Add enough water to cover beans by 2 inches. Cover and bake until beans are tender but not broken, stirring occasionally and adding more water if necessary to keep moist, about 3 hours. Cool to room temperature. (*Can be prepared 2 days ahead. Cover and refrigerate.*)

Chop 6 fresh sage leaves. Add to beans with 6 tablespoons oil. Season with salt and generous amount of pepper. Serve at room temperature.

Lentils and Carrots with Marjoram

If there is any of this delicious side dish left over, turn it into a soup for the next night by thinning with broth or cream.

2 to 4 servings; can be doubled or tripled

2 tablespoons olive oil
1 large onion, chopped
2 large carrots, sliced into rounds
2 large garlic cloves, minced
1 cup (rounded) dried lentils

2 cups (or more) canned chicken broth
1 teaspoon dried marjoram, crumbled
Salt and freshly ground pepper

Heat oil in heavy medium saucepan over medium heat. Add onion and sauté until soft, about 8 minutes. Add carrots and garlic and stir 2 minutes. Add lentils, then 2 cups broth. Cover and simmer until lentils are just tender and broth is absorbed, uncovering at end if necessary to evaporate liquid, or adding more broth if too dry, 45 minutes to 1 hour. Mix in marjoram. Season with salt and pepper.

Broccoli and Carrots in Garlic Oil

*The vegetables are mari-
nated in a chili-and-garlic
oil and then tossed with
some fresh lemon juice just
before serving.*

8 servings

1½ pounds carrots, peeled and cut
diagonally into ¼-inch-thick
slices
1 large bunch broccoli, cut into
florets with 2-inch-long stalks

6 tablespoons olive oil

8 small dried red chilies
1 teaspoon mustard seeds
12 medium garlic cloves, halved

Salt
2 tablespoons fresh lemon juice

Bring large pot of salted water to boil. Add carrots and cook until almost tender,
about 5 minutes. Transfer to bowl of ice water using slotted spoon. Add broccoli
to pot and cook until almost tender, about 2 minutes. Drain. Refresh in ice
water. Drain vegetables well. Transfer to large bowl.

Heat oil in heavy medium skillet over medium-high heat. Add chilies and
cook 30 seconds. Add mustard seeds and stir until chilies brown and seeds
darken, about 30 more seconds. Add garlic. Reduce heat to low and sauté until
golden brown, about 1 minute. Pour oil into small bowl. Cool completely. (*Can
be prepared 8 hours ahead. Chill vegetables. Store oil at room temperature.*)

Discard chilies and garlic; pour oil over vegetables. Season with salt. Cover
and let stand 4 hours at room temperature. Add lemon juice and toss to coat just
before serving.

Brussels Sprouts with Prosciutto and Leeks

16 servings

4 pounds brussels sprouts, outer
leaves removed, halved lengthwise

10 tablespoons (1¼ sticks) unsalted
butter
3 medium leeks (white and pale
green parts only), cut into ¼-inch
pieces

6 ounces thinly sliced prosciutto,
cut julienne
Salt and freshly ground pepper

Cook brussels sprouts in large pot of boiling salted water until just tender, about
5 minutes. Drain. Refresh under cold water and drain again. (*Can be prepared
1 day ahead. Wrap in kitchen towel and then plastic bag; refrigerate.*)

Melt butter in heavy large deep skillet over medium heat. Add leeks and
sauté until softened, about 5 minutes. Add brussels sprouts and sauté 5 minutes.
Add prosciutto and toss to combine. Season with salt and pepper. Transfer to
platter and serve.

Sweet-and-Sour Cabbage

6 servings

¼ cup (½ stick) unsalted butter
1 onion, thinly sliced
½ cup balsamic vinegar*
2 tablespoons golden brown sugar
6 whole cloves
6 juniper berries

1 2-pound head red cabbage, finely
shredded
2 tablespoons dark unsulfured
molasses
Salt and freshly ground pepper

Melt butter in heavy large skillet over medium heat. Add onion and sauté until
translucent, about 3 minutes. Add vinegar, sugar, cloves and juniper berries and

bring to boil, stirring constantly. Mix in cabbage. Reduce heat to low. Cover and cook until cabbage is very tender and almost no liquid remains in skillet, stirring occasionally, about 40 minutes. Mix in molasses. Season with salt and pepper. (*Can be prepared 1 day ahead. Cover and refrigerate. Rewarm over low heat.*)

*Available at specialty foods stores, Italian markets and some supermarkets.

Corn Fritters

These crisp fritters can— surprisingly—be made up to five hours ahead.

Makes about 25

2 10-ounce packages frozen whole kernel corn
2 tablespoons (¼ stick) unsalted butter
2 tablespoons sugar

¼ cup unbleached all purpose flour
¼ cup matzo meal or unsalted cracker crumbs

1¼ teaspoons salt
1 teaspoon baking powder
¼ teaspoon cayenne pepper
    Freshly ground pepper
2 eggs, beaten to blend
2 tablespoons whipping cream
1½ tablespoons chopped fresh chives

    Corn oil (for frying)

Cook corn in saucepan of boiling water until tender, about 5 minutes. Drain well. Melt butter in heavy large skillet over medium heat. Add corn and sauté 3 minutes. Add sugar and stir 2 minutes. Transfer corn to small bowl using slotted spoon. Set aside.

Mix dry ingredients in large bowl. Stir in eggs, cream, chives and corn.

Heat 1 inch oil in heavy large skillet to 350°F. Carefully drop batter by heaping tablespoons into oil. Cook in batches until deep golden brown, about 3 minutes per side. Transfer to paper towels using slotted spoon and drain. (*Can be prepared 5 hours ahead. Cool. Place on cookie sheet and cover with plastic wrap; let stand at room temperature. Before serving, remove plastic and bake fritters in 350°F oven until heated through.*) Serve hot.

Sautéed Greens with Garlic and Lemon

To get a head start, blanch the beans and rinse, drain and wrap greens tightly in paper towels. Refrigerate them for up to one day before sautéing.

6 servings

½ pound green beans, trimmed and halved diagonally

6 tablespoons olive oil (preferably extra-virgin)
3 large garlic cloves, finely chopped
1 pound escarole, trimmed
1 pound fresh spinach, stemmed

¼ pound arugula
1 tablespoon minced fresh marjoram or 1 teaspoon dried, crumbled
    Salt and freshly ground pepper
1 large lemon

Blanch beans in large saucepan of boiling water until tender but still firm to bite, about 3 minutes. Drain well.

Heat oil in heavy large skillet over medium heat. Add garlic and stir 20 seconds. Add escarole and cook 2 minutes. Add spinach and arugula and cook until wilted, stirring occasionally, about 2 minutes. Add beans and marjoram and stir until heated through. Season with salt and pepper. Grate lemon peel directly over.

Roasted New Potatoes and Shallots with Caraway

2 servings

4 small red potatoes, quartered
lengthwise
5 large shallots, peeled

2 tablespoons olive oil
½ teaspoon caraway seeds
Salt and freshly ground pepper

Position rack in center of oven and preheat to 400°F. Mix all ingredients in small shallow baking pan. Bake until potatoes are tender, stirring occasionally, about 45 minutes. Serve hot.

Gratin of Potatoes and Celery Root

If celery root is unavailable, just use all potatoes.

4 servings

1 garlic clove, crushed

1 cup whipping cream
¾ cup milk
1½ pounds boiling potatoes, peeled
and cut into 1/16-inch-thick slices

Salt and freshly ground pepper
Freshly grated nutmeg
¾ pound celery root, peeled and cut
into 1/16-inch-thick slices

Preheat oven to 450°F. Rub 9½-inch-diameter pie dish with 3-inch-high sides with garlic. Discard garlic. Butter dish generously and set aside.

Bring cream and milk to boil in heavy medium saucepan. Arrange half of potatoes in prepared dish. Season with salt, pepper and nutmeg. Cover with celery root. Season with salt, pepper and nutmeg. Top with remaining potatoes in overlapping slices. Season with salt. Pour milk mixture over. Bake 20 minutes. Reduce oven to 400°F. Bake until potatoes and celery root are tender when pierced with knife and liquid has thickened, about 40 more minutes.

Potatoes with Sausage and Leeks

Serve either warm or at room temperature.

8 servings

4 large leeks (white and pale green
parts only)
4 cups chicken stock or canned
broth

4 teaspoons Dijon mustard
¼ cup red wine vinegar
2 large garlic cloves, flattened
½ cup olive oil (preferably extra-
virgin)

Salt and freshly ground pepper

12 medium-size red new potatoes
(about 4 pounds)

1 pound smoked kielbasa sausage,
cut into ⅛-inch-thick rounds

Fresh chervil or parsley

Cut pale green part of leeks into thin rounds. Coarsely chop white part of leeks. Boil chicken stock and white part of leeks in large saucepan until liquid is reduced to 1¼ cups, about 30 minutes. Strain through sieve, pressing on leeks with back of spoon; discard cooked leeks. (*Can be prepared 1 day ahead. Refrigerate stock and pale green sections of leeks separately.*)

Place mustard in small bowl. Whisk in vinegar and garlic. Gradually whisk in oil in slow steady stream. Season dressing with salt and pepper. (*Can be prepared 6 hours ahead. Cover and let stand at room temperature.*)

Place potatoes in large saucepan. Add enough water to cover. Salt water.

Bring to boil. Reduce heat and simmer until potatoes are tender, about 30 minutes. Drain and cool slightly. Peel warm potatoes and cut into ¼-inch-thick rounds. Transfer to large bowl.

Meanwhile, bring reduced stock to boil in large saucepan. Reduce heat to medium. Add reserved pale green leeks and sausage and cook 5 minutes. Drain sausage and leeks, reserving stock.

Pour 1 cup hot stock over potatoes; toss gently. (Reserve any remaining stock for another use.) Add leeks and sausage to potatoes and toss. Remove garlic from dressing. Pour dressing over potatoes and toss gently. Adjust seasoning. Transfer to platter. Garnish with chervil or parsley.

Butternut Squash with Apples and Cranberries

Delicious with roast turkey.

8 servings

1 large butternut squash

4 Granny Smith apples, peeled, cored and chopped

½ cup sugar

2 cups cranberries

½ cup (1 stick) butter, melted

Preheat oven to 350°F. Cut squash in half. Place cut side down on baking sheet. Bake until tender, about 1 hour. Maintain oven temperature.

Meanwhile, combine apples with ¼ cup sugar in heavy medium saucepan over medium heat. Cook until juices evaporate, stirring frequently, about 12 minutes. Set aside. Combine cranberries with remaining ¼ cup sugar in another heavy medium saucepan over medium heat. Cook until juices evaporate, stirring frequently, about 4 minutes.

Peel skin off squash. Cut squash into 2-inch pieces and place in 12 × 9-inch baking dish. Mix in apples and cranberries. Pour butter over and toss. Bake until heated through, about 10 minutes. Serve hot.

Herbed Zucchini and Crookneck Squash

A delicious side dish with grilled lamb chops or steak.

4 servings

¼ cup olive oil

1 tablespoon chopped fresh oregano or 1½ teaspoons dried, crumbled

1 tablespoon chopped fresh rosemary or 1½ teaspoons dried, crumbled

1 tablespoon chopped fresh thyme or 1½ teaspoons dried, crumbled
Salt and freshly ground pepper

4 small zucchini, halved lengthwise

2 small yellow crookneck squash, halved lengthwise

Combine oil and herbs. Season with salt and pepper. Pat zucchini and crookneck squash dry. Brush with seasoned oil. Marinate 30 minutes.

Prepare barbecue (medium-high heat) or preheat broiler. Grill zucchini and squash until cooked through, brushing often with seasoned oil, about 4 minutes per side. Serve hot.

 *Grains*

Quick Broccoli Risotto

2 servings; can be doubled
or tripled

3 cups canned low-salt chicken
broth
2 tablespoons (¼ stick) butter
1 onion, minced
⅔ cup Arborio* or other short-
grain rice

1 pound broccoli, cut into small
florets (florets only)
⅔ cup freshly grated Romano
cheese (about 3 ounces)
Salt and freshly ground pepper

Bring broth to simmer in small saucepan. Reduce heat to low and keep warm. Melt butter in heavy medium saucepan over medium-low heat. Add onion and cook until tender, stirring occasionally, about 6 minutes. Add rice and stir until opaque, about 2 minutes. Add ½ cup broth; adjust heat so that liquid simmers slowly. Cook for 20 minutes, continuing to add broth ½ cup at a time and simmering until each addition is absorbed, stirring occasionally. Add broccoli and remaining broth. Cover and simmer gently until broccoli is just crisp-tender, rice is just tender and liquid is creamy, about 12 minutes. Stir in cheese. Season with salt and pepper and serve.

*Arborio is an Italian short-grain rice. Available at Italian markets and many specialty foods stores.

Baked Rice with Sour Cream, Chilies and Corn

8 servings

2 poblano chilies*

2 cups water
1½ teaspoons butter
1 teaspoon salt
1 cup rice

1 tablespoon vegetable oil
¼ cup plus 2 tablespoons chopped
onion

1 garlic clove, minced
¾ cup drained canned whole-
kernel corn
½ cup sour cream
¼ cup chopped fresh cilantro
2¼ cups grated white cheddar cheese
(about 9 ounces)

Char chilies over gas flame or in broiler until blackened on all sides. Wrap in paper bag and let stand 10 minutes to steam. Peel and seed. Rinse if necessary; pat dry. Chop chilies.

Bring water to boil in heavy medium saucepan. Add butter and salt. Mix in rice. Reduce heat to low, cover and cook until rice is tender, about 25 minutes. Transfer rice to large bowl and cool, fluffing occasionally with fork.

Butter 8-cup shallow baking dish. Heat vegetable oil in heavy medium skillet over medium heat. Add ¼ cup onion and garlic and sauté until onion is translucent, about 5 minutes. Add chopped chilies and sauté 1 minute. Mix chili mixture and corn into rice. Combine sour cream, cilantro and remaining 2 tablespoons onion in small bowl. Add to rice and mix well. Stir in cheese. Transfer rice mixture to prepared dish.

Preheat oven to 325°F. Bake rice until sides are light brown and mixture is heated through, about 25 minutes.

*A fresh green chili, sometimes called a fresh *pasilla*, available at Latin American markets.

Rice and Lentil Griddle Cakes

8 servings

2¼ cups salted water
1 cup short-grain rice
½ cup red lentils*

3 tablespoons butter
1 medium onion, minced
2 tablespoons minced shallot
2 eggs, beaten to blend

¼ teaspoon freshly grated nutmeg
Salt and freshly ground pepper

¼ cup all purpose flour
½ teaspoon dried thyme, crumbled
½ teaspoon salt
1 tablespoon corn oil

Bring 2¼ cups salted water to boil in heavy medium saucepan. Add rice. Cover, reduce heat and simmer until all water is absorbed, about 20 minutes. Rinse lentils. Place in heavy small saucepan. Cover with cold water. Bring to boil. Reduce heat and simmer until just tender, about 5 minutes. Drain. Combine 2 cups cooked rice and 1 cup cooked lentils in medium bowl. Cool. (*Can be prepared 1 day ahead. Chill.*)

Melt 2 tablespoons butter in heavy medium skillet over medium-low heat. Add onion and shallot and cook until tender, stirring occasionally, about 8 minutes. Add to rice. Mix in eggs and nutmeg. Season with salt and pepper. (*Can be prepared 12 hours ahead. Chill.*)

Combine flour, thyme, ½ teaspoon salt and pepper on plate. Shape rice mixture into 2-inch-diameter, ½-inch-thick patties. Dust with flour mixture. Melt remaining 1 tablespoon butter with oil on griddle or in heavy large skillet over medium heat. Add patties (in batches if necessary; do not crowd) and cook until brown and crisp, about 5 minutes per side. Serve immediately.

*Available at Indian and Middle Eastern markets. If unavailable, use green lentils and cook until tender, about 30 minutes.

Wild Rice and Barley with Mushrooms

6 servings

1 small onion, quartered

½ cup (1 stick) unsalted butter
1¼ cups wild rice (8 ounces)
2 tablespoons pearl barley
3½ to 4 cups canned beef broth

1 teaspoon minced fresh thyme or
¼ teaspoon dried, crumbled
¼ teaspoon freshly ground pepper

8 ounces small mushrooms

Mince onion in processor.

Melt ¼ cup butter in heavy medium skillet over medium heat. Add onion and cook until soft, stirring occasionally, about 8 minutes. Mix in rice and barley. Add 4 cups beef broth, thyme and pepper and bring to boil. Reduce heat, cover and simmer until liquid is absorbed, stirring occasionally, about 1¼ hours. (**Or to microwave:** Melt ¼ cup butter in 3-quart microwave casserole on High. Add onion and cook uncovered on High until soft, about 1 minute. Add rice, barley, 3½ cups broth, thyme and pepper. Cover tightly and cook on High 25 minutes. Reduce to Medium and cook until most of liquid is absorbed, about 40 minutes. Let stand, covered, until all liquid is absorbed, about 10 minutes.)

Meanwhile, prepare mushrooms: Insert medium slicer in processor. Place mushrooms on their sides in feed tube, fitting closely. Slice using light pressure.

Melt remaining ¼ cup butter in heavy medium skillet over medium heat. Add mushrooms and cook until soft, stirring frequently, about 5 minutes. (**Or to** microwave: Melt remaining ¼ cup butter in shallow 10-inch microwave dish on High. Add mushrooms. Cook uncovered on High until mushrooms are tender, stirring twice, 4 to 5 minutes.)

Stir mushrooms into cooked rice. (*Can be prepared 2 days ahead. Cover and refrigerate. Rewarm on stove over medium heat or in microwave on High, stirring occasionally.*) Serve hot.

Jalapeño Cheese Grits

This is great with roast chicken or lamb.

4 servings

2 cups milk
1 cup water
1 cup instant grits
2 tablespoons (¼ stick) butter
1 jalapeño chili, seeded and minced
2 teaspoons Worcestershire sauce
2 teaspoons minced garlic

1 teaspoon freshly ground pepper
Dash of hot pepper sauce (such as Tabasco)
Salt
12 ounces Monterey Jack cheese with jalapeños, shredded

Cook all ingredients except cheese in heavy medium saucepan over medium-high heat until thickened, stirring frequently, about 30 minutes. Add cheese and cook until thickened to consistency of soft mashed potatoes, stirring frequently, about 10 minutes. Transfer grits to bowl. Serve hot.

Spiced Couscous

4 servings

2 cups chicken stock or canned broth
⅓ cup dried currants

½ teaspoon salt
⅛ teaspoon ground allspice
1 cup quick-cooking couscous

Bring first 4 ingredients to boil in medium saucepan. Add couscous and boil 2 minutes, stirring constantly. Remove from heat, cover and let stand 5 minutes. Fluff with fork and serve.

 Breads

Corn Sticks with Bacon

You can bake these in batches if you have only one corn stick pan.

Makes about 42

2¼ cups yellow cornmeal
¾ cup all purpose flour
1½ tablespoons baking powder
1 teaspoon salt
2¼ cups milk
½ cup pure maple syrup
4 eggs, room temperature

1 egg yolk
12 bacon slices, cooked until crisp, crumbled
¾ cup chopped pecans (about 2¼ ounces)

Vegetable oil

Preheat oven to 350°F. Place corn stick pans in oven and heat while preparing batter. Sift cornmeal, flour, baking powder and salt into large bowl. Mix milk, syrup, eggs and yolk in medium bowl. Mix into dry ingredients. Fold in bacon and chopped pecans.

Brush pans with oil. Spoon batter into molds, filling almost to top. Bake until golden brown, about 25 minutes. Remove from pans. (*Can be prepared 8 hours ahead. Cool on rack. Wrap in foil. Reheat in 350°F oven until warmed through, 5 minutes.*) Serve hot.

Garlic Hearts

Use a heart-shaped cutter for these little rolls. Nice with Italian food, naturally.

Makes about 36

2 envelopes dry yeast
Pinch of sugar
6¼ cups (about) unbleached all purpose flour
1 cup warm water (105°F to 115°F)

1 cup milk
2 eggs
2 tablespoons olive oil
1 tablespoon whole wheat flour
1 tablespoon cornmeal or whole wheat flour

1 tablespoon buckwheat flour or whole wheat flour
2 teaspoons salt

Garlic Oil
¼ cup olive oil
3 garlic cloves, pressed

Coarse salt (optional)

Sprinkle yeast, sugar and 1 tablespoon all purpose flour over warm water in small bowl; stir to dissolve. Let stand until foamy, about 10 minutes.

Whisk milk, eggs, oil, whole wheat flour, cornmeal, buckwheat flour and salt in large bowl. Add 1 cup all purpose flour and yeast mixture. Stir vigorously until smooth, about 3 minutes. Mix in enough all purpose flour ½ cup at a time to form soft dough. Knead dough on lightly floured surface until smooth and elastic, adding more flour if necessary, about 5 minutes (dough will be sticky).

Grease large bowl. Add dough, turning to coat entire surface. Cover bowl with plastic. Let dough rise in warm area until doubled, about 1 hour.

For garlic oil: Heat oil in heavy small saucepan until just warm. Stir in garlic.

Preheat oven to 400°F. Line 2 baking sheets with parchment. Punch dough down. Knead on lightly floured surface until smooth. Let rest 10 minutes. Roll half of dough out on lightly floured surface to thickness of ¾ inch. Cut dough using 3-inch heart cutter (or other shape). Transfer rolls to prepared sheet, spacing 1 inch apart. Reserve scraps. Repeat rolling and cutting with second half of dough. Gather and reroll scraps. Cut additional rolls.

Gently brush rolls with garlic oil and sprinkle with coarse salt if desired. Bake until golden brown, about 15 minutes. Serve immediately.

Lemon Butter Crust Buns

Makes 20

1 envelope dry yeast
Pinch of sugar
½ cup warm water (105°F to 115°F)

¾ cup warm milk (105°F to 115°F)
½ cup (1 stick) unsalted butter, melted
1 egg
1 egg yolk

1 tablespoon grated lemon peel
2 teaspoons salt
4 cups (about) unbleached all purpose flour

Lemon Butter
¼ cup (½ stick) unsalted butter
1½ teaspoons grated lemon peel

Sprinkle yeast and sugar over warm water in small bowl; stir to dissolve. Let stand until foamy, about 10 minutes.

Combine warm milk and next 5 ingredients in bowl of heavy-duty mixer (dough can be also mixed by hand). Add yeast mixture and 1½ cups flour. Mix on medium speed until smooth and creamy, about 3 minutes. Mix in enough flour ½ cup at a time to form soft dough. Knead dough on lightly floured surface until smooth and elastic, adding more flour if necessary, about 5 minutes.

Grease large bowl. Add dough, turning to coat entire surface. Cover bowl with plastic. Let dough rise in warm area until doubled, about 1¼ hours.

For lemon butter: Melt butter with lemon peel in heavy small saucepan over low heat. Set aside.

Grease 12-inch springform pan or earthenware baking dish. Gently punch dough down. Knead on lightly floured surface until smooth. Divide into 20 equal pieces. Roll each piece into ball, pulling edges under to create smooth top. Place rolls rounded side up with sides just touching in prepared pan. Cover loosely with plastic and let rise in warm draft-free area until almost doubled, about 20 minutes.

Preheat oven to 375°F. Gently brush rolls with lemon butter. Bake until golden brown, about 35 minutes. Cool slightly on rack before serving.

Power Pear-Oat Muffins

Breakfast for the nineties: satisfying muffins packed with whole grains, fruits and high-fiber yams. The muffins freeze beautifully.

Makes 12

¾ cup whole wheat flour
½ cup plus 2 tablespoons firmly packed dark brown sugar
⅓ cup finely chopped pitted dates
¼ cup raisins
¼ cup rolled oats
¼ cup sunflower seeds (unsalted), toasted
3 tablespoons oat bran*
3 tablespoons toasted wheat germ
1 teaspoon baking soda
1 teaspoon ground allspice

½ teaspoon baking powder
½ teaspoon salt
½ teaspoon ground ginger
½ cup vegetable oil
⅓ cup shredded bran cereal (such as All-Bran)
2 eggs
2 teaspoons vanilla extract
1 large pear, peeled, cored and finely chopped
1 cup grated peeled yam or sweet potato (about 4 ounces)

Preheat oven to 375°F. Grease twelve ½-cup muffin cups. Mix first 13 ingredients in medium bowl. Combine oil, bran cereal, eggs and vanilla in large bowl. Let stand until bran absorbs liquid, about 3 minutes. Using electric mixer, beat bran cereal mixture until thick. Beat in pear and yam. Fold in dry ingredients; do not overmix (batter will be thick and lumpy).

Divide batter among prepared muffin cups. Bake until tester inserted in centers comes out clean, about 25 minutes. Serve warm. (*Can be prepared ahead. Cool completely on rack. Wrap tightly and refrigerate 3 days, or freeze up to 1 month. Rewarm in 350°F oven.*)

*Available at natural foods stores. Rolled oats can be substituted.

Apricot Pecan Bread

Use any remaining apricot puree on toast.

Makes 1 loaf

12 fresh apricots, pitted
½ cup (1 stick) butter, room temperature
1 cup plus 2 tablespoons sugar
2 eggs, beaten to blend
⅓ cup chopped pecans
1½ cups all purpose flour

1 teaspoon baking soda
½ teaspoon salt
½ teaspoon cinnamon
½ teaspoon ground ginger
½ teaspoon ground allspice
¼ teaspoon baking powder

Preheat oven to 325°F. Butter 9 × 5-inch loaf pan. Puree apricots in blender on processor. Set aside.

Cream butter with sugar in large bowl. Stir in eggs. Mix in 1 cup apricot puree and pecans. Sift together flour and remaining ingredients. Mix into batter. Pour into prepared pan. Bake until tester inserted in center comes out clean, about 45 minutes. Cool 10 minutes in pan on rack. Invert onto rack and cool completely. (*Can be prepared 1 day ahead. Wrap tightly and refrigerate.*)

Cinnamon Raisin Bread

Nothing matches home-made bread. The aroma alone is reason enough to bake it. This one is sensational—generously studded with plump raisins and swirled with cinnamon and sugar.

Makes 1 loaf

Bread
1 envelope dry yeast
¼ cup (or more) warm water (105°F to 115°F)
3 tablespoons sugar

2½ cups (or more) bread flour
3 tablespoons unsalted butter or margarine, cut into 6 pieces, room temperature

¾ teaspoon salt
⅔ cup evaporated milk
¾ cup raisins

Topping
5 tablespoons sugar
1½ teaspoons cinnamon
¼ cup (½ stick) unsalted butter or margarine

For bread: Sprinkle yeast over ¼ cup warm water in small bowl. Add 1 teaspoon sugar and stir to dissolve. Let stand until foamy, about 5 minutes.

Combine 2½ cups flour, butter or margarine, salt, remaining sugar and yeast mixture in processor. With machine running, pour evaporated milk through feed tube and process until dough forms. If dough sticks to bowl, add more flour through feed tube 1 tablespoon at a time, incorporating each addition before adding next. If dough is dry, add water through feed tube 1 teaspoon at a time, incorporating each addition before adding next. Process until smooth and elastic, about 40 seconds. Add raisins and process just until combined, 4 or 5 seconds.

Transfer dough to large plastic bag. Seal tightly, leaving space for dough to rise. Let dough rise in warm draft-free area until doubled in volume, about 2 hours. (*Can be prepared 1 day ahead. Punch dough down, cover tightly with plastic wrap and refrigerate.*)

For topping: Butter 7-cup loaf pan. Mix 1 tablespoon sugar and ¼ teaspoon cinnamon in small bowl. Sprinkle light layer in pan. Reserve remaining cinnamon-sugar mixture. Melt butter in heavy small saucepan over low heat. Add remaining 4 tablespoons sugar and 1¼ teaspoons cinnamon. Stir just until sugar dissolves.

Punch dough down. Knead on lightly floured surface until smooth. Divide into 24 pieces. Spoon 2 tablespoons butter mixture into bottom of pan. Add

12 dough pieces in single layer. Spoon about 2 tablespoons of butter mixture over dough and add second layer of dough pieces. Reserve remaining butter mixture. Cover dough and let rise in warm draft-free area until almost doubled in volume, about 50 minutes (this rising time will be longer if dough has been refrigerated).

Position rack in center of oven and preheat to 350°F. Bake bread until well browned, about 40 minutes. Let cool in pan 5 minutes. Using small knife, cut between pan and bread. Transfer bread to rack. Brush with remaining butter mixture and sprinkle with remaining cinnamon-sugar mixture. Serve warm or at room temperature.

Pesto and Cheese French Bread

2 servings; can be doubled or tripled

½ cup mayonnaise
½ cup freshly grated Romano or Parmesan cheese (about 2 ounces)

2 teaspoons prepared pesto sauce
½ 1-pound French bread loaf

Combine first 3 ingredients in small bowl. (*Can be prepared 1 day ahead. Cover tightly and refrigerate.*)

Preheat broiler. Halve bread lengthwise. Broil cut side up until beginning to brown. Spread each half generously with mayonnaise mixture. Broil until bubbling and beginning to brown, watching carefully. Cut crosswise into 1½-inch pieces and serve.

Black Bread

Makes 2 loaves

¾ cup water
½ cup cornmeal
⅓ cup cold water
3 ounces unsweetened chocolate, chopped
¼ cup instant coffee powder
1 tablespoon butter
1 tablespoon salt

2 envelopes dry yeast
1¼ cups warm water (105°F to 115°F)

¾ cup dark molasses
2 cups rye flour
1 cup whole wheat flour
2½ cups (about) unbleached all purpose flour

Cornmeal

1 egg white beaten with 1 tablespoon water (glaze)

Bring ¾ cup water to boil in heavy medium saucepan. Combine ½ cup cornmeal and ⅓ cup cold water in small bowl and gradually stir into boiling water. Stir until very thick, about 1 minute. Remove from heat. Add chocolate, coffee powder, butter and salt and stir until chocolate melts. Let cool to lukewarm.

Sprinkle yeast over 1¼ cups warm water in large bowl; stir to dissolve. Mix in molasses and cornmeal mixture, then rye and whole wheat flours. Mix in enough all purpose flour ½ cup at a time to form firm but sticky dough. Turn dough out onto floured pastry cloth. Knead until firm and elastic, adding more all purpose flour if very sticky, about 10 minutes.

Grease 2 medium bowls. Divide dough in half and form into balls. Place 1 in each bowl, turning to coat entire surface. Cover each with plastic. Let rise in warm draft-free area until doubled in volume, about 1¾ hours.

Grease two 8-inch-diameter cake pans; sprinkle with cornmeal. Punch each dough ball down. On lightly floured surface, knead each until smooth. Form into balls. Transfer to prepared pans and flatten slightly. Cover pans and let dough rise in warm draft-free area until almost doubled in volume, about 45 minutes.

Position rack in lowest third of oven and preheat to 375°F. Brush loaves with glaze. Bake until loaves sound hollow when tapped on bottom, about 55 minutes. Transfer to racks and cool. (*Can be prepared ahead. Wrap tightly and store at room temperature 1 day or freeze up to 3 weeks. Thaw at room temperature. Rewarm in 350°F oven about 15 minutes.*) Serve warm.

6 ❦ Desserts

Whether you're a fan of old-fashioned desserts or more contemporary creations, you'll find a variety of sweet treats here to fill the bill—there's even a selection of great classics updated for today's tastes. Traditionalists will love desserts like Raisin Rice Pudding, made with a hint of cinnamon; Triple Strawberry Sundaes, homemade strawberry ice cream layered with sliced berries and strawberry sauce; and Fudge-slathered Fudge Cake, a chocoholic's dream come true.

For an irresistible twist on tradition, you might try Raspberry Salzburger Nockerl, a fast, foolproof soufflé—our rendition includes a layer of raspberry jam. In the Peach Cobbler with Blueberries and Bing Cherries, the cherries add a sweet, colorful note to a dessert that celebrates the best of summer. And for a delicious surprise, there's Chocolate Hazelnut Strudel, a luscious layering of crunchy hazelnut praline, buttery pastry and creamy chocolate filling.

We end the chapter with a collection of cookies—just the thing for those occasions that call for a small bite of something sweet. With recipes as easy and as tempting as Walnut Lace Cookies, Caramel Almond Cashew Bars and Macadamia Nut Brownies, you'll find yourself taking *many* small bites.

🍎 *Fruit Desserts*

Fig, Melon and Mint Salad

The refreshing dessert fruit salad updated.

2 servings; can be doubled or tripled

3/4 cup plain yogurt
1 tablespoon honey
1 1/2 teaspoons fresh lime juice
1/3 honeydew melon, peeled, seeded and thinly sliced

4 fresh figs or dried Calimyrna figs, quartered
2 teaspoons chopped fresh mint
2 tablespoons chopped walnuts

Combine first 3 ingredients in small bowl. (*Can be prepared 2 days ahead. Cover and refrigerate.*)

Arrange melon slices in ring on plates. Place figs in center. Spoon yogurt dressing over. Sprinkle each with mint and walnuts, then serve.

Fresh Pears with Port Zabaglione

Port is substituted for the traditional Marsala.

2 servings; can be doubled or tripled

2 egg yolks
2 tablespoons sugar
1/4 cup Port, Marsala or cream Sherry

1 large pear, halved, cored and sliced

Whisk yolks and sugar in top of double boiler (off heat) until thick and pale yellow. Set over simmering water. Whisk in Port. Whisk until mixture triples in volume and holds shape in spoon. Arrange pear slices in fan pattern on plates. Spoon zabaglione over. Serve immediately.

Cranberry and Raspberry Fool

Pureed berries are swirled into a puff of whipped cream for a refreshing, simple dessert. To show off the beautiful color of the fruit, serve this in clear goblets.

4 servings

1 1/2 cups cranberries
1 1/2 cups fresh raspberries or frozen unsweetened raspberries, thawed
1/2 cup plus 2 tablespoons sugar

2 tablespoons water
2 teaspoons framboise liqueur*
1 1/4 cups chilled whipping cream

Puree berries and 1/2 cup sugar in processor.

Transfer puree to heavy medium saucepan. Add 2 tablespoons water and cook over medium heat until thick puree forms, stirring frequently, about 25 minutes. Remove from heat. (**Or to microwave:** Transfer puree to 1 1/2-quart microwave-safe dish. Cook uncovered on High until thick, stirring once, about 10 minutes.) Press through fine sieve set over bowl to remove seeds. Stir framboise liqueur into puree. Refrigerate until well chilled.

Using electric mixer, whip cream until frothy. Add remaining 2 tablespoons sugar and whip until peaks form. Gently swirl cream into chilled berry mixture; do not mix thoroughly. Divide among 4 goblets. (*Can be prepared 3 hours ahead. Cover and refrigerate.*) Serve dessert chilled.

*A raspberry liqueur available at some liquor stores and specialty foods stores.

Sweet Plum Cream

6 servings

1 cup ruby Port
½ cup sugar
¾ pound ripe purple-fleshed plums, quartered, pitted

2 tablespoons fresh lemon juice

1 teaspoon grated lemon peel
¾ cup chilled whipping cream, whipped to peaks
6 ripe purple-fleshed plums, pitted, thinly sliced

Cook Port, sugar and ¾ pound plums in heavy nonaluminum saucepan over medium heat, stirring until sugar dissolves. Increase heat and bring to boil. Reduce heat and simmer until plums are very soft, about 15 minutes. Remove from heat and cool slightly.

Puree plum mixture in processor. Strain back into same saucepan, pressing with back of spoon. Add lemon juice and peel. Simmer until plum sauce is reduced to 1¼ cups, stirring frequently, about 10 minutes. Cool. Cover and refrigerate until well chilled.

Pour ½ cup plum sauce into small bowl. Fold in whipped cream. Divide sliced plums among 6 goblets. Spoon remaining plum sauce over. Top each with dollop of plum cream.

Peach Cobbler with Blueberries and Bing Cherries

6 servings

Biscuit Topping
¾ cup unbleached all purpose flour
3 tablespoons sugar
1½ teaspoons baking powder
½ teaspoon cinnamon
¼ teaspoon cream of tartar
⅛ teaspoon salt
3 tablespoons chilled unsalted butter, cut into 6 pieces
¼ cup sour cream

Fruit
4 large ripe peaches (about 2 pounds), peeled, pitted, cut into ½-inch wedges

⅓ cup plus 2 teaspoons sugar
1½ tablespoons quick-cooking tapioca
1 tablespoon fresh lemon juice
¼ teaspoon cinnamon
1 cup fresh blueberries
1 cup fresh Bing cherries (about 6 ounces), halved, pitted

Vanilla Cream*

Position rack in center of oven and then preheat to 400°F.

For topping: Combine flour, sugar, baking powder, cinnamon, cream of tartar and salt in processor. Add butter and cut in until mixture resembles coarse meal. Add sour cream and blend just until dough begins to come together. Do not overprocess; do not form ball.

Transfer to large plastic bag. Working through bag, form dough into ball; flatten into circle slightly larger than diameter of 6-cup soufflé dish or deep casserole. Chill while preparing fruit.

For fruit: Cook peaches, ⅓ cup sugar, tapioca, lemon juice and cinnamon in heavy medium skillet over medium heat just until liquid simmers, stirring occasionally, about 4 minutes. Remove from heat. Add blueberries and cherries. Transfer fruit mixture to 6-cup soufflé dish or deep casserole.

Place dough atop fruit and gently tuck edges under. Sprinkle with remaining 2 teaspoons sugar. Bake until crust is browned, about 30 minutes. Let cool

1 hour. (*Can be prepared 8 hours ahead. Cover and refrigerate. To reheat, place cobbler in cold oven, heat to 350°F and bake 12 to 15 minutes.*) Serve warm with Vanilla Cream.

*Vanilla Cream

Makes about 1²/₃ cups

1 3-inch piece vanilla bean, split lengthwise

1½ cups sour cream
¼ cup powdered sugar

Scrape seeds from vanilla bean into sour cream. Mix in sugar. (*Can be prepared 2 days ahead. Cover and chill.*)

Prune and Armagnac Compote with Ice Cream

Delicious on its own, even better over ice cream.

4 servings

1½ cups water
¾ cup sugar
3 orange slices
1 cinnamon stick
1 12-ounce box moist pitted prunes

3 tablespoons Armagnac, Cognac or brandy (optional)

Chocolate or vanilla ice cream
Sliced toasted almonds

Simmer water, sugar, orange slices and cinnamon in heavy medium saucepan 15 minutes, stirring until sugar dissolves. Add prunes and simmer until tender, about 20 minutes. Remove from heat and mix in Armagnac. (*Can be prepared 3 days ahead; refrigerate.*)

Serve compote warm or at room temperature over chocolate or vanilla ice cream. Top with nuts.

❧ Custards, Puddings and Soufflés

Maple Crème Caramel

These individual custards are a snap to make and can be baked a day ahead.

6 servings

1⅓ cups pure maple syrup

2 cups milk (do not use lowfat or nonfat)

3 large eggs
2 egg yolks

Preheat oven to 350°F. Cook 1 cup syrup in heavy 2-quart saucepan over medium-low heat until reduced to ¾ cup, stirring constantly, about 10 minutes. Immediately pour syrup into six ¾-cup ramekins or soufflé dishes.

Scald milk in heavy large saucepan. Whisk eggs, yolks and remaining ⅓ cup syrup in medium bowl to blend. Gradually whisk in hot milk. Strain custard. Ladle into syrup-lined ramekins. Place ramekins in large baking pan. Add enough boiling water to pan to come halfway up sides of ramekins. Bake until custards move slightly in center when pan is shaken, about 35 minutes.

Remove custards from water. Cover and refrigerate until well chilled. (*Can be prepared 1 day ahead.*) Run small sharp knife around custards to loosen. Unmold onto plates (some of syrup may have crystallized) and serve.

Bittersweet Chocolate Terrine with Vanilla Custard Sauce

A rich chocolate mousse with a hazelnut pastry bottom, all encased in a bittersweet chocolate glaze.

12 servings

Mousse
- 12 ounces bittersweet (not unsweetened) or semisweet chocolate, chopped
- ¾ cup (1½ sticks) unsalted butter
- 6 large egg yolks
- 8 large egg whites, room temperature
- 3 tablespoons sugar

Pastry
- ⅔ cup toasted hazelnuts (about 3 ounces)
- ½ cup unbleached all purpose flour
- 2 tablespoons sugar
- 5 tablespoons chilled unsalted butter, cut into small pieces

- 1 egg yolk
- 3 teaspoons (about) whipping cream

Glaze
- 6 ounces bittersweet (not unsweetened) or semisweet chocolate, chopped
- ¼ cup (½ stick) unsalted butter
- 1 tablespoon light corn syrup
- ⅔ cup whipping cream
- ¼ cup Cognac

- 12 toasted hazelnuts

Vanilla Custard Sauce*

For mousse: Line 9 × 5-inch rectangular loaf pan with 2 pieces of parchment extending 1 inch over long and short sides. Melt chocolate with butter in top of double boiler over barely simmering water, stirring until smooth. Remove from over water. Cool 5 minutes. Whisk in yolks 1 at a time.

Using electric mixer, beat whites in large bowl until soft peaks begin to form. Gradually add sugar and beat until stiff but not dry. Fold half of whites into cooled chocolate to lighten. Gently fold in remaining whites. Pour mousse into prepared pan. Cover with plastic and refrigerate overnight.

For pastry: Finely grind hazelnuts in processor. Blend in flour and sugar. Add butter and cut in using on/off turns until mixture has sandy texture. Blend in yolk and enough cream to form dough that just begins to come together. Gather dough into square; flatten into rectangle. Wrap in plastic and chill 1 hour.

Preheat oven to 350°F. Roll dough out between sheets of parchment to 9 × 5-inch rectangle. Peel off top sheet of parchment. Transfer dough on parchment to cookie sheet. Bake until pastry is firm and beginning to brown, about 15 minutes. Cool pastry on sheet. Refrigerate 1 hour.

For glaze: Melt chocolate and butter with corn syrup in heavy medium saucepan over low heat, stirring until smooth. Scald cream with Cognac in heavy small saucepan. Pour into chocolate; mix well. Cool slightly.

Carefully place pastry atop mousse. Place cake rack over terrine. Invert terrine onto rack. Peel off parchment. Using serrated knife, carefully cut away any excess pastry around base of terrine. Place terrine on rack over cookie sheet. Pour lukewarm glaze over terrine, spreading gently to coat top and sides. Arrange nuts down center of terrine. Chill until glaze sets, about 1 hour. (*Can be prepared 1 day ahead.*)

Run small sharp knife around base of terrine to loosen. Transfer terrine to serving plate. Cut into slices using warm knife. Transfer to plates. Spoon custard around each piece and serve.

*Vanilla Custard Sauce

Makes about 3 cups

2 cups half and half
2/3 cup milk (do not use lowfat or nonfat)
1 vanilla bean, split lengthwise

5 egg yolks
2/3 cup sugar
Pinch of salt

Combine half and half and milk in heavy medium saucepan. Scrape in seeds from vanilla bean; add pod. Bring mixture to simmer. Remove from heat. Cover and let steep 40 minutes.

Whisk yolks, sugar and salt in medium bowl to blend. Bring half and half mixture to boil again. Gradually whisk some into yolks. Return mixture to saucepan and stir over medium-low heat until custard thickens and leaves path on back of spoon when finger is drawn across, about 8 minutes; do not boil. Strain into bowl. Cover and refrigerate until well chilled. (*Sauce can be prepared up to 3 days ahead.*)

Peach Crème Brûlées with Cinnamon Topping

A rich creamy custard is layered with fresh peaches and a crisp topping. All the components can be made a day ahead—just assemble and broil before serving. Or refrigerate the desserts for up to one hour after broiling and serve chilled.

8 servings

Custards
4 cups whipping cream
1/4 cup sugar
9 large egg yolks
1 teaspoon vanilla extract

Peaches
1 cup water
3/4 cup sugar
3 ripe peaches, peeled, pitted, thinly sliced

Topping
1/2 cup all purpose flour
1/4 cup firmly packed golden brown sugar
1/4 cup sugar
1/2 teaspoon cinnamon
1/2 cup (1 stick) chilled unsalted butter, cut into small pieces

For custards: Preheat oven to 350°F. Stir cream and sugar in heavy large saucepan over medium heat until sugar dissolves. Increase heat and bring to simmer. Whisk yolks in large bowl to blend. Gradually whisk in cream mixture. Mix in vanilla. Strain custard through sieve into bowl. Ladle custard into eight 1-cup soufflé cups or ramekins. Place cups in large baking pan. Add enough hot water to pan to come halfway up sides of cups. Bake until edges are set but centers still move slightly when pan is shaken, about 30 minutes. Remove custards from water. Cover and refrigerate overnight.

For peaches: Stir water and sugar in heavy medium saucepan over low heat until sugar dissolves. Increase heat and bring to boil. Place peaches in bowl; pour syrup over. Cool. (*Can be prepared 1 day ahead. Cover and chill.*)

For topping: Mix flour, both sugars and cinnamon in processor. Add butter and cut in using on/off turns until mixture resembles coarse crumbs. (*Can be prepared 1 day ahead. Chill.*)

Preheat broiler. Drain peaches. Pat dry with paper towels. Arrange peaches decoratively atop custards. Sprinkle topping over. Broil until topping is light golden brown, about 2 minutes. Serve at room temperature or refrigerate custards until cold, about 1 hour.

Raisin Rice Pudding

6 to 8 servings

6 cups milk
1 cup sugar
¼ cup (½ stick) unsalted butter
1 cup short-grain rice (such as Calrose)
2 3-inch-long cinnamon sticks
1 3-inch-long piece vanilla bean

2 egg yolks beaten with ¼ cup water
1½ cups raisins
Cinnamon

Bring first 3 ingredients to boil in heavy large pot, stirring until sugar dissolves. Add rice, cinnamon sticks and vanilla and bring to boil. Reduce heat to medium-low and cook 8 minutes, stirring occasionally. Stir in yolk mixture. Simmer 10 minutes. Cool, cover and refrigerate until well chilled, stirring occasionally, at least 5 hours. (*Can be prepared 1 day ahead.*)

Bring large saucepan of water to simmer. Add raisins and cook 3 minutes. Drain raisins and cool completely.

Remove cinnamon sticks and vanilla bean from pudding. Mix in raisins. Ladle rice pudding into bowls. Sprinkle with cinnamon and serve.

Bread Pudding with Currants and Maple Syrup

Cardamom lends a delicious nuance to this quick dessert. Any extra makes a nice breakfast.

4 to 6 servings

⅓ cup dried currants
2 tablespoons brandy or hot water

6 cups 1-inch cubes French bread (about ½ pound)
1 cup half and half
1 cup milk (do not use nonfat or lowfat)

2 eggs
¾ cup sugar
1 tablespoon vanilla extract
1½ teaspoons grated orange peel
½ teaspoon ground cardamom
Maple syrup

Preheat oven to 325°F. Butter 9 × 5-inch glass loaf pan. Place currants in small bowl. Add brandy and let soak while preparing pudding.

Place bread in large bowl. Pour half and half and milk over and stir gently with rubber spatula. Let stand 5 minutes until soaked through.

Mix eggs, sugar, vanilla, orange peel and cardamom in another bowl. Add currants with their soaking liquid. Pour over bread and mix gently with rubber spatula. Transfer to prepared pan. Bake pudding until knife inserted in center comes out clean, about 1¼ hours. Cool slightly. Serve hot, warm or at room temperature, pouring maple syrup over each serving.

Raspberry Salzburger Nockerl

About 20 minutes to a sweet soufflé.

2 to 4 servings

¼ cup raspberry jam
3 eggs, separated
Pinch of cream of tartar
¼ cup sugar

1 teaspoon vanilla extract
1 teaspoon grated orange peel
1½ tablespoons all purpose flour
Powdered sugar

Preheat oven to 350°F. Butter 9-inch glass pie plate. Spread jam over bottom of plate. Beat whites with cream of tartar in large bowl until soft peaks form. Gradually add ¼ cup sugar and continue beating until stiff but not dry.

Whisk yolks, vanilla and orange peel in medium bowl to blend. Whisk in flour. Mix in ¼ of whites. Return to whites and gently fold in. Spoon mixture atop jam in 4 mounds. Bake until golden, 15 minutes. Top with sugar.

❦ Frozen Desserts

French Quarter Chocolate Ice Cream

The robust flavor of molasses and the hint of bourbon give this ice cream a real southern accent. Be sure to use light unsulfured molasses rather than blackstrap, which is too strong.

Makes about 1 quart

½ cup light unsulfured molasses
4 extra-large egg yolks
1 tablespoon dark brown sugar
  Pinch of ground ginger
  Pinch of cinnamon
  Pinch of salt
1 cup whipping cream
6 ounces bittersweet (not unsweetened) or semisweet chocolate, finely chopped

3 tablespoons chilled unsalted butter, cut into pieces
1 cup chilled whipping cream
2 tablespoons bourbon

  Chocolate-dipped Pecans*

Mix first 6 ingredients in medium bowl. Bring 1 cup cream to simmer in heavy medium saucepan. Gradually whisk into molasses mixture. Return to saucepan and stir over medium heat until custard thickens and leaves path on back of spoon when finger is drawn across, about 3 minutes; do not boil. Remove from heat. Add chopped chocolate and butter and stir until smooth. Pour into medium bowl. Mix in 1 cup chilled cream and bourbon. Cover and chill.

Transfer custard to ice cream maker and process according to manufacturer's instructions. Freeze in covered container several hours or overnight. (*Can be prepared 3 days ahead.*)

Scoop ice cream into bowls. Top with Chocolate-dipped Pecans.

*Chocolate-dipped Pecans

Delicious on their own or as a decoration for cakes, cookies and ice cream.

Makes 15

1 ounce bittersweet (not unsweetened) or semisweet chocolate, chopped

1½ teaspoons bourbon
15 toasted pecan halves

Line large baking sheet with waxed paper. Melt chocolate in small metal bowl set over saucepan of simmering water, stirring until smooth. Mix in bourbon. Remove from over water. Dip 1 end of 1 pecan halfway into chocolate, tilting bowl if necessary. Place on prepared sheet, flat side down. Repeat with remaining nuts and chocolate. Chill until chocolate hardens. (*Can be prepared 1 day ahead.*)

Clockwise from lower left: Chestnut Soup; Sweet-and-Sour Cabbage; Roast Goose with Apricot and Rice Stuffing; Steamed Broccoli and Roasted New Potatoes (recipes not included); Caramel Almond Tart

Irwin Horowitz

Victor Scocozza

Coconut Macadamia Cream Tart; Chocolate Harvest Cake; Pear and Raisin Pie with Pecan Crust

Chicken, Endive and Roquefort Salad; Parsley, Sage, Rosemary and Thyme Chicken

Lemon Cheesecake with Gingersnap Crust

*Smoked Salmon and Endive
Salad; Filet Mignon with
Mustard Cream Sauce;
Roasted New Potatoes
and Shallots with Caraway*

Myron Beck

Mile-High Whipped Cream Cake with Fresh Fruit; Fudge-slathered Fudge Cake

Walnut Praline Ice Cream

The ideal summer treat for walnut lovers.

Makes about 1³/₄ quarts

4 **cups milk**	1 **cup sugar**
1 **cup coarsely chopped walnuts**	1 **cup whipping cream**
12 **egg yolks**	**Walnut Praline***

Scald milk with walnuts in heavy medium saucepan. Remove from heat and let steep for 10 minutes.

Whisk yolks and sugar to blend in medium bowl. Reheat milk mixture. Gradually whisk half of milk mixture into yolks. Return to saucepan. Stir over low heat until mixture thickens and leaves path on back of spoon when finger is drawn across, about 10 minutes; do not boil. Strain into medium bowl. Stir in whipping cream. Refrigerate until chilled (or chill over bowl of ice and water, whisking occasionally).

Transfer custard to ice cream maker and process according to manufacturer's instructions, adding 1 cup praline when ice cream is almost set. Freeze in covered container several hours. (*Can be prepared 4 days ahead. If frozen solid, soften in refrigerator before serving.*)

Sprinkle remaining praline over scoops of ice cream before serving.

*Walnut Praline

Try this nutty homemade topping over purchased ice cream, too.

Makes about 1½ cups

½ **cup sugar**	1 **cup walnuts**
¼ **cup water**	

Lightly oil baking sheet. Cook sugar and water in heavy small saucepan over low heat, stirring until sugar dissolves. Increase heat and boil without stirring until mixture begins to color, brushing down any sugar crystals on sides of pan with wet pastry brush. Continue cooking, swirling pan gently, just until mixture turns rich caramel color, about 7 minutes. Remove from heat. Add walnuts and stir until well coated. Immediately pour onto prepared sheet. Cool completely. Break into 2-inch pieces. Coarsely chop in processor using on/off turns. (*Can be prepared 1 month ahead. Refrigerate airtight.*)

Cherry Ice Cream in Chocolate Cups

Small scoops of the ice cream are served in rich chocolate cups and garnished with more cherries.

Makes about 1½ quarts

3 **cups whipping cream**	3½ **cups fresh cherries, pitted, or**
8 **egg yolks**	2 **1-pound bags frozen**
1¼ **cups sugar**	**unsweetened pitted cherries,**
	thawed, drained, patted dry
1½ **tablespoons kirsch (clear cherry brandy)**	
	Chocolate Cups*
	Additional cherries

Scald cream in heavy medium saucepan. Remove from heat. Whisk yolks and sugar to blend in medium bowl. Gradually whisk half of hot cream into yolks. Return to saucepan. Stir over low heat until mixture thickens and leaves path on back of spoon when finger is drawn across, about 5 minutes; do not boil. Strain into medium bowl. Refrigerate custard to chill (or chill over bowl of ice and water, whisking occasionally).

Add kirsch to chilled custard. Puree custard with 3½ cups cherries in batches in processor. Strain through sieve into bowl, pressing to extract all puree.

Transfer custard to ice cream maker and process according to manufacturer's instructions. Freeze in covered container several hours. (*Can be prepared 4 days ahead. If ice cream is frozen solid, soften slightly in refrigerator before serving.*) Set 1 chocolate cup on each plate. Place several miniscoops of ice cream in each. Garnish with cherries.

*Chocolate Cups

Molded around oranges, these tasty cups make excellent "bowls" for ice cream.

Makes 6

6 oranges

1½ pounds semisweet chocolate, coarsely chopped

Line baking sheet with waxed paper or plastic. Wrap each orange with plastic wrap, keeping plastic as smooth as possible. Melt chocolate in top of double boiler over barely simmering water, stirring occasionally until smooth. Remove from over water. Let stand 5 minutes. Dip lower 1½ inches of 1 wrapped orange into chocolate. Place on baking sheet chocolate side down. Repeat with remaining oranges. Refrigerate until chocolate sets, about 20 minutes.

Carefully remove chocolate and plastic wrap from oranges. Gently separate plastic from chocolate cups. Reserve oranges for another use. Refrigerate chocolate cups in airtight container until ready to use. (*Chocolate cups can be prepared 3 days ahead.*)

Triple Strawberry Sundaes

Strawberry ice cream is layered in parfait glasses with sliced berries and strawberry sauce. Whipped cream and mint garnish this refreshing summery sweet.

8 servings

Ice Cream
2½ cups coarsely chopped hulled strawberries (about 1⅓ one-pint baskets)
1 cup sugar

2¼ cups whipping cream
½ vanilla bean, split lengthwise
6 large egg yolks
1 tablespoon framboise liqueur* (optional)

Sauce
1½ cups coarsely chopped hulled strawberries (about ⅔ one-pint basket)

¼ cup grenadine
3 tablespoons sugar
Fresh lemon juice

1 one-pint basket strawberries, sliced
2 tablespoons sugar
Whipped cream
8 strawberries
Fresh mint sprigs

For ice cream: Place berries in small bowl and sprinkle with ½ cup sugar. Let stand 30 minutes. Pulse in processor until medium-coarse puree forms.

Scald ¾ cup cream in heavy medium saucepan. Scrape in seeds from vanilla bean; add pod. Whisk yolks with remaining ½ cup sugar in medium bowl to blend. Whisk ½ of hot cream mixture into yolks. Return to saucepan and stir until custard thickens and leaves path on back of spoon when finger is drawn across, about 5 minutes; do not boil. Strain into bowl. Mix in remaining 1½ cups cream, strawberry puree and liqueur. Chill custard.

Transfer custard to ice cream maker. Process according to manufacturer's instructions. Transfer to container. Cover and freeze overnight.

For sauce: Cook first 3 ingredients in heavy small saucepan over low heat until berries begin to break up, stirring occasionally, about 5 minutes. Puree in processor. Add lemon juice to taste. Refrigerate sauce until cold.

Mix sliced berries and 2 tablespoons sugar in small bowl. Alternate scoops of ice cream, berries and sauce in each of 8 glasses. Top each with whipped cream, whole berry and mint sprig.

*A raspberry liqueur available at some liquor stores and specialty foods stores.

White Chocolate and Turkish Coffee Parfait

A creamy frozen dessert. Ideal for entertaining, it can be made well in advance, leaving only a quick decoration of piped whipped cream for the last minute.

4 servings

3/4 cup whipping cream
3 ounces imported white chocolate, finely chopped

1 tablespoon instant espresso coffee powder
1/8 teaspoon ground cardamom
1/8 teaspoon cinnamon
    Pinch of ground ginger
2/3 cup chilled whipping cream

8 large egg yolks

1/2 cup sugar
1/2 cup water
    Pinch of cream of tartar
2 teaspoons light corn syrup

2 teaspoons coffee liqueur
4 1/2 teaspoons light rum
1/8 teaspoon vanilla extract

    Sweetened whipped cream
    Crushed hard coffee candies

Bring 3/4 cup cream to simmer in heavy small saucepan over very low heat. Add white chocolate and stir until melted and smooth. Pour mixture into bowl. Refrigerate until very thick, stirring occasionally, about 3 hours.

Combine coffee, cardamom, cinnamon and ginger in medium bowl. Gradually add 2/3 cup cream, stirring to dissolve coffee. Chill well.

Using electric mixer, beat yolks in large bowl until pale yellow and slowly dissolving ribbon forms when beaters are lifted. Cook sugar, water and cream of tartar in heavy small saucepan over low heat, stirring until sugar dissolves. Increase heat and boil without stirring until syrup registers 238°F on candy thermometer (soft-ball stage), tilting pan to submerge thermometer tip, about 5 minutes. Gradually beat hot syrup into yolks in slow steady stream. Beat in 1 teaspoon corn syrup. Continue beating until mixture is completely cool and very light, about 5 minutes. Divide parfait base between 2 bowls.

Mix liqueur, 2 teaspoons rum and remaining 1 teaspoon corn syrup into coffee cream. Using electric mixer, beat coffee cream to peaks. Fold into half of parfait base. Beat white chocolate cream with remaining 2 1/2 teaspoons rum and vanilla to soft peaks. Fold into remaining half of parfait base. Divide half of coffee parfait among four 8-ounce parfait or slender wine glasses. Divide half of white chocolate parfait among glasses, spooning atop coffee parfait. Repeat layering. Freeze until firm, about 4 hours. (*Can be prepared 2 days ahead.*)

Spoon whipped cream into pastry bag fitted with large star tip. Pipe cream decoratively atop each parfait. Sprinkle with crushed candy and serve.

Candy-studded Ice Cream Sandwiches

Big cookies studded with Raisinets, Goobers and Reese's Pieces (or whatever your favorite candies are) and sandwiched with premium ice cream. Never has so little kitchen time afforded so much sweet satisfaction to so many.

Makes 15 ice cream cookie sandwiches and about 8 extra cookies

2½ cups unbleached all purpose flour
2½ cups rolled oats
1¼ teaspoons salt
1¼ teaspoons baking soda
1¼ teaspoons baking powder
1¼ cups Raisinets
1¼ cups Goobers, M & M's chocolate-covered peanuts, M & M's or peanuts
1¼ cups Reese's Pieces

1¼ cups (2½ sticks) unsalted butter, room temperature
1½ cups firmly packed golden brown sugar
⅔ cup plus 3 tablespoons sugar
3 eggs

1 half-gallon carton vanilla ice cream, softened slightly

Preheat oven to 350°F. Grease 2 baking sheets. Combine first 5 ingredients in large bowl. Mix in Raisinets, Goobers and Reese's Pieces. Using electric mixer, cream butter with sugars in large bowl until light and fluffy. Mix in eggs 1 at a time. Add dry ingredients and stir until just combined.

Drop batter by ¼ cupfuls onto prepared sheets, spacing 2 inches apart. Flatten each into 2¾-inch round. Bake until golden brown, about 12 minutes. Cool cookies on sheets 5 minutes. Transfer to waxed paper and cool completely. Refrigerate cookies until well chilled, approximately 1 hour.

Place large baking sheet in freezer. Sandwich ½ cup ice cream between 2 cookies, pressing slightly to bring ice cream to edge of sandwich. Place cookie sandwich on baking sheet in freezer. Repeat with remaining cookies and ice cream, forming 14 more. Leave sandwiches on baking sheet until frozen solid, about 1 hour. Wrap individually in plastic wrap and store in freezer. (*Can be prepared up to 3 days ahead. Soften slightly in refrigerator before serving.*) Store remaining cookies in airtight container at room temperature.

Hazelnut and Almond Crunch Ice Cream Loaf with Strawberry Sauce

Use your favorite vanilla ice cream. The loaf can be prepared a week ahead.

8 servings

½ cup (1 stick) unsalted butter
½ cup sugar
1½ teaspoons light corn syrup
1½ teaspoons water
⅓ cup blanched almonds
⅓ cup toasted husked hazelnuts

1 quart vanilla ice cream

1 cup chilled whipping cream, whipped to peaks

Toasted husked hazelnuts
Toasted blanched almonds
Fresh strawberries (optional)
Strawberry Sauce*

Lightly oil baking sheet. Melt butter and sugar in heavy medium saucepan over low heat, stirring constantly until sugar dissolves. Increase heat to medium-high. Mix in corn syrup and water. Boil until syrup registers 270°F (soft-crack stage) on candy thermometer, stirring occasionally, about 10 minutes. Add ⅓ cup almonds and ⅓ cup hazelnuts and stir to coat. Pour mixture onto prepared sheet. Cool completely. Break into 1-inch pieces. Coarsely chop praline in processor.

Soften ice cream in large bowl. Fold in whipped cream and praline. Pour into 8½ × 4½ × 2¾-inch loaf pan. Cover and freeze overnight. (*Ice cream loaf can be prepared 1 week ahead.*)

Run small sharp knife around pan to loosen loaf. Dip briefly into hot water. Unmold onto chilled platter. Cut into slices. Arrange slices on plates. Garnish with hazelnuts, almonds and strawberries. Pour sauce over; serve.

*Strawberry Sauce

Balsamic vinegar adds an intriguing touch of acidity.

Makes about 1¾ cups

1 pint fresh strawberries, hulled, or 2 cups frozen unsweetened strawberries, thawed
2 tablespoons powdered sugar

1 tablespoon strawberry preserves
1½ teaspoons balsamic vinegar*

Puree berries in processor. Blend in sugar, preserves and vinegar. (*Can be prepared 1 day ahead; refrigerate.*)

Pour puree into heavy small saucepan. Cook over low heat until heated through. Serve sauce warm.

*Available at specialty foods stores, Italian markets and some supermarkets.

🍎 Pies, Tarts and Pastries

Caramel Almond Tart

Offer a selection of grapes alongside this chewy, candylike treat.

6 servings

Pastry
1½ cups all purpose flour
2 tablespoons sugar
Pinch of salt
½ cup (1 stick) chilled unsalted butter, cut into pieces
1 egg yolk
½ teaspoon almond extract
3 tablespoons (about) ice water

1 egg white, beaten to blend

Filling
¾ cup sugar
½ cup (1 stick) unsalted butter

2 tablespoons honey
½ cup whipping cream
1¾ cups sliced blanched almonds (about 8 ounces)
1 tablespoon Grand Marnier or other orange liqueur
¼ teaspoon almond extract

Sweetened whipped cream
Assorted fresh grapes

For pastry: Butter 9-inch-diameter tart pan with removable bottom. Mix flour, sugar and salt in processor. Add butter and cut in using on/off turns until mixture resembles coarse meal. Blend in yolk and extract. Blend in enough water by tablespoons to form dough that just comes together. Gather dough into ball; flatten into disk. Roll dough out on lightly floured surface to ⅛-inch-thick round. Transfer dough to prepared pan. Trim overhang to ½ inch. Fold overhang in to form double edge; press firmly. Pierce bottom of crust with fork. Refrigerate at least 30 minutes. (*Can be prepared 1 day ahead. Cover and refrigerate.*)

Preheat oven to 350°F. Line tart shell with foil. Fill with dried beans or pie weights. Bake 15 minutes. Remove foil and weights. Lightly brush crust with egg white. Bake until crust is light golden brown, about 15 more minutes. Cool completely on rack.

For filling: Preheat oven to 375°F. Cook sugar, butter and honey in heavy 2-quart saucepan over low heat, stirring until sugar dissolves. Increase heat to medium and cook until sugar is golden brown, stirring frequently, about 3 minutes. Remove from heat. Stir in cream (mixture will bubble). Return to heat and stir until well blended. Mix in nuts, Grand Marnier and almond extract. Remove from heat. Let stand 15 minutes. Gently ladle almond filling into crust. Bake until filling bubbles vigorously all over, about 20 minutes.

Cool tart in pan on rack until set, about 4 hours. (*Can be prepared 1 day ahead. Cover tart with plastic wrap and let stand at room temperature.*)

Remove tart from pan. Cut into wedges. Serve with dollops of whipped cream. Pass grapes separately.

Coconut Macadamia Cream Tart

An elegant version of coconut cream pie, with macadamias added for interest.

8 servings

Crust
²/₃ cup roasted unsalted macadamia nuts*
1½ cups unbleached all purpose flour
¼ cup sugar
½ teaspoon salt
½ cup (1 stick) chilled unsalted butter, cut into pieces
1 egg yolk

Filling
4 cups milk
2 cups packed sweetened shredded coconut

1½ teaspoons unflavored gelatin
2 teaspoons dark rum
8 large egg yolks
5 tablespoons sugar
Pinch of salt

1 cup chilled whipping cream, whipped to peaks

¾ cup sweetened shredded coconut, toasted
¾ cup coarsely chopped unsalted macadamia nuts

For crust: Finely chop nuts in processor using on/off turns. Transfer to large bowl. Mix in flour, sugar and salt. Add butter and cut in until mixture resembles coarse meal. Mix in yolk. Press dough over bottom and up sides of 11-inch-diameter tart pan with removable bottom. Cover and refrigerate 30 minutes. (*Can be prepared 1 day ahead.*)

For filling: Bring milk and 2 cups coconut to boil in large saucepan. Cover and remove from heat. Steep 1 hour.

Line sieve with several layers of dampened cheesecloth. Place sieve over heavy medium saucepan. Pour coconut mixture through cheesecloth. Gather up sides and press to extract milk. Boil coconut milk until reduced to 2 cups. (*Can be prepared 1 day ahead. Cool, cover and refrigerate.*)

Preheat oven to 375°F. Bake crust until golden brown, about 30 minutes. Cool completely on rack.

Sprinkle gelatin over rum in small bowl. Whisk yolks, sugar and salt in medium bowl. Bring coconut milk to boil in heavy medium saucepan. Gradually whisk into yolks. Return mixture to saucepan and stir over medium-low heat until custard thickens and forms path on back of spoon when finger is drawn across; do not boil. Pour into bowl. Add gelatin mixture and stir until dissolved. Refrigerate until thickened but not set, stirring frequently.

Fold whipped cream into coconut filling. Pour into crust. Refrigerate until set, at least 2 and up to 6 hours.

Sprinkle toasted coconut around outer edges and center of tart. Sprinkle nuts in ring around coconut in center of tart. Cut into wedges and serve.

*Available at some specialty foods stores and some natural foods stores. If unavailable, rinse salted nuts briefly under running water. Drain and pat dry.

Apples and Almond Custard in Pastry

Homey and delicious.

8 servings

Crust

- 2½ cups all purpose flour
- ½ cup sugar
- ½ teaspoon salt
- ¼ teaspoon baking powder
- 1 cup (2 sticks) chilled unsalted butter, cut into pieces
- 3 large egg yolks
- 1 teaspoon vanilla extract

Apples

- ¾ cup (1½ sticks) unsalted butter
- ¾ cup sugar
- 6 large Golden Delicious apples, peeled, quartered, cored

Custard

- 4 ounces almond paste
- 2 large eggs
- 1 cup half and half
- 1 teaspoon vanilla extract
  Generous pinch of cinnamon

For crust: Mix first 4 ingredients in large bowl. Add butter and cut in until mixture resembles coarse meal. Beat yolks with vanilla to blend. Pour over flour mixture. Stir until dough comes together. Cover dough with plastic wrap and let rest 20 minutes.

Press dough into bottom and 1¼ inches up sides of 9 × 13-inch glass baking dish. Cover and refrigerate at least 1 hour. (*Can be prepared 1 day ahead.*)

For apples: Melt butter in heavy large skillet over medium-high heat. Add sugar and stir until syrup turns golden brown. Add apples and cook until tender but not mushy, turning apples over occasionally, about 10 minutes. Cool apples in caramel in skillet. (*Can be prepared 1 day ahead. Cover apple mixture and let stand at room temperature.*)

Preheat oven to 375°F. Bake crust until edges just begin to color, about 15 minutes. Cool slightly on rack. Maintain oven temperature.

Meanwhile, prepare custard: Remove apples from caramel in skillet. Boil caramel until reduced to ½ cup, stirring occasionally and skimming fat off surface, about 10 minutes. Place almond paste in bowl. Using electric mixer, gradually beat in caramel, eggs, half and half, vanilla and cinnamon.

Arrange apples rounded side up in rows in crust. Pour custard over apples. Bake until custard is set and top browns, about 50 minutes. Cool slightly on rack.

Fresh Lime Pie in Almond-Gingersnap Crust

You can assemble this refreshing pie the day before. Round out the dessert menu with bowls of fresh blueberries, strawberries and raspberries accompanied by lightly sweetened plain yogurt.

10 servings

Crust

- 1¼ cups roasted salted almonds (about 6 ounces)
- 3 tablespoons sugar
- 1 cup ground gingersnap cookies (about 18)
- ½ teaspoon almond extract
- 6 tablespoons (¾ stick) unsalted butter, melted

Filling

- ¾ pound whole milk ricotta cheese, drained if necessary
- ¼ cup powdered sugar
- 3 tablespoons sour cream
- 1½ teaspoons coarsely chopped crystallized ginger
- 1 teaspoon vanilla extract
- 1¼ teaspoons unflavored gelatin
- 2 tablespoons cold water
- 8 egg yolks
- 1 cup sugar
- 1½ cups strained fresh lime juice
- 4 teaspoons grated lime peel
- 3 tablespoons unsalted butter, cut into pieces

Topping

- 1 cup chilled whipping cream
- 2 tablespoons powdered sugar
- ¼ teaspoon almond extract

For crust: Preheat oven to 350°F. Butter 10-inch glass pie dish. Coarsely chop almonds in processor using on/off turns. Transfer ¼ cup nuts to small bowl; reserve. Add sugar to remaining nuts in processor and grind finely. Add cookie crumbs. Mix almond extract into butter. Pour over mixture in processor. Blend using on/off turns until combined. Press crumb mixture firmly onto bottom and up sides of prepared dish. Bake until slightly crisp and brown, about 12 minutes. Cool completely.

For filling: Blend ricotta, powdered sugar, sour cream, ginger and vanilla in processor. Spread in pie shell. Refrigerate until firm, about 1 hour.

Sprinkle gelatin over water in small cup. Let stand 10 minutes to soften. Using electric mixer, beat yolks with 1 cup sugar in medium bowl until pale yellow and slowly dissolving ribbon forms when beaters are lifted. Add lime juice and 3 teaspoons lime peel. Set bowl over saucepan of simmering water and stir until mixture leaves path on back of spoon when finger is drawn across, about 7 minutes. Add gelatin mixture and stir to dissolve. Add butter and stir until completely melted.

Cool lime mixture. Pour over ricotta. Cover and refrigerate until well chilled. (*Can be prepared 1 day ahead. Cover and refrigerate pie and 1 teaspoon lime peel separately. Store reserved nuts in plastic bag at room temperature.*)

For topping: Whip cream with powdered sugar and ¼ teaspoon almond extract in large bowl to soft peaks.

Spoon topping into pastry bag fitted with star tip. Pipe cream around edge of pie or spread cream completely over filling. (*Can be prepared 3 hours ahead. Cover and refrigerate.*) Sprinkle reserved ¼ cup almonds and 1 teaspoon lime peel over before serving.

Strawberry White Chocolate Mousse Tart

An elegant dessert. If you don't have a square pan, use a ten-inch round one.

8 servings

Pastry

- 1¾ cups all purpose flour
- ¼ cup firmly packed golden brown sugar
- 2½ teaspoons grated orange peel
  Pinch of salt
- 11 tablespoons chilled unsalted butter, cut into pieces
- 2 tablespoons fresh orange juice
- 1 egg yolk
- ½ teaspoon vanilla extract

- 2 ounces imported white chocolate (such as Tobler or Lindt), very finely chopped

Mousse

- 6 ounces imported white chocolate (such as Tobler or Lindt), chopped
- ¼ cup whipping cream
- 1 large egg white, room temperature
- 1 tablespoon sugar
- ½ cup chilled whipping cream, whipped to stiff peaks
- 2 tablespoons Grand Marnier or other orange liqueur

- 2 large strawberries with stems
- 20 (about) strawberries, hulled
- ½ cup strawberry jam

For pastry: Mix first 4 ingredients in large bowl. Add butter and cut in until mixture resembles fine meal. Blend orange juice with yolk and vanilla in small bowl. Add enough juice mixture to dry mixture by teaspoons to form dough that just comes together. Gather dough into ball; flatten into square.

Position rack in center of oven and preheat to 375°F. Roll dough out between sheets of plastic wrap to ⅛-inch-thick square. Trim dough to 11-inch square. Peel off top sheet of plastic. Transfer dough to 9-inch square tart pan with removable bottom. Trim edges and crimp. Freeze 15 minutes.

Line tart shell with foil; fill with dried beans or pie weights. Bake until sides are set, about 10 minutes. Remove foil and beans. Bake crust until golden brown, about 18 minutes. Sprinkle 2 ounces white chocolate over crust. Let stand 1 minute. Spread chocolate with back of spoon over bottom and up sides of tart. Transfer to rack and cool.

For mousse: Melt white chocolate with ¼ cup cream in heavy small saucepan over very low heat, stirring constantly. Pour into bowl. Let stand until just cool. Beat egg white in small bowl until soft peaks form. Gradually add sugar and beat until stiff but not dry. Fold whipped cream, 1 tablespoon Grand Marnier and egg white into chocolate mixture. Spoon mousse into prepared crust, spreading evenly. Refrigerate until mousse is set, about 2 hours. (*Can be prepared 1 day ahead.*)

Fan all strawberries by making several lengthwise cuts in each starting ¼ inch from base and extending through tip. Fan with fingertips. Bring jam and remaining 1 tablespoon Grand Marnier to boil in heavy small saucepan, stirring constantly. Transfer to processor and puree. Brush thin layer of jam over mousse. Place 2 fanned berries with stems at opposite corners of tart. Arrange remaining berries in rows atop mousse, overlapping slightly and revealing fanned edges. Brush berries with jam. (*Can be prepared 4 hours ahead. Cover and refrigerate.*)

Pear and Raisin Pie with Pecan Crust

This heartwarming pie is a natural with scoops of vanilla ice cream.

8 servings

Crust
- ¾ cup coarsely chopped toasted pecans (about 3 ounces)
- 1¾ cups unbleached all purpose flour
- 3 tablespoons sugar
- ½ teaspoon salt
- ½ cup (1 stick) chilled unsalted butter, cut into pieces
- 3 tablespoons chilled solid vegetable shortening, cut into pieces
- 2 tablespoons (about) ice water

Filling
- ¾ cup water
- ¾ cup raisins

- 2¼ pounds firm but ripe pears, peeled, cored, cut into eighths
- ½ cup firmly packed golden brown sugar
- 1 tablespoon quick-cooking tapioca
- ¼ teaspoon cinnamon
- 3 tablespoons unsalted butter, melted
- 1 tablespoon fresh lemon juice

- 1 egg yolk beaten with 2 teaspoons whipping cream (glaze)
- ¼ cup coarsely chopped pecans (about 1 ounce)

For crust: Finely grind pecans with flour in processor. Blend in sugar and salt. Transfer to large bowl. Add butter and shortening and work with fingertips until mixture resembles coarse meal. Mix in enough water just to bind dough. Gather dough into 2 balls, 1 slightly smaller than the other. Flatten into disks. Wrap separately in plastic and refrigerate 30 minutes. (*Can be prepared 1 day ahead. Let dough stand 2 hours at room temperature to soften slightly before continuing.*)

For filling: Simmer water and raisins in small saucepan until only 2 tablespoons liquid remain in pan, about 25 minutes. Cool completely.

Preheat oven to 400°F. Toss raisins and their liquid with pears in large bowl. Mix in sugar, tapioca and cinnamon, then butter and lemon juice.

Roll larger dough piece out on sheet of lightly floured plastic wrap to 12-inch round. Invert dough into 9-inch pie dish with 1¼-inch sides. Press into bottom and up sides of dish. Remove plastic. Trim overhanging dough. Gather trimmings together. Roll out on lightly floured surface to thickness of ⅛ inch.

Cut out leaf shapes. Roll smaller dough piece out on sheet of lightly floured plastic to 10-inch round.

Spoon filling into pie crust. Top with 10-inch pastry round. Crimp edges decoratively to seal. Brush pastry leaves with water and arrange atop pie. Brush top (not edges) with some of glaze. Cut slit in center. Bake 40 minutes, covering edges with foil if browning too quickly. Brush top (not edges) with glaze again. Sprinkle with nuts. Reduce oven temperature to 350°F. Bake 10 more minutes. Cool slightly. (*Can be prepared 4 hours ahead.*)

Visions of Sugarplums

This elegant nut and dried fruit tart is decorated with chocolate-glazed sugarplums. It can be prepared a day ahead.

10 servings

Crust
1½ cups all purpose flour
¼ cup sugar
10½ tablespoons chilled unsalted butter, cut into pieces
1 egg yolk
1 tablespoon whipping cream, chilled

Filling
½ cup walnuts, coarsely chopped
¼ cup raisins
¼ cup golden raisins
¼ cup dried apricots, cut into ½-inch pieces
¼ cup dried pineapple, cut into ½-inch pieces
¼ cup brandy

Caramel
1 cup plus 2 tablespoons sugar
¾ cup water
¾ cup plus 2 tablespoons whipping cream
5 tablespoons unsalted butter

Chocolate Glaze*

Sugarplums**

For crust: Mix flour and sugar in large bowl. Add butter and cut in until mixture resembles coarse meal. Mix yolk with cream to blend. Add to flour mixture and stir until dough comes together. Gather dough into 2 balls, 1 slightly smaller than the other. Flatten into disks. Wrap separately in plastic and refrigerate 30 minutes. (*Can be prepared 1 day ahead. Let dough soften slightly at room temperature before continuing.*)

For filling: Combine all ingredients in medium metal bowl. Let mixture soak at least 2 and up to 6 hours.

Roll larger dough piece out on floured surface to 12-inch round. Roll dough up on rolling pin and transfer to 9-inch round tart pan with removable bottom. Trim and finish edges. Roll second dough piece out to 10-inch round. Transfer to cookie sheet. Refrigerate tart shell and round 1 hour.

For caramel: Cook sugar and water in heavy medium saucepan over medium-low heat, stirring until sugar dissolves. Increase heat and bring to boil, brushing down sides of pan with wet pastry brush. Boil mixture without stirring until amber color, swirling pan occasionally, about 10 minutes. Add cream and butter and whisk to combine (mixture will bubble up). Continue cooking until candy thermometer registers 238°F (soft-ball stage). Pour caramel into medium metal bowl. Cool to room temperature, about 1 hour.

Preheat oven to 350°F. Line cookie sheet with parchment or foil. Spread fruit and nut mixture evenly in crust. Pour caramel over. Press dough round on top. Trim off excess. Pierce in several places with tip of small sharp knife.

Place tart on parchment-lined sheet. Bake until crust is golden brown, about 35 minutes. (Some caramel may leak out.) Cool on rack, about 6 hours.

Turn tart over onto rack. Set over rimmed cookie sheet. Spoon some Chocolate Glaze over sides of tart. Set aside ½ cup glaze. Pour remaining glaze over tart. Smooth top and sides of tart with spatula if necessary.

Line small cookie sheet with waxed paper. Rewarm reserved ½ cup glaze in top of double boiler over simmering water until just lukewarm, stirring occasionally. Grasp one sugarplum between thumb and index finger. Dip halfway into glaze. Remove from glaze and allow excess to drip back into pan. Place on prepared sheet, chocolate side up. Repeat with remaining sugarplums. Refrigerate sugarplums until glaze is set, about 30 minutes.

Garnish top of tart with glazed sugarplums. (*Can be prepared 1 day ahead. Cover and refrigerate.*) Cut into wedges and serve at room temperature.

*Chocolate Glaze

Makes about 1½ cups

10 ounces semisweet chocolate, chopped
½ cup hot whipping cream

¼ cup (½ stick) unsalted butter, room temperature

Melt chocolate in top of double boiler over simmering water, stirring until smooth. Remove from over water. Whisk in cream and butter. (*Can be prepared 1 day ahead. Cover and let stand at room temperature. Whisk over simmering water until melted before continuing.*) Let glaze stand until just cool to touch.

**Sugarplums

Makes about twenty-five ½-inch balls

¼ cup walnuts
¼ cup dried apricots
2 tablespoons golden raisins
2 tablespoons sweetened shredded coconut

2 tablespoons pitted dates
1 tablespoon brandy
¼ cup sugar

Finely chop first 5 ingredients in processor; do not puree. Transfer to small bowl; mix in brandy. Form mixture into ½-inch balls by rolling teaspoonfuls between hands. Roll balls in sugar. (*Can be prepared 1 day ahead. Store at room temperature in airtight container.*)

Chocolate Peanut Butter "Quiche"

Chocolate and peanut butter in a dessert quiche. It will keep up to two days.

16 servings

Crust
1¼ cups sifted all purpose flour
3½ tablespoons sugar
¼ teaspoon salt
6 tablespoons (¾ stick) chilled unsalted butter, diced
1½ tablespoons beaten egg

Chocolate Topping
1½ cups whipping cream
4 ounces bittersweet (not unsweetened) or semisweet chocolate, chopped
2 ounces unsweetened chocolate, finely chopped

½ cup firmly packed golden brown sugar
3 egg yolks

Peanut Butter Filling
1 cup plus 3 tablespoons creamy peanut butter (do not use old-fashioned style or freshly ground)
½ cup firmly packed golden brown sugar
1 cup chilled whipping cream
1 large egg yolk

Lightly crushed peanut brittle (optional)

For crust: Mix flour, sugar and salt in processor. Add butter and cut in until mixture resembles coarse meal. Add egg and blend until dough just begins to come together. Gather dough into ball. Flatten into 5- to 6-inch round. Roll dough out between sheets of plastic wrap to 12-inch round. Peel off top sheet of plastic. Invert dough into 10-inch-diameter fluted quiche dish with 1¼-inch-high sides. Press dough into crevices, using plastic as aid. Peel off plastic. Trim excess dough. Refrigerate crust until firm, about 1 hour. (*Can be prepared 1 day ahead.*)

Position rack in center of oven and preheat to 350°F. Lightly butter 12-inch foil round. Place buttered side down in dough-lined quiche dish, pressing into crevices. Fill with dried beans or pie weights. Bake 15 minutes. Carefully remove beans and foil. Bake crust until golden brown, piercing bottom with fork if dough puffs, about 10 more minutes. Cool crust on rack.

For chocolate topping: Bring cream to simmer in heavy medium saucepan. Remove from heat. Add both chocolates and stir until melted. Add sugar and stir to dissolve. Cool to lukewarm. Mix in yolks and cool completely.

For peanut butter filling: Mix peanut butter and sugar in processor. With machine running, gradually add 1 cup cream through feed tube. Add yolk and process until smooth, stopping occasionally to scrape down sides of bowl.

Preheat oven to 325°F. Spoon 2 cups peanut butter filling over bottom of crust; smooth top. Cover and refrigerate remaining filling. Spread chocolate topping over. Bake until outer edges of filling puff and center moves only slightly when shaken, about 32 minutes. Transfer to rack and cool completely. Cover and refrigerate until very firm, about 4 hours. (*Can be prepared up to 2 days ahead.*)

Spoon remaining peanut butter filling into pastry bag fitted with small star tip. Pipe 16 rosettes of peanut butter around outer edge of quiche. Sprinkle with peanut brittle if desired. Let stand 15 minutes before serving.

Apple Cider Tartlets

These elegant little tarts can be prepared four hours ahead. Just top with sautéed apple slices and, before serving, broil quickly until nicely caramelized.

6 servings

Pastry
- 1½ cups unbleached all purpose flour
- 2 tablespoons sugar
- ½ teaspoon salt
- ½ cup (1 stick) chilled unsalted butter, cut into pieces
- 1 egg yolk
- 4 teaspoons (about) whipping cream

Filling
- 3 cups apple cider
- 1 cinnamon stick
- ¾ cup firmly packed golden brown sugar

- Pinch of salt
- 2 large eggs
- 2 large egg yolks
- 2 tablespoons (¼ stick) unsalted butter
- 1 teaspoon vanilla extract

Caramelized Apples
- ¼ cup (½ stick) unsalted butter
- ½ cup sugar
- ½ teaspoon cinnamon
- 3 tart green apples, peeled, cored and cut into ¼-inch-thick slices

Whipped Sour Cream Topping*

For pastry: Combine flour, sugar and salt in processor. Add butter and cut in using on/off turns until mixture resembles coarse crumbs. Mix in yolk and enough cream by teaspoons to form dough that just comes together. Gather dough into ball; flatten into disk. Wrap in plastic and refrigerate 1 hour.

Preheat oven to 350°F. Roll dough out on lightly floured surface to thickness of ⅛ inch. Roll dough onto rolling pin and unroll over six 4½-inch-diameter tartlet pans with ¾-inch-high sides, allowing dough to drape into pans. Run rolling pin over dough to trim edges. Press dough into pans. Line crusts with foil or parchment. Fill with dried beans or pie weights. Bake until crust edges are light brown, about 15 minutes. Remove foil and beans. Bake crusts until golden brown, about 5 minutes more. Transfer to rack and cool. (*Can be prepared 1 day ahead. Wrap tartlets in pans with plastic wrap and store at room temperature.*)

For filling: Preheat oven to 350°F. Boil cider with cinnamon in heavy medium nonaluminum saucepan until reduced to 1½ cups, about 15 minutes. Discard cinnamon. Reduce heat to low. Add brown sugar and salt to cider and stir until sugar dissolves. Whisk eggs and yolks in large bowl to blend. Gradually whisk in hot cider mixture. Add butter and vanilla and whisk until butter melts. Ladle ⅓ cup filling into each tart shell (reserving any remainder for another use). Bake until filling no longer moves in center when pans are shaken, about 20 minutes. Cool on racks. (*Can be prepared 4 hours ahead. Let stand at room temperature until ready to use.*)

For apples: Melt butter in heavy large skillet over medium heat. Add sugar and stir until dissolved. Mix in cinnamon. Add apples and sauté until tender, about 15 minutes. Cool apples in skillet for 20 minutes.

Preheat broiler. Arrange apple slices in overlapping spiral atop each tart. Broil until apples caramelize, about 1 minute. Serve tarts warm or at room temperature with sour cream topping.

*Whipped Sour Cream Topping

Makes about 1½ cups

⅔ cup chilled whipping cream
¼ cup chilled sour cream

1 tablespoon sugar

Using electric mixer, whip cream, sour cream and sugar in medium bowl to soft peaks. (*Can be prepared 4 hours ahead. Cover and refrigerate.*)

Chocolate Hazelnut Strudels

This makes two strudels. If you're baking for six or fewer, freeze the extra one.

Makes 2 strudels; about 6 servings each

Chocolate Filling
¼ cup sugar
1½ tablespoons cornstarch
1½ tablespoons all purpose flour
1 cup milk
1 large egg
1 large egg yolk
1½ ounces imported bittersweet (not unsweetened) chocolate, finely chopped
1½ ounces unsweetened chocolate, finely chopped

1 tablespoon unsalted butter
2 teaspoons Frangelico liqueur or dark rum
⅛ teaspoon vanilla extract

Pastry
Hazelnut Praline*
⅔ cup ground husked toasted hazelnuts (about 3 ounces)
10 phyllo pastry sheets
1 cup (2 sticks) unsalted butter, melted

For filling: Mix first 3 ingredients in heavy small saucepan. Gradually whisk in milk. Add egg and yolk. Boil 2 minutes, stirring constantly. Reduce heat to medium-low and cook until custard thickens to consistency of peanut butter, stirring constantly, about 2 minutes. Pour into bowl. Add both chocolates and butter and whisk until smooth. Stir in Frangelico and vanilla. Press plastic wrap onto surface of filling. Refrigerate until chilled. (*Can be prepared 2 days ahead.*)

For pastry: Mix ⅔ cup Hazelnut Praline and ground nuts in small bowl. Arrange 1 pastry sheet on work surface (keep remainder covered with damp towel). Brush pastry with melted butter. Sprinkle evenly with 1 tablespoon praline-nut mixture. Top with second pastry sheet. Brush lightly with melted butter. Sprinkle evenly with 1 tablespoon praline-nut mixture. Continue layering with 3 more pastry sheets. Starting 3 inches in from one long side, sprinkle 1 tablespoon praline-nut mixture in 14-inch-long line.

Mix ¾ cup Hazelnut Praline into chocolate filling. Spoon ½ of chocolate filling atop 14-inch-long praline-nut line. Sprinkle 1 tablespoon praline-nut mixture over filling. Starting at filled side, gently and loosely roll pastry up jelly roll style, forming strudel. Brush top, sides and bottom with melted butter. Place seam side down on heavy large baking sheet. Tuck pastry ends under to enclose filling completely. Repeat with remaining pastry, butter, praline-nut mixture and filling, forming second strudel. Cover strudels with plastic wrap and refrigerate at least 4 hours. (*Can be prepared ahead. Refrigerate overnight or wrap tightly and freeze up to 2 weeks. Defrost overnight in refrigerator before baking.*)

Position rack in center of oven and preheat to 375°F. Remove plastic wrap. Bake strudels until golden brown, about 25 minutes. Sprinkle each with 1 tablespoon praline. Cool 1½ hours on sheet. Trim ends. Cut each strudel into 1-inch-thick rounds.

*Hazelnut Praline

You can use this on ice cream, too.

Makes about 1⅔ cups

1 cup sugar	1 cup husked toasted hazelnuts
6 tablespoons water	(about 4½ ounces)

Lightly oil small baking sheet. Cook sugar and water in heavy small saucepan over low heat, stirring until sugar dissolves. Increase heat and boil without stirring until syrup turns deep golden brown. Mix in nuts. Pour praline onto prepared sheet. Cool completely. Break praline into 2-inch pieces. Finely grind in processor. (*Can be prepared 2 weeks ahead; refrigerate airtight.*)

Pumpkin-Buttermilk Doughnuts with Maple Sugar

These old-fashioned cake doughnuts taste as good as they look.

Makes about 18

3½ cups sifted all purpose flour	2 large eggs
1 tablespoon baking powder	⅔ cup canned solid pack pumpkin
1 teaspoon baking soda	⅔ cup buttermilk
1 teaspoon salt	½ cup maple sugar* or firmly
½ teaspoon cinnamon	packed golden brown sugar
½ teaspoon ground ginger	½ cup sugar
¼ cup (½ stick) unsalted butter, room temperature ·	Vegetable oil (for deep frying)
¾ cup sugar	

Resift flour with baking powder, soda, salt, cinnamon and ginger in large bowl. Using electric mixer, cream butter in large bowl until fluffy. Gradually add ¾ cup sugar and beat until fluffy. Add eggs 1 at a time, beating well after each addition. Beat in ¼ cup dry ingredients. Add pumpkin and buttermilk and mix until thoroughly combined. Add remaining dry ingredients and stir until just blended (dough will be slightly sticky). Cover and chill at least 3 hours or overnight.

Combine maple sugar and ½ cup sugar in paper bag.

Roll dough out on lightly floured surface to thickness of ¼ to ⅓ inch. Using lightly floured 3½-inch doughnut cutter (or 3-inch-round cookie cutter and 1-inch-round cookie cutter for center hole), cut out doughnuts and doughnut holes. Transfer to floured board. Let stand 10 minutes.

Heat 4 inches oil in deep fryer or heavy large saucepan to 365°F. Add ¼ of doughnuts and doughnut holes and cook until golden brown, turning once, about 5 minutes. Transfer to paper towels using slotted spoon and drain 3 minutes. Immediately transfer to paper bag containing sugar mixture. Shake to coat. Arrange on racks. Repeat process with remaining doughnuts and doughnut holes in 3 more batches. (*Can be prepared 1 day ahead. Store in airtight container.*)

* Available at natural foods stores and some specialty foods stores.

 Cakes

Instant Cassata

A sublime dessert easy enough to prepare right before serving. It keeps well, too, so you can make it up to a day ahead. Even easier, spoon the chocolate-cherry sauce over vanilla ice cream.

4 servings

²⁄₃ cup ricotta cheese
2 tablespoons sugar
¼ teaspoon vanilla extract
½ 10¾-ounce frozen pound cake, thawed

3 ounces semisweet chocolate, chopped
6 tablespoons cherry preserves
2 tablespoons unsalted butter
2 tablespoons brandy

Mix ricotta, sugar and vanilla in small bowl. Cut cake horizontally into 4 layers. Place bottom layer on plate. Spread with ⅓ of ricotta. Top with second layer and spread with ⅓ of ricotta. Repeat layering, ending with cake.

Melt chocolate with preserves and butter in heavy small saucepan over low heat, stirring until smooth. Mix in brandy. (*Can be prepared 1 day ahead. Cover cake and refrigerate. Cover sauce and let stand at room temperature. Rewarm sauce over low heat, stirring.*)

Cut cake crosswise into 4 slices. Arrange cut side down on plates. Spoon warm sauce over and serve.

Flash-in-the-Pan Birthday Cake

Here is your cake and ice cream in one easy-to-prepare dessert—no baking required. Organized cooks can make it two days before the celebration.

Makes 1 large cake

1 1-pound frozen pound cake, thawed
2 pints coffee ice cream, softened slightly
1⅓ cups prepared hot fudge topping

4 1.2-ounce packages chocolate-covered English toffee (such as Heath bars), chopped

1 cup chilled whipping cream, whipped to peaks

Cut pound cake into ⅓-inch-thick slices. Halve each diagonally, forming triangles. Line bottom of 9-inch springform pan with cake by arranging some triangles, points facing in, around bottom edge of pan. Fill in center with more triangles, then cut additional pieces to fill in any remaining spaces. Spread half of ice cream over cake. Freeze until firm, about 1 hour.

Spread half of fudge topping over ice cream. Sprinkle with half of chopped candy. Repeat layering with remaining cake, ice cream, fudge topping and candy, freezing after adding ice cream. Cover tightly and freeze until ice cream is set, about 30 minutes. (*Can be prepared up to 2 days ahead.*)

Remove pan sides. Place cake on platter. Spread some of whipped cream over sides of cake. Spoon remaining cream into pastry bag fitted with medium star tip. Pipe cream in rosettes around upper edge of cake.

Mile-High Whipped Cream Cake with Fresh Fruit

This dramatic, extrava-gantly tall "shortcake" is lots of fun for a party. You can use just about any fruit that is available. The cake layers and glaze can be made a day ahead.

12 servings

Cake
2 cups all purpose flour
2 teaspoons baking powder
½ teaspoon salt
3 large eggs, room temperature
1⅓ cups sugar
2 teaspoons vanilla extract
1 cup milk (do not use lowfat or nonfat)
¼ cup (½ stick) unsalted butter, melted, lukewarm

Glaze
½ cup peach jam
¼ cup Grand Marnier or other orange liqueur

Filling
2 large navel oranges
2 medium bananas, peeled and sliced
⅔ cup diced peeled peaches
2 tablespoons fresh lemon juice
1 1-pint basket strawberries, hulled and quartered

2 cups chilled whipping cream
⅓ cup sugar
1 teaspoon vanilla extract

Strawberries with stems

For cake: Preheat oven to 350°F. Grease bottoms of three 8-inch-diameter cake pans with 1½-inch-high sides. Line bottoms of pans with waxed paper, then grease paper.

Mix flour, baking powder and salt in medium bowl. Using electric mixer, beat eggs in large bowl until foamy. Gradually add sugar and beat until pale yellow and slowly dissolving ribbon forms when beaters are lifted. Beat in vanilla. Mix in dry ingredients alternately with milk beginning and ending with dry ingredients. Mix in butter.

Divide batter among prepared pans; smooth tops. Bake until edges are golden brown and toothpick inserted in centers comes out clean, about 20 minutes. Cool cakes in pans on racks. Run small sharp knife around pan sides to loosen. Turn cakes out onto racks; peel off paper. (*Cakes can be prepared 1 day ahead. Wrap each tightly in plastic and store at room temperature.*)

For glaze: Melt jam in heavy medium saucepan over low heat. Remove from heat. Mix in Grand Marnier. (*Can be prepared 1 day ahead. Cool. Cover and let stand at room temperature.*)

For filling: Remove peel and white pith from oranges. Working over bowl, cut between membranes with small sharp knife to release segments. Drain well. Pat dry with paper towels. Toss bananas and peaches with lemon juice in large bowl. Drain off excess liquid. Add orange segments and quartered strawberries and toss gently.

Whip cream to soft peaks in large bowl. Gradually add sugar and vanilla and beat until stiff. Spoon 1 cup whipped cream into pastry bag fitted with medium star tip; refrigerate.

Rewarm glaze over low heat, stirring constantly. Place 1 cake layer on plate. Brush ⅓ of glaze over cake. Spoon ½ of fruit over, allowing some to show around cake edges. Spread ¾ cup whipped cream over. Top with second cake layer. Brush with ⅓ of glaze. Spoon remaining fruit over, allowing some to show around cake edges. Spread ¾ cup whipped cream over. Top with third cake layer. Brush with remaining glaze. Spread ¾ cup whipped cream over. Pipe cream in pastry bag decoratively atop cake. Refrigerate for 30 minutes.

Arrange fresh strawberries decoratively atop cake and serve.

Orange Hazelnut Roulade

Offer this light, orange- and cream-filled jelly roll cake with coffee. If desired, the cake can be topped with additional whipped cream before serving. The extra orange curd is delicious over waffles.

8 servings

Orange Curd
 2 **cups fresh orange juice**
 8 **large egg yolks**
 6 **tablespoons sugar**
 2 **large eggs**
 2 **tablespoons fresh lemon juice**
 ¾ **cup (1½ sticks) unsalted butter, cut into pieces**
 2 **tablespoons grated orange peel**

Cake
 1½ **cups husked toasted hazelnuts (about 7½ ounces)**
 2 **tablespoons unbleached all purpose flour**

 6 **large eggs, separated, room temperature**
10 **tablespoons sugar**
 ½ **teaspoon vanilla extract**
 1 **teaspoon grated orange peel**
 ½ **teaspoon cream of tartar**
 ⅛ **teaspoon salt**

 ⅔ **cup whipping cream**
 1 **tablespoon powdered sugar**
 ½ **teaspoon vanilla extract**

 Powdered sugar
 Toasted hazelnuts
 Candied Orange Peel* (optional)

For curd: Boil orange juice in heavy medium saucepan until reduced to ⅔ cup. Whisk yolks, sugar and eggs in large bowl. Gradually whisk in orange juice, lemon juice, then butter and peel. Set bowl over saucepan of boiling water and stir until custard thickens to consistency of yogurt, about 12 minutes; do not boil. Pour into another bowl. Press plastic wrap onto surface of curd to prevent skin from forming. Refrigerate overnight. (*Can be prepared 2 days ahead.*)

For cake: Preheat oven to 300°F. Butter 11 × 17-inch jelly roll pan. Line with parchment. Butter and flour parchment. Coarsely grind 1½ cups nuts with flour in processor. Using electric mixer, beat yolks with 5 tablespoons sugar in medium bowl until pale yellow and slowly dissolving ribbon forms when beaters are lifted. Stir in ½ teaspoon vanilla and orange peel. Using clean dry beaters, beat whites with cream of tartar and salt in large bowl until peaks form. Gradually add remaining 5 tablespoons sugar and beat until stiff but not dry. Fold whites into yolk mixture. Gently fold in ground hazelnut and flour mixture.

Spread batter evenly in prepared pan. Bake until toothpick inserted in center comes out clean, about 30 minutes. Run small sharp knife around pan sides if necessary to loosen cake. Slide cake on parchment onto rack. Cool completely. (*Can be prepared 1 day ahead. Return to pan, cover with plastic wrap and let stand at room temperature.*)

Slide cake on parchment onto work surface. Loosen cake from parchment using heavy large knife as aid.

Whip cream with 1 tablespoon powdered sugar and ½ teaspoon vanilla in small bowl until soft peaks form. Spoon ¾ cup whipped cream into pastry bag fitted with medium star tip; refrigerate. Spread all but ¾ cup curd over cake, leaving ¾-inch border (reserve remaining curd for another use). Spread remaining whipped cream over curd. Starting at one long side and using parchment as aid, roll cake up jelly roll style. Transfer to platter seam side down. (*Can be prepared 3 hours ahead. Cover and refrigerate.*)

Just before serving, sift powdered sugar over cake; trim ends. Pipe cream decoratively down center of cake. Top with hazelnuts and candied peel.

*Candied Orange Peel

Makes about ⅔ cup

 Peel from 1 large orange, cut julienne

 ½ **cup water**
 2 **tablespoons sugar**

Blanch peel in saucepan of boiling water 1 minute. Drain. Repeat blanching and draining twice.

Line baking sheet with waxed paper. Cook ½ cup water and sugar in heavy small saucepan over medium-low heat, stirring until sugar dissolves. Add peel and simmer until almost no liquid remains in pan, about 10 minutes. Transfer peel to prepared sheet, separating into strips. Cool completely. (*Can be prepared 2 days ahead. Cover and let stand at room temperature.*)

Aspen Chocolate Cream Cake

Layers of chocolate-chip-studded chocolate cake alternate with layers of vanilla-flavored pastry cream and sliced strawberries. You can make the cake in the morning and garnish the top with strawberries just before serving.

10 servings

Pastry Cream Filling
- ⅔ cup milk
- 1 1-inch piece vanilla bean, split lengthwise
- 2 egg yolks
- 2 tablespoons sugar
- 1 tablespoon all purpose flour

Cake
- 2 cups cake flour
- 1 teaspoon baking soda
- ½ teaspoon salt
- 1½ cups sugar
- ½ cup unsweetened cocoa powder
- 1 cup buttermilk
- ½ cup (1 stick) unsalted butter, room temperature
- ½ cup firmly packed golden brown sugar
- 2 eggs
- 1½ teaspoons vanilla extract
- 1 cup semisweet chocolate chips

Chocolate Icing
- 8 ounces semisweet chocolate, chopped
- 2 ounces unsweetened chocolate, chopped
- 12 tablespoons (1½ sticks) unsalted butter, room temperature
- 6 ounces semisweet chocolate
- 2½ 1-pint baskets strawberries, hulled

For pastry cream: Scald milk with vanilla bean in heavy medium saucepan. Whisk yolks, sugar and flour in medium bowl. Gradually whisk in hot milk. Return mixture to saucepan. Bring to boil over medium heat, whisking constantly. Reduce heat to medium-low and stir until pastry cream is very thick and smooth, about 1 minute. Transfer to small bowl. Remove vanilla bean. Press plastic wrap onto surface of cream and refrigerate until well chilled. (*Can be prepared 3 days ahead.*)

For cake: Preheat oven to 350°F. Grease and flour three 8-inch-diameter cake pans. Sift first 3 ingredients into medium bowl. Mix 1 cup sugar and cocoa in another bowl. Gradually stir ½ cup buttermilk into cocoa mixture. Using electric mixer, cream butter, brown sugar and remaining ½ cup sugar in large bowl until fluffy. Beat in eggs and vanilla. Beat in cocoa mixture. Mix in dry ingredients alternately with remaining ½ cup buttermilk, beginning and ending with dry ingredients. Fold in chocolate chips.

Divide batter among prepared pans. Bake until toothpick inserted into centers comes out clean, about 30 minutes. Cool in pans on rack 10 minutes. Turn cakes out onto racks and cool completely. (*Can be prepared 1 day ahead. Wrap separately in plastic and store at room temperature.*)

For icing: Melt 8 ounces semisweet and 2 ounces unsweetened chocolate in top of double boiler over simmering water, stirring until smooth. Remove from over water and cool to room temperature, about 20 minutes. Using electric mixer, beat butter until fluffy. Gradually beat in melted chocolate.

Line cookie sheet with waxed paper. Using vegetable peeler, shave 6 ounces semisweet chocolate onto sheet.

Slice 1 basket of strawberries into ⅛-inch-thick slices. Place 1 cake layer on cardboard round or platter. Spread ½ of pastry cream over. Distribute ½ of strawberry slices over filling. Top with second cake layer. Spread with remaining pastry cream and top with remaining strawberry slices. Top with last cake layer. Spread top and sides of cake with chocolate icing. Gently press chocolate shavings onto sides of cake. (*Can be prepared 8 hours ahead. Refrigerate. Let cake stand for 3 hours at room temperature before continuing.*)

Slice remaining strawberries into ⅛-inch-thick slices. Place strawberry slices on top of cake in concentric circles, tips pointing toward outer edge of cake and overlapping slightly. Cut chocolate cake into wedges and serve.

Fudge-slathered Fudge Cake

A moist, dense dessert. Begin making the cake a day ahead of serving.

12 servings

Cake
½ cup (1 stick) unsalted butter
3 tablespoons brandy
6 ounces bittersweet (not unsweetened) or semisweet chocolate, chopped
¾ cup walnuts (about 3 ounces)
2 tablespoons all purpose flour

6 large eggs, separated, room temperature
Pinch of salt
½ cup sugar
1 teaspoon vanilla extract

Frosting
1½ cups sugar
1 cup whipping cream
6 ounces unsweetened chocolate, finely chopped
½ cup (1 stick) unsalted butter, cut into pieces
1 teaspoon vanilla extract

1 cup chopped walnuts (about 4 ounces)

For cake: Preheat oven to 350°F. Lightly grease two 8-inch square baking pans with 2-inch-high sides. Line with foil, extending over sides. Grease and flour foil. Tap out excess flour. Melt butter in heavy medium saucepan over low heat. Add brandy and chocolate and stir until chocolate melts and mixture is smooth. Cool. Finely grind walnuts with flour in processor.

Using electric mixer, beat whites with salt in large bowl until soft peaks just begin to form. Gradually add ¼ cup sugar and beat until stiff but not dry. Beat yolks in medium bowl with remaining ¼ cup sugar until pale yellow and slowly dissolving ribbon forms when beaters are lifted. Beat in vanilla and chocolate mixture. Add ground nut mixture and beat until just blended. Fold ¼ of whites into batter to lighten. Gently fold in remaining whites. Divide batter between prepared pans; smooth tops. Bake until tops spring back lightly when touched in center and cakes begin to pull away from pan sides, about 30 minutes. Cool cakes in pans on racks overnight.

For frosting: Stir sugar and cream in heavy 2½-quart saucepan over medium heat until sugar dissolves and mixture comes to boil. Reduce heat to low and cook for 10 minutes without stirring (mixture will bubble), occasionally washing down sugar crystals from sides of pan with moistened pastry brush. Pour mixture into bowl. Add chocolate, butter and vanilla and stir until melted. Cool frosting to room temperature, stirring occasionally, about 1½ hours. Refrigerate until thick enough to spread, stirring occasionally, about 40 minutes.

Lift cakes from pans using foil sides as aid. Trim any uneven edges. Invert 1 cake onto plate. Remove foil.

Spread 1¼ cups frosting over cake layer. Top with second cake layer. Remove foil. Spread remaining frosting over top and sides of cake. Press walnuts on sides of cake. Let cake stand at least 1 hour at room temperature. (*Can be prepared 1 day ahead. Refrigerate.*) Serve at room temperature.

Chocolate Harvest Cake

Dried fruit and bittersweet chocolate combine in a luscious layer cake.

10 servings

Cake
- ¾ cup unbleached all purpose flour
- ¼ cup unsweetened cocoa powder
- 1½ teaspoons baking powder
- 3 large eggs
- ½ cup sugar
- 1 teaspoon vanilla extract
- 3 tablespoons unsalted butter, melted, lukewarm

Fruit Filling
- ¾ cup water
- 15 pitted prunes
- 12 dried apricots
- 2 tablespoons brandy
- ½ cup (1 stick) unsalted butter, room temperature

Chocolate Ganache*

Chocolate Glaze**
- 1½ cups toasted walnuts, chopped
- 3 dried apricots
- 3 pitted prunes

For cake: Preheat oven to 350°F. Butter and flour 9-inch-diameter cake pan with 1½-inch-high sides. Sift ¾ cup flour with cocoa and baking powder into medium bowl. Whisk eggs and sugar in large metal bowl. Set over saucepan of boiling water and whisk eggs until warm to touch. Remove bowl from over water.

Using electric mixer, beat egg mixture until it whitens and more than triples in volume, about 5 minutes. Mix in vanilla. Sift dry ingredients over. Gently fold into egg mixture until just incorporated. Add butter and fold in until just incorporated; do not overmix. Pour batter into prepared pan. Bake until cake begins to pull away from sides of pan and toothpick inserted in center comes out clean, about 20 minutes. Invert cake onto rack and cool.

For fruit filling: Bring first 3 ingredients to boil in heavy medium saucepan. Reduce heat and simmer until liquid is reduced to 2 tablespoons, stirring occasionally, about 15 minutes. Puree mixture in blender with brandy. Cool completely in blender. Add butter to puree and blend until smooth.

Cut cake horizontally into 3 layers using serrated knife. Place bottom cake layer on 9-inch cardboard round or cake pan bottom. Set aside ½ cup ganache for cake top and sides. Spread half of remaining ganache over bottom cake layer. Spread scant ½ cup fruit filling over. Top with middle cake layer. Spread with other half of ganache. Spread scant ½ cup fruit filling over. Cover with top cake layer. Spread remaining fruit filling over top of cake. Refrigerate 30 minutes.

Spread reserved ½ cup ganache over top and sides of cake. Refrigerate until ganache is firm, about 1 hour.

Place cake on rack set over rimmed baking sheet. Spoon some of glaze over sides of cake. Pour remaining glaze over top of cake. Smooth top and sides with spatula if necessary. Let stand 30 minutes. Press toasted walnuts onto sides of cake using palm of hand.

Roll 3 dried apricots and 3 pitted prunes out on lightly oiled surface to thickness of ⅛ inch. Cut into assorted leaf shapes. Arrange in cluster atop cake. (*Can be prepared 1 day ahead; refrigerate. Let cake stand 3½ hours at room temperature before serving.*)

*Chocolate Ganache

A rich, chocolaty filling, good in any cake.

Makes about 1⅓ cups

- 1 cup whipping cream
- 5 ounces bittersweet (not unsweetened) or semisweet chocolate, chopped

Bring cream to boil in heavy small saucepan. Remove pan from heat. Add chocolate and stir until melted. Pour into bowl; refrigerate overnight.

Just before using, beat with electric mixer until just fluffy, about 5 seconds.

**Chocolate Glaze

Makes about 1⅛ cups

½ **cup (1 stick) unsalted butter, cut into pieces**
4 **ounces bittersweet (not unsweetened) or semisweet chocolate, chopped**

1 **tablespoon light corn syrup**

Melt butter and chocolate in heavy small saucepan over low heat, stirring until smooth. Mix in corn syrup. (*Can be prepared 1 day ahead. Cover and let stand at room temperature. Whisk over low heat until melted before continuing.*) Let glaze stand until just cool to touch, about 20 minutes. Use immediately.

Lemon Cheesecake with Gingersnap Crust

12 servings

Crust
20 **vanilla wafer cookies**
10 **gingersnap cookies**
3 **tablespoons sugar**
1 **tablespoon grated lemon peel**
¼ **cup (½ stick) unsalted butter, melted**

Filling
1 **tablespoon plus ¾ teaspoon unflavored gelatin**
¼ **cup cold water**
Peel from 2 lemons, removed with vegetable peeler

1 **1-inch piece fresh ginger, peeled**
¾ **cup plus 2 tablespoons sugar**
Generous pinch of salt
3 **large egg yolks**
¾ **cup milk (do not use lowfat or nonfat)**

12 **ounces cream cheese, room temperature**
⅓ **cup fresh lemon juice**
1½ **cups chilled whipping cream**
Lemon Curd*

Fresh mint sprigs

For crust: Position rack in center of oven and preheat to 350°F. Lightly oil 9-inch-diameter springform pan. Finely grind vanilla wafers and gingersnaps with sugar and lemon peel in processor. Add butter and blend well. Sprinkle crumbs over bottom of prepared pan; press to form bottom crust. Bake until golden brown, 12 minutes. Cool.

For filling: Sprinkle gelatin over cold water in small bowl. Let stand 10 minutes to soften. Mince lemon peel and ginger with sugar and salt in processor until lemon peel and ginger are as fine as sugar. Add yolks and blend until light and fluffy. Scald milk in heavy medium saucepan. With processor running, add milk through feed tube and blend well. Return mixture to saucepan. Stir over medium-low heat until mixture thickens and leaves path on back of spoon when finger is drawn across, about 12 minutes; do not boil. Add gelatin mixture to custard and stir until dissolved. Strain into bowl, pressing on solids with back of spoon. Chill until thickened but not set, stirring often, about 20 minutes.

Blend cream cheese and lemon juice in processor until smooth. Add custard and blend until smooth. Pour into large bowl. Whip cream in medium bowl to soft peaks. Gently fold into filling. Pour half of filling over crust. Spoon half of curd by tablespoonfuls over filling. Swirl mixtures together using tip of knife. Pour remaining filling over. Spoon remaining curd over by tablespoonfuls. Swirl mixtures together using tip of knife. Refrigerate at least 4 hours or overnight.

Run knife around sides of cake. Release pan sides. Garnish with mint.

*Lemon Curd

Makes about 1 cup

¼ teaspoon unflavored gelatin
1 teaspoon water
1 tablespoon grated lemon peel
½ cup sugar

¼ cup fresh lemon juice
3 large egg yolks
6 tablespoons (¾ stick) unsalted butter

Sprinkle gelatin over water in small cup. Let stand 10 minutes to soften. Mince lemon peel with sugar in processor until lemon peel is as fine as sugar. Transfer to heavy small saucepan. Mix in lemon juice and yolks, then butter. Stir over medium heat until very thick, about 5 minutes; do not boil. Pour into bowl. Add gelatin and stir to dissolve. Cool completely, stirring frequently, about 1 hour.

Maple, Walnut and Date Cheesecake

Creamy and utterly decadent. This cheesecake is ideal for a party as it can be prepared up to two days ahead. The sauce would also be good over ice cream.

10 servings

Crust
20 vanilla wafer cookies
12 pitted dates, coarsely chopped
2 cups toasted walnuts (about 8 ounces)
3 tablespoons butter, melted

Filling
2 8-ounce packages cream cheese, room temperature
1 cup maple sugar or firmly packed golden brown sugar
½ cup pure maple syrup
6 large egg yolks
2 large eggs
2 cups whipping cream

Topping
2 cups sour cream
¼ cup maple sugar or firmly packed golden brown sugar

Maple, Date and Walnut Sauce*

For crust: Preheat oven to 350°F. Finely grind cookies in processor. With machine running, gradually add dates and blend until finely chopped. Add walnuts and grind coarsely using on/off turns. Add butter and blend using on/off turns until mixture resembles coarse meal. Press crumbs in bottom and 1½ inches up sides of 10-inch-diameter springform pan. Bake until slightly puffed and golden brown, about 12 minutes. Cool crust on rack. Maintain oven temperature.

For filling: Wrap foil around bottom and 2 inches up outside of crust-lined pan. Using electric mixer, beat cream cheese with sugar until sugar dissolves. Add syrup, yolks and eggs and beat until just blended. Mix in cream. Pour filling into crust. Set cheesecake in large baking pan. Add enough hot water to pan to come 1½ inches up sides of cheesecake. Bake until sides are set and center 4 inches of cheesecake move slightly when pan is shaken, about 70 minutes. Remove cheesecake from water. Maintain oven temperature.

Meanwhile, prepare topping: Mix sour cream and sugar in small bowl. Let stand 5 minutes. Stir until sugar dissolves. Spoon over cheesecake. Bake 5 minutes. Cool cheesecake completely on rack. Cover and refrigerate overnight. (*Can be prepared 2 days ahead.*)

Run small sharp knife around pan sides if necessary to loosen. Release pan sides. Transfer cheesecake to platter. Spoon some of sauce over center. Serve with remaining sauce.

* Maple, Date and Walnut Sauce

Makes about 2 cups

1 cup pure maple syrup
¾ cup chopped pitted dates

¾ cup coarsely chopped toasted
   walnuts (about 3 ounces)

Mix all ingredients in bowl.

 Cookies

Walnut Lace Cookies

Makes about 12

2 tablespoons (¼ stick) unsalted
   butter
⅓ cup firmly packed golden brown
   sugar
2 tablespoons whipping cream

2 teaspoons light corn syrup
½ cup finely chopped walnuts,
   preferably black (about
   2½ ounces)
1 tablespoon all purpose flour

Preheat oven to 350°F. Lightly butter 2 nonstick cookie sheets. Melt 2 tablespoons butter with sugar, cream and corn syrup in heavy small saucepan over
low heat, stirring until sugar dissolves. Add nuts and flour and bring to boil,
stirring constantly. Drop half of batter by tablespoonfuls onto prepared sheets,
spacing evenly. Bake until cookies are bubbly and golden brown, about 8 minutes. Cool slightly. Gently slide cookies off sheets using spatula. Transfer to
racks and cool. Repeat with remaining batter. (*Can be prepared 6 hours ahead.
Store in airtight container between sheets of waxed paper.*)

Walnut-Pepper Biscotti

*Don't be put off by the
title—the pepper adds a
nice "bite." These make a
terrific dessert to serve with
a glass of sweet white wine,
red wine or espresso.*

Makes about 3½ dozen

1¾ cups all purpose flour
½ teaspoon baking soda
½ teaspoon baking powder
⅛ teaspoon salt
1½ teaspoons freshly ground pepper
½ cup (1 stick) unsalted butter,
   room temperature

1 cup sugar
2 large eggs, room temperature
2 teaspoons grated orange peel
1½ teaspoons vanilla extract
¼ teaspoon almond extract
1½ cups walnuts, lightly toasted and
   coarsely chopped (about 6 ounces)

Sift first 4 ingredients into medium bowl. Mix in pepper. Using electric mixer,
cream butter in another bowl until light. Gradually add sugar and beat until
fluffy. Mix in eggs 1 at a time. Mix in orange peel and vanilla and almond
extracts. Mix in walnuts. Add dry ingredients and mix just until blended. Cover
dough with plastic and refrigerate until chilled. (*Can be prepared 1 day ahead.*)

Preheat oven to 350°F. Butter and flour 2 baking sheets. Divide dough into
3 pieces. Using lightly floured hands, roll each piece into 1½-inch-wide log on
lightly floured surface. Arrange 2 logs on one sheet, spacing 5 inches apart.
Arrange third log on second sheet. Bake until logs are light brown, about
20 minutes (logs will spread during baking). Cool slightly on pan. Cut logs on
baking sheet crosswise on diagonal into ¾-inch-wide slices. Turn cut side down
on baking sheets. Bake until golden brown, about 15 minutes. Transfer to racks
and cool. Store in airtight container.

Honey and Lemon Madeleines

The perfect treat to have with tea.

Makes about 2 dozen 3-inch cookies

Melted butter
2 large eggs
⅓ cup honey
¼ cup sugar
1½ teaspoons grated lemon peel
⅛ teaspoon ground cloves

½ teaspoon vanilla extract
1 cup sifted all purpose flour
¾ cup (1½ sticks) unsalted butter, melted and cooled to lukewarm

Sugar

Preheat oven to 400°F. Generously brush madeleine pan* with melted butter; dust with flour. Combine eggs and next 4 ingredients in bowl of electric mixer. Set over saucepan of simmering water and stir until lukewarm. Remove from over water and beat until pale yellow and tripled in volume. Add vanilla. On low speed gradually mix in flour, scraping bowl occasionally. Transfer ⅓ of batter to medium bowl. Gradually fold ¾ cup melted butter into batter in medium bowl (do not fold in water at bottom of butter). Return mixture to remaining batter and gently fold in.

Transfer batter to glass measuring cup. Pour into madeleine molds, filling almost to top. Bake until cookies are golden brown and springy to touch, turning pan halfway through cooking, about 12 minutes. Invert pan onto rack. Gently pry out cookies with knife tip. Sprinkle with sugar. Wipe out molds, grease with melted butter, dust with flour and repeat with remaining batter. Cool. Store in airtight container.

*A metal mold with scallop shell-shaped indentations, available at specialty cookware stores.

Hazelnut Thumbprint Cookies

This recipe doubles easily. Fill half the cookies with orange marmalade and the other half with raspberry preserves for a nice mix.

Makes about 2 dozen

1 cup sifted all purpose flour
⅛ teaspoon salt
½ cup (1 stick) unsalted butter, room temperature
⅓ cup sugar
1 egg yolk

¾ teaspoon vanilla extract
¾ cup toasted hazelnuts, coarsely ground (about 4 ounces)

Orange marmalade and/or raspberry preserves

Preheat oven to 350°F. Combine flour and salt in small bowl. Using electric mixer, cream butter in large bowl until fluffy. Add sugar and beat until light and fluffy. Mix in yolk and vanilla. Mix in dry ingredients and nuts.

Form dough into 1-inch balls. Arrange on ungreased baking sheet, spacing 1½ inches apart. Make depression in center of each using fingertip or handle of wooden spoon. Bake 10 minutes. Fill depressions with marmalade and/or preserves. Continue baking until cookies begin to color, about 10 minutes. Cool on rack. Store airtight.

Toffee Crunch Fans

Chopped toffee candy is folded into a classic short-bread dough, which is patted out into a round and scored into fans.

Makes 12

¾ cup (1½ sticks) unsalted butter, room temperature
⅓ cup packed dark brown sugar
¾ teaspoon vanilla extract
1½ cups all purpose flour

¼ cup cornstarch
¼ teaspoon salt
2 1.2-ounce packages chocolate-covered English toffee bars (such as Heath Bars), chopped

Preheat oven to 350°F. Using electric mixer, cream butter until light. Add brown sugar and vanilla and beat until light and fluffy. Combine flour, cornstarch and salt. Add to butter and mix until beginning to gather together. Mix in toffee.

Grease 10-inch glass pie dish. Press dough into bottom of pie dish, building edges ½ inch up sides. Use fork to crimp edges. Cut into 12 wedges, using ruler as guide and cutting all the way through dough. Pierce each wedge 3 times with fork. Bake until barely firm to touch and beginning to color, about 30 minutes. Recut wedges. Cool in pie dish on rack. (*Store airtight.*)

Lime Almond Squares

Lime replaces lemon in this new take on a classic, made simple by the processor.

Makes 16

Crust
- 1 cup all purpose flour
- ¼ cup firmly packed golden brown sugar
- ¼ teaspoon salt
- 6 tablespoons (¾ stick) well-chilled unsalted butter, cut into ½-inch pieces
- ¼ cup toasted slivered almonds

Filling
- ¾ cup sugar
- 2 eggs
- 3 tablespoons fresh lime juice
- 1 tablespoon grated lime peel
- ½ teaspoon baking powder
- Pinch of salt

Powdered sugar
Lime-peel curls (optional)

For crust: Preheat oven to 350°F. Line 8-inch square baking pan with foil; butter foil. Mix flour, sugar and salt in processor. Add butter and nuts and blend until fine meal forms. Press into bottom of prepared pan. Bake until golden brown, about 20 minutes.

Meanwhile, prepare filling: Blend ¾ cup sugar, eggs, lime juice, 1 tablespoon grated lime peel, baking powder and salt in processor until smooth.

Pour filling onto hot crust. Bake until filling begins to brown and is just springy to touch, about 20 minutes. Cool completely in pan on rack.

Lift foil and cookies from pan. Gently peel foil from edges. Cut into 16 squares. (*Can be prepared 1 day ahead. Wrap tightly and refrigerate.*) Sift powdered sugar over. Garnish each with lime peel. Serve at room temperature.

Caramel Almond Cashew Bars

Makes about 40

Pastry
- 1½ cups (3 sticks) unsalted butter, room temperature
- ⅔ cup sugar
- 2½ teaspoons grated lemon peel
- 3 cups all purpose flour
- ½ cup cornstarch
- ½ teaspoon salt

Topping
- 10 tablespoons (1¼ sticks) unsalted butter
- ½ cup plus 2 tablespoons firmly packed dark brown sugar
- ⅓ cup honey
- 1½ cups toasted blanched whole almonds (about 8 ounces)
- 1½ cups salted roasted cashews (about 8 ounces)
- 2½ tablespoons whipping cream

For pastry: Preheat oven to 350°F. Line 9 × 13-inch glass baking dish with foil. Using electric mixer, cream butter. Add sugar and lemon peel and beat until light and fluffy. Combine flour, cornstarch and salt in small bowl; mix to blend. Add to butter and mix until beginning to gather together. Turn out onto sheet of waxed paper; form into rectangle. Cover with another sheet of waxed paper. Roll out to 10 × 15-inch rectangle. Refrigerate 10 minutes.

Transfer pastry to prepared dish, discarding waxed paper. Fold and press as necessary to form 1-inch-high edges. Pierce all over with fork. Bake until beginning to color, piercing with fork if pastry puffs during baking (edges will recede), about 40 minutes. Remove from oven; maintain oven at 350°F.

For topping: Combine first 3 ingredients in heavy medium saucepan. Whisk over medium-high heat until mixture comes to boil. Boil without whisking until mixture thickens and bubbles enlarge, about 1 minute. Mix in almonds and cashews. Remove from heat and mix in whipping cream.

Spread topping in crust. Bake until caramel bubbles, about 20 minutes. Cool in pan on rack. Remove from pan, using foil as aid. Cut into 1½-inch squares. (*Store in airtight container.*)

Orange-Ginger Brownies

Candied orange peel and crystallized ginger add a sophisticated touch to these fudgy brownies. They're best the day they are baked, but you can wrap them individually and store them in an airtight container for up to three days.

Makes 2 dozen

4 ounces unsweetened chocolate, chopped
½ cup (1 stick) unsalted butter
1 tablespoon instant espresso powder
3 eggs
1½ cups sugar

1 teaspoon vanilla extract
¼ teaspoon almond extract
Pinch of salt
¾ cup sifted all purpose flour
⅓ cup finely chopped candied orange peel
⅓ cup finely chopped crystallized ginger

Preheat oven to 350°F. Butter and flour 12 × 7-inch glass baking dish. Melt chocolate and butter with espresso powder in top of double boiler over barely simmering water, stirring until smooth. Cool slightly.

Beat eggs to blend in medium bowl. Mix in sugar, vanilla and almond extracts and salt. Mix in chocolate mixture. Add flour and stir until combined. Mix in orange peel and ginger.

Spread batter in prepared pan. Bake until brownies are firm around edges and tester inserted in center comes out with only a few crumbs, about 25 minutes. Do not overcook. Cool on rack. Cut into 24 pieces. (*Can be prepared 3 days ahead. Wrap brownies individually and store in airtight container.*)

Macadamia Nut Brownies

Wrap leftovers in plastic to keep fresh for the rest of the week (if they last that long).

Makes about 9

3 ounces unsweetened chocolate
6 tablespoons (¾ stick) unsalted butter
2 teaspoons instant espresso powder
2 large eggs

1 cup sugar
¾ teaspoon vanilla extract
½ cup sifted all purpose flour
¾ cup salted macadamia nuts, coarsely chopped

Preheat oven to 350°F. Butter and flour 8-inch square baking pan. Melt chocolate and butter with espresso powder in top of double boiler over barely simmering water; stir until smooth. Remove from over water. Cool mixture slightly.

Whisk eggs in medium bowl until foamy. Whisk in sugar, then vanilla. Mix in melted chocolate. Add flour and mix just until blended. Fold in nuts. Spread batter in prepared pan. Bake until just springy to touch and tester inserted in center comes out with a few crumbs, about 25 minutes. Cool. Cut into squares.

🍎 Index

Almond(s). *See also* Caramel Almond
  and Cashews, Tabasco-flavored, 2
  Custard and Apples in Pastry, 95
  and Hazelnut Crunch Ice Cream Loaf
    with Strawberry Sauce, 92
  Lime Squares, 113
Appetizer, 2–8
  Avocado Pâté with Parsley and
    Pistachios, 2
  Bagels, Toasted Mini, with Smoked
    Salmon and Caviar, 5
  Black Olives with Cilantro, Garlic and
    Lemon, 2
  Blue Cheese Dip with Garlic and
    Bacon, Warm, 3
  California Nachos, 6
  Clams with Horseradish Salsa, 8
  Coconut Chicken Bites, 7
  Cranberry-glazed Brie, 4
  Green Onion and Red Pepper Tart, 63
  Herbed Phyllo Purses with Camembert
    and Walnuts, 4
  Marmalade-glazed Chicken Wings, 7
  Ratatouille French Bread Pizzas, 6
  Shrimp, Grilled, with Asparagus and
    Garlic Mayonnaise, 8
  Smoked Salmon Cream with
    Crudités, 3
  Tabasco-flavored Almonds and
    Cashews, 2
  Tomato Croutons with Bacon and
    Basil, 5
  White Bean Dip with Roasted Garlic
    Gremolata, 3
Apple(s)
  and Almond Custard in Pastry, 95
  Cider Tartlets, 100
  and Cranberries, Butternut Squash
    with, 72
Apricot Pecan Bread, 78
Apricot and Rice Stuffing, Roast Goose
  with, 55
Aram Sandwiches, 33
Artichoke Heart, Chick-Pea and
  Romaine Salad, 17
Artichoke and Smoked Turkey Salad, 21
Asparagus Soup, Chilled, 10
Aspen Chocolate Cream Cake, 106
Avocado, Chili and Bitter Greens
  Salad, 16
Avocado Pâté with Parsley and
  Pistachios, 2
Bagels, Toasted Mini, with Smoked
  Salmon and Caviar, 5
Barbecue Sauce, Rattlesnake Club, 48

Barley and Wild Rice with
  Mushrooms, 74
Beans. *See* Black Bean, Green Beans,
  White Beans
Beef, 37–42
  Brisket with Aromatic Vegetables, 39
  Cottage Pie, 41
  Cowboy Steak with Red Chili Onion
    Rings, 37
  Filet Mignon with Mustard Cream, 36
  Flank Steak, Grilled, with Spicy Garlic
    Sauce, 36
  Flank Steak Stuffed with Sausage, Basil
    and Cheese, 38
  Meat Loaf with Sun-dried
    Tomatoes, 40
  and Noodle Soup, Oriental, 13
  Short Ribs of, Deviled, 38
  Skirt Steak, Onion and Bell Pepper
    Sandwiches, 34
  Steak Salad, Marinated Mongolian, 20
  Steak and Spicy Tomato-Vegetable
    Sauce, Rigatoni with, 27
  Stew, Southwest, 40
Birthday Cake, Flash-in-the-Pan, 103
Biscotti, Walnut-Pepper, 111
Bitter Greens. *See* Greens, Bitter
Black Bean and Squash Stew with
  Cilantro Pesto, Spicy, 65
Black Bread, 79
Black Olives. *See* Olives
Blue Cheese Dip with Garlic and Bacon,
  Warm, 3
Blueberries and Bing Cherries, Peach
  Cobbler with, 83
Bluefish with Fried Capers and
  Spinach, 58
Bow Ties with Shrimp and Scallops, 25
Bread, 75–80
  Apricot Pecan, 78
  Black, 79
  Cinnamon Raisin, 78
  Corn and Goat Cheese Soufflé, 62
  Corn Sticks with Bacon, 75
  French, Pesto and Cheese, 79
  Garlic Hearts (Rolls), 76
  Lemon Butter Crust Buns, 76
  Power Pear-Oat Muffins, 77
  Pudding with Currants and Maple
    Syrup, 87
Brie, Cranberry-glazed, 4
Broccoli and Carrots in Garlic
  Oil, 69
Broccoli Risotto, Quick, 73
Brownies. *See* Cookies

Brussels Sprouts with Prosciutto and
  Leeks, 69
Butternut Squash. *See* Squash

Cabbage, Sweet-and-Sour, 69
Cake, 103–11
  Aspen Chocolate Cream, 106
  Cassata, Instant, 103
  Cheesecake, Lemon, with Gingersnap
    Crust, 109; Lemon Curd for, 110
  Cheesecake, Maple, Walnut and
    Date, 110
  Chocolate Harvest, 108
  Flash-in-the-Pan, Birthday, 103
  Fudge-slathered Fudge, 107
  Mile-High Whipped Cream, with
    Fresh Fruit, 104
  Orange Hazelnut Roulade, 105
California Nachos, 6
Candied Orange Peel, 105
Candy-studded Ice Cream
  Sandwiches, 92
Caramel Almond Cashew Bars, 113
Caramel Almond Tart, 93
Carrots and Broccoli in Garlic Oil, 69
Carrots and Lentils with Marjoram, 68
Cashews and Almonds, Tabasco-
  flavored, 2
Cassata, Instant, 103
Celery Root and Potatoes, Gratin, 71
Cheese Soup, Santa Fe, 12
Cheesecake. *See* Cake
Cherries, Bing, and Blueberries, Peach
  Cobbler with, 83
Cherry Ice Cream in Chocolate Cups, 89
Chestnut Soup, 11
Chick-Pea, Artichoke Heart and
  Romaine Salad, 17
Chicken, 50–54
  Breasts with Mushroom-Sherry
    Sauce, 50
  Coconut Bites, 7
  Coq au Vin Kebabs, 52
  Corn and Escarole Soup, 13
  Endive and Roquefort Salad, 19
  Lime Ginger, with Tomato and Green
    Pepper Salsa, 51
  Moroccan-spiced, with Lemon and
    Carrots, 52
  Parsley, Sage, Rosemary and Thyme, 54
  Prairie Grilled, 54
  Sandwiches with Three-Onion
    Relish, 33
  Sauté in Tomato-Vinegar Sauce, 50
  Sesame-coated Fried, 53

Stir-fried, with Onion and Hoisin
Sauce, 51
Wings, Marmalade-glazed, 7
Chili, Red, Onion Rings, 37
Chili, Vegetarian, 64
Chocolate
Bittersweet, Terrine with Vanilla
Custard Sauce, 85
Cake, Fudge-slathered Fudge, 107
Cream Cake, Aspen, 106
Cups, 90
-dipped Pecans, 88
Glaze, 99
Harvest Cake, 108; Ganache, 108;
Glaze, 109
Hazelnut Strudels, 101
Ice Cream, French Quarter, 88
Peanut Butter "Quiche," 99
White, Mousse Strawberry Tart, 96
White, and Turkish Coffee Parfaits, 91
Chutney, Spiced Fruit, 49
Cilantro Pesto, 66
Cinnamon Raisin Bread, 78
Clams with Horseradish Salsa, Iced, 8
Coconut Chicken Bites, 7
Coconut Macadamia Cream Tart, 94
Compote, Prune and Armagnac, with
Ice Cream, 84
Cookies, 111–114
Brownies, Macadamia Nut, 114
Brownies, Orange-Ginger, 114
Caramel Almond Cashew Bars, 113
Hazelnut Thumbprint, 112
Honey and Lemon Madeleines, 112
Lime Almond Squares, 113
Toffee Crunch Fans, 112
Walnut Lace, 111
Walnut-Pepper Biscotti, 111
Coq au Vin Kebabs, 52
Corn
Bread and Goat Cheese Soufflé, 62
Fritters, 70
Sticks with Bacon, 75
Cottage Pie, 41
Couscous, Spiced, 75
Cranberry(ies)
and Apples, Butternut Squash with, 72
-glazed Brie, 4
and Raspberry Fool, 82
Crème. See Custard
Croutons, Tomato, with Bacon and
Basil, 5
Custard. See also Mousse, Pudding
Apples and Almond in Pastry, 95
Maple Crème Caramel, 84
Peach Crème Brûlées with Cinnamon
Topping, 86
Sauce, Vanilla, 86

Dessert, 82–93. See also Kind of Dessert

Dessert Topping
Chocolate Glaze, 99, 109
Hazelnut Praline, 102
Maple, Date and Walnut Sauce, 111
Strawberry Sauce, 93
Vanilla Cream, 84; Custard Sauce, 86
Walnut Praline, 89
Whipped Sour Cream, 101
Dip
Blue Cheese, with Garlic and Bacon, 3
Smoked Salmon Cream with
Crudités, 3
White Bean, with Roasted Garlic
Gremolata, 3
Doughnuts, Pumpkin-Buttermilk with
Maple Sugar, 102
Dressing. See Mayonnaise, Vinaigrette

Eggs, Baked with Peppers and
Mushrooms, 63
Enchiladas, Shrimp, con Queso, 61
Endive
Chicken and Roquefort Salad, 19
Curly, Fennel, Radicchio and Apple
Salad, 15
and Smoked Salmon Salad, 17
and Spinach Salad with Stilton
Vinaigrette, 16

Farfalle with Bitter Greens and
Sausage, 26
Fettuccine with Cream, Basil and
Romano Cheese, 24
Fig, Melon and Mint Salad, 82
Filet Mignon. See Beef
Fish, 57–60. See also Shellfish
Bluefish with Fried Capers and
Spinach, 58
Red Snapper with Chili-Corn
Sauce, 59
Salmon with Garlic Mayonnaise, 58
Salmon in Vodka Cream Sauce with
Green Peppercorns, 58
Sea Bass with Garlic Herb Oil, 57
Swordfish, Broiled with Olives and
Thyme, 59
Tuna, Grilled with Salade Niçoise, 60
Whitefish, Grilled, with Pepper,
Tomatillos and Cilantro, 60
Flank Steak. See Beef
Flash-in-the-Pan Birthday Cake, 103
French Quarter Chocolate Ice Cream, 88
Frozen Dessert, 88–93
Candy-studded Ice Cream
Sandwiches, 92
Cherry Ice Cream in Chocolate
Cups, 89
Flash-in-the-Pan Birthday Cake, 103
French Quarter Chocolate Ice Cream, 88

Hazelnut Almond Crunch Ice Cream
Loaf with Strawberry Sauce, 92
Strawberry Sundaes, Triple, 90
Walnut Praline Ice Cream, 89
White Chocolate and Turkish Coffee
Parfait, 91
Fruit, Chutney, Spiced, 49
Fruit Dessert, 82–84. See also Name of
Fruit
Fudge-slathered Fudge Cake, 107

Garlic Hearts (Rolls), 76
Garlic-studded Racks of Lamb, 45
Goat Cheese and Corn Bread Soufflé, 62
Goose, Roast, with Apricot and Rice
Stuffing, 55
Greek-style Pasta Salad, 17
Green Bean, Potato, Tomato and Onion
Salad, 18
Green Beans with Browned Butter and
Balsamic Vinegar, 68
Green Onion and Red Pepper Tart, 63
Green Peppers. See Peppers
Greens
Bitter, Avocado and Chili Salad, 16
Bitter, Farfalle with Sausage and, 26
Sautéed with Garlic and Lemon, 70
Summer, and Herbs, Salad of, 15
Grits, Jalapeño Cheese, 75

Hazelnut
and Almond Crunch Ice Cream Loaf
with Strawberry Sauce, 92
Orange Roulade, 105
Praline, 102
Thumbprint Cookies, 112
Honey and Lemon Madeleines, 112

Ice Cream, 88–93. See also Frozen
Dessert

Jalapeño Cheese Grits, 75

Lamb, 44–47
Cottage Pie, 41
Garlic-studded Racks of, 45
Grilled, and Melon Kebabs, 44
Ragout, Spring, 46
Shanks in Cilantro Sauce, 46
Stock, 45
White Beans and Tomatoes, Rigatoni
with, 26
Lasagne with Roasted Red and Green
Bell Peppers, 29
Leeks and Sausage, Potatoes with, 71
Lemon Butter Crust Buns, 76
Lemon Cheesecake with Gingersnap
Crust, 109; Lemon Curd for, 110
Lentil and Rice Griddle Cakes, 74
Lentils and Carrots with Marjoram, 68

Lime
  Almond Squares, 113
  Ginger Chicken with Tomato and
    Green Pepper Salsa, 51
  Pie, in Almond-Gingersnap Crust, 95
Linguine, Spicy, Red Peppers Stuffed
  with, 25

Macadamia Coconut Cream Tart, 94
Macadamia Nut Brownies, 114
Madeleines, Honey and Lemon, 112
Mahimahi Fillets. See Bluefish
Maple Crème Caramel, 84
Maple, Walnut and Date Cheesecake, 110
Margarita Shrimp, 61
Marinated Mongolian Steak Salad, 20
Marmalade-glazed Chicken Wings, 7
Mayonnaise, Chive, 21; Garlic, 41
Meat Loaf with Sun-dried Tomatoes, 40
Mediterranean Tuna Salad, 22
Melon, Fig and Mint Salad, 82
Mile-High Whipped Cream Cake with
  Fresh Fruit, 104
Molasses-and-Bourbon-glazed Pork with
  Yams and Turnips, 47
Moroccan-spiced Chicken with Lemon
  and Carrots, 52
Mousse, Bittersweet Chocolate Terrine
  with Vanilla Custard Sauce, 85
Mousse Tart, Strawberry White
  Chocolate, 96
Muffins, Power Pear-Oat, 77
Mushroom and Pasta Soup, 12
Mussels, and Vermicelli, Provençal
  Tomato Soup with, 14
Mustard Vinaigrette, 20

Nachos, California, 6
Noodles, Spicy Sesame Chinese, 18

Olives, Black, with Cilantro, Garlic and
  Lemon, 2
Onion Rings, Red Chili, 37
Orange-Ginger Brownies, 114
Orange Hazelnut Roulade, 105
Oriental Beef and Noodle Soup, 13
Oriental Dipping Sauce, 53

Parmesan Béchamel Sauce, 29
Parsley, Sage, Rosemary and Thyme
  Chicken, 54
Pasta, 24–30
  Bow Ties with Shrimp and Scallops, 25
  Farfalle wth Bitter Greens and
    Sausage, 26
  Fettuccine with Cream, Basil and
    Romano Cheese, 24
  with Gorgonzola and Walnut Sauce, 24
  Lasagne with Roasted Red and Green
    Bell Peppers, 29

Linguine, Spicy, Red Peppers Stuffed
  with, 25
  and Mushroom Soup, 12
  Noodles, Spicy Sesame Chinese, 18
  Rigatoni with Lamb, White Beans and
    Tomatoes, 26
  Rigatoni with Sliced Steak and Spicy
    Tomato-Vegetable Sauce, 27
  Rolls Stuffed with Ricotta, Spinach
    and Prosciutto, 30
  Salad, Greek-style, 17
  Shells, Spinach-stuffed with Tomato
    Concassé, 28
Pastries. See Doughnuts, Strudel
Pastry Crust, Butter-Flake, 64
Pâté, Avocado, with Parsley and
  Pistachios, 2
Peach Cobbler with Blueberries and Bing
  Cherries, 83
Peach Crème Brûlées with Cinnamon
  Topping, 86
Peanut Butter Chocolate "Quiche," 99
Pear(s)
  Fresh, with Port Zabaglione, 82
  -Oat Muffins, Power, 77
  and Raisin Pie with Pecan Crust, 97
Pecan Apricot Bread, 78
Pecans, Chocolate-dipped, 88
Peppers
  Bell, Roasted Red and Green, Lasagne
    with, 29
  Red, and Green Onion Tart, 63
  Red, Stuffed with Spicy Linguine, 25
Pesto and Cheese French Bread, 79
Pesto, Cilantro, 66
Phyllo Purses, Herbed, with Camembert
  and Walnuts, 4
Pies and Tarts, 93–101
  Apple Cider Tartlets, 100
  Apples and Almond Custard in
    Pastry, 95
  Caramel Almond Tart, 93
  Chocolate Peanut Butter "Quiche," 99
  Coconut Macadamia Cream Tart, 94
  Green Onion and Red Pepper, 63;
    Butter-Flake Pastry Crust, 64
  Lime Pie, in Almond-Gingersnap
    Crust, 95
  Pear and Raisin with Pecan Crust, 97
  Strawberry White Chocolate
    Mousse, 96
  Visions of Sugarplums, 98
Pizza(s), 31–32
  Grilled Tomato with Herbs, 32; Dough
    Rounds, 32
  Ratatouille French Bread, 6
  Thin-crusted with Bacon, Brie and
    Muenster Cheese, 31
Plum Cream, Sweet, 83
Pork, 47–50. See also Sausage

Baby Back Ribs with Barbecue
  Sauce, 48
Chops with Garlic and Mushrooms, 47
Crown Roast of, with Fruit
  Chutney, 49
Molasses-and-Bourbon-glazed, with
  Yams and Turnips, 47
Potato(es)
  and Celery Root, Gratin of, 71
  Roasted, and Shallots with Caraway, 71
  with Sausage and Leeks, 71
  Shrimp and Cucumber Salad with Dill
    Dressing, 22
  Tomato, Green Bean and Onion
    Salad, 18
Power Pear-Oat Muffins, 77
Prairie Grilled Chicken, 54
Prosciutto and Fontina Sandwiches, 34
Provençal Tomato Soup with Mussels and
  Vermicelli, 14
Prune and Armagnac Compote with Ice
  Cream, 84
Pudding, Bread, with Currants and
  Maple Syrup, 87
Pudding, Raisin Rice, 87
Pumpkin-Buttermilk Doughnuts with
  Maple Sugar, 102

Radicchio, Curly Endive, Fennel and
  Apple Salad, 15
Raisin
  Cinnamon Bread, 78
  and Pear Pie with Pecan Crust, 97
  Rice Pudding, 87
Raspberry and Cranberry Fool, 82
Raspberry Salzburger Nockerl, 87
Ratatouille French Bread Pizzas, 6
Red Peppers. See Peppers
Red Snapper with Chili-Corn Sauce, 59
Rice. See also Wild Rice
  Apricot Stuffing, Roast Goose with, 55
  Baked with Sour Cream, Chilies and
    Corn, 73
  Broccoli Risotto, Quick, 73
  and Lentil Griddle Cakes, 74
  Pudding, Raisin, 87
  Salad, Tuscan-style with Ham, 20
Rigatoni with Lamb, White Beans and
  Tomatoes, 26
Rigatoni with Sliced Steak and Spicy
  Tomato-Vegetable Sauce, 27
Risotto, Quick Broccoli, 73
Rolls, Garlic Hearts, 76

Salad, 15–22
  Avocado, Chili and Bitter Greens, 16
  Chick-Pea, Artichoke Heart and
    Romaine, 17
  Chicken, Endive and Roquefort, 19
  Chinese Noodles, Spicy Sesame, 18

Fig, Melon and Mint (Dessert), 82
Greek-style Pasta, 17
Green Bean, Potato, Tomato and
    Onion, 18
Marinated Mongolian Steak, 20
Mediterranean Tuna, 22
Radicchio, Curly Endive, Fennel and
    Apple, 15
Shrimp, Potato and Cucumber with
    Dill Dressing, 22
Smoked Salmon and Endive, 17
Smoked Turkey and Artichoke, 21
Spinach and Endive with Stilton
    Vinaigrette, 16
of Summer Greens and Herbs, 15
Tuscan-style Rice with Ham, 20
Salad Dressing. *See* Mayonnaise,
    Vinaigrette
Salmon. *See also* Smoked Salmon
    with Garlic Mayonnaise, 58
    Grilled, with Salade Niçoise, 60
    in Vodka Cream Sauce with Green
        Peppercorns, 58
Salsa Cruda, 62
Salsa, Fresh Vegetable, 10
Salzburger Nockerl, Raspberry, 87
Sandwiches, 33–34
    Aram (with Lavash), 33
    Chicken with Three-Onion Relish, 33
    Grilled Prosciutto and Fontina, 34
    Skirt Steak, Onion and Bell Pepper, 34
Santa Fe Cheese Soup, 12
Sauce. *See also* Dessert Topping
    Barbecue, Rattlesnake Club, 48
    Cilantro Pesto, 66
    Oriental Dipping, 53
    Parmesan Béchamel, 29
    Salsa. *See* Salsa
    Vegetable Herb, 39
    Vinaigrette. *See* Vinaigrette
Sausage
    Farfalle with Bitter Greens and, 26
    -filled Soft Tacos, Spicy, 49
    and Leeks, Potatoes with, 71
Sea Bass with Garlic Herb Oil, 57
Sea Bass, Grilled with Salade Niçoise, 60
Sesame Chinese Noodles, Spicy, 18
Sesame-coated Fried Chicken, 53
Shellfish. *See* Clams, Mussels, Shrimp
Shells, Spinach-stuffed with Tomato
    Concassé, 28
Short Ribs of Beef, Deviled, 38
Shrimp
    Enchiladas con Queso, 61
    Grilled, with Dilled Asparagus and
        Garlic Mayonnaise, 8
    Margarita, 61
    Potato and Cucumber Salad with Dill
        Dressing, 22
    and Scallops, Bow Ties with, 25
Smoked Salmon
    and Caviar, Toasted Mini Bagels, 5

and Endive Salad, 17
Cream with Crudités, 3
Snow Pea Soup with Shrimp,
    Cream of, 14
Soufflé, Corn Bread and Goat Cheese, 62
Soufflé, Raspberry Salzburger
    Nockerl, 87
Soup, 10–14
    Asparagus, Chilled, 10
    Cheese, Santa Fe, 12
    Chestnut, 11
    Chicken, Corn and Escarole, 13
    Oriental Beef and Noodle, 13
    Pasta and Mushroom, 12
    Provençal Tomato, with Mussels and
        Vermicelli, 14
    Snow Pea with Shrimp, Cream of, 14
    Summer Garden, 11
    Zucchini, with Fresh Vegetable Salsa,
        Cold, 10
Sour Cream Whipped Topping, 101
Southwest Beef Stew, 40
Spinach and Endive Salad with Stilton
    Vinaigrette, 16
Spinach-stuffed Shells with Tomato
    Concassé, 28
Squash
    and Black Bean Stew with Cilantro
        Pesto, Spicy, 65
    Butternut, with Apples and
        Cranberries, 72
    Crookneck, and Zucchini, Herbed, 72
Steak. *See* Beef
Stir-fried Chicken with Onion and
    Hoisin Sauce, 51
Stock, Goose, 56
Strawberry
    Sauce, 93
    Sundaes, Triple, 90
    White Chocolate Mousse Tart, 96
Strudels, Chocolate Hazelnut, 101
Sugarplums (Dried Fruit), 99
Sun-dried Tomato Vinaigrette, 30
Sun-dried Tomatoes, Meat Loaf with, 40
Sweet-and-Sour Cabbage, 69
Swordfish, Broiled with Olives and
    Thyme, 59
Swordfish, Grilled with Salade
    Niçoise, 60

Tabasco-flavored Almonds and Cashews, 2
Tacos, Soft, Spicy Sausage-filled, 49
Tart. *See* Pies and Tarts
Toffee Crunch Fans, 112
Tomato. *See also* Sun-dried Tomato
    Croutons with Bacon and Basil, 5
    Soup, Provençal, with Mussels and
        Vermicelli, 14
Tuna, Grilled with Salade Niçoise, 60
Tuna, Salad, Mediterranean, 22
Turkey
    Cutlets Piccata, 57

Scaloppine with Red Pepper Cream
    Sauce, 56
Smoked, and Artichoke Salad, 21
Tuscan-style Rice Salad with Ham, 20

Vanilla Cream (Dessert Topping), 84
Vanilla Custard Sauce, 86
Veal, 42–44
    Chops with Apple Bourbon Sauce, 42
    "Dino," 43
    with Roquefort Cream and Oven-fried
        Potatoes, 43
Vegetable(s), 63–73. *See also* Name of
    Vegetable
    Aromatic, Beef Brisket with, 39
    Herb Sauce, 39
    Salsa, Fresh, 10
    Summer Garden Soup, 11
    Vegetarian Chili, 64
Vinaigrette
    Creamy, 18
    Mustard, 19
    Stilton, 16
    Sun-dried Tomato, 30
Visions of Sugarplums, 98

Walnut
    Lace Cookies, 111
    -Pepper Biscotti, 111
    Praline Ice Cream, 89
White Bean(s)
    Dip with Roasted Garlic Gremolata, 3
    Rigatoni with Lamb, Tomatoes and, 26
    with Sage, Garlic and Olive Oil, 68
White Chocolate. *See* Chocolate
Whitefish, with Marinated Peppers,
    Tomatillos and Cilantro, 60
Wild Rice and Barley with
    Mushrooms, 74

Yellowtail Fillets. *See* Bluefish

Zucchini and Crookneck Squash,
    Herbed, 72
Zucchini Soup with Fresh Vegetable
    Salsa, Cold, 10

News '89

The Year of Food and Entertaining in Review

Trends & New Products

Foods & Info by Mail

Books

Restaurants & People

Getaways

For the Kitchen & Table

Diet News

🍂 Trends & New Products

After 20 years, Prosciutto di Parma is back in the United States at your deli. September was the arrival date for the first shipment, which began its four-hundred-day air-curing last July.

In a competition to celebrate the centennial of the Eiffel Tower, 24 art schools in the United States submitted 47 poster designs under sponsorship of Food and Wines from France. Measuring 14 by 34 inches, the winning poster is by Juan Alberto Castillo of Northern Illinois University. It has been reproduced and is $3.50 from Food and Wines from France, Poster Fulfillment Center, 200 North 12th Street, Newark, NJ 07107.

Southern California microbiologists have developed a way to grow truffles indoors. They market their product in the form of truffle paste, dried ground truffles, truffle olive oil and truffle stock. The complete line is available from California Truffle Company, telephone (916) 661-3505.

In order to introduce Stolichnaya Cristall in the U.S., the Soviet Mission to the United Nations in New York opened its doors for the first time to the American food press. Petrossian's sevruga caviar abounded, the airiest blini were served and, of course, the smooth-as-silk vodka flowed. It was a truly memorable first.

Get your vegetable garden in gear with a new series of seed collections called Gourmet Gardens, from the English firm of Thompson & Morgan. Five collections—French, Italian, Chinese, Tex-Mex and Cajun-Creole—are offered, with each containing 10 packets of seeds, 20 planting pellets and a 22-page booklet with 20 recipes and com-

plete instructions for planting a 20x 20-foot garden. Each "garden" costs $19.95 plus $1.50 for shipping from Thompson & Morgan, P.O. Box 1308, Jackson, NJ 08527; (201) 363-2225.

A whole new line of treats, including jams, preserves and cookies, comes straight across the Atlantic from the London company of Burberrys. Crisp, thin shortbread, apple plum chutney, rhubarb ginger preserves and a savory plum pudding are a few of the offerings. Look for the products at specialty foods and department stores.

Top ten among the bridal set: The number-one preferred wedding gift, according to a Krups survey, is dishes; second, linens and bedding; tied for third are pots and pans and toasters; fourth, towels; fifth, silverware and cutlery; sixth, televisions; seventh, vacuum cleaners; tied for eighth are washing machines, dryers and irons; tied for ninth are coffee makers and bedroom sets; tenth is a microwave.

World famous for nearly three hundred years and the joy of collectors for almost as long, Quimper ceramic dishware can now be matched to fabrics and wall coverings. The French folk art designs of traditionally garbed peasants, colorful flowers and farm animals are now on the American market courtesy of Sandpiper Studios, a division of Design Directions. Whether you collect original Quimper or reproductions, you can now have a kitchen or dining room coordinated with your plates, pitchers and bowls. For more information on the Quimper Collection, contact Seabrook Wall Coverings, Inc., 1325 Farmville Rd., Memphis, TN 38122; (901) 320-3500.

If the bitterness of walnut skins bothers you, try Honey Forest brand roasted skinless ones. With a completely natural patented process, the fine skins of the shelled walnuts are removed, making for a sweeter nut. Plain dry-roasted or honey-roasted nuts come in ten-ounce cans for $4.50 per can (minimum order of four) from Penutech Corp., 15334 East Valley Blvd., Industry, CA 91746.

New to the U.S. is the Bouvet collection of sparkling wines. Bouvet-Ladubay is the second-oldest sparkling wine-producing establishment in Saumur, in France's Loire valley. Bottles of Bouvet Signature Brut, Rosé, Saphir Vintage Brut and Rubis range in price from about $11 to $14. The most interesting of the quartet is the Rubis, a *méthode champenoise* red wine with hints of raspberry and violet. Look for them in wine shops nationwide.

Believe it. There's now a faux smoked salmon that's a blend of Pacific fish and smoked salmon. Mox Lox tastes terrific, has a delicate texture and, at less than $3 for a three-ounce package, is a steal when compared to the real thing. Another bonus: only 50 calories per package. Look for it in your local supermarket.

It may be commonplace in years to come, but for now the Burns Sun Oven looks like a peek at the future. The completely solar-powered, portable unit is available for $99.50 plus shipping from Burns-Milwaukee, 4010 West Douglas Avenue, Milwaukee, WI 53209; (414) 438-1234.

Style-conscious food lovers' alert! Hermès has reissued a witty classic scarf pattern called "A la Gloire de la Cuisine Française." It was created by fourth-generation Hermès chairman Robert Dumas in 1943, during World War II. A steady diet of wartime rations inspired his fashionable tribute to French food. The silk-twill scarf shows two chefs watching over a

tempting array of fish, fruit, desserts and wine. Available at Hermès stores nationwide for $175.

Fax your food? You bet. It's the office lunch of the twenty-first century, say the proprietors of Kate Mantilini, the upscale Beverly Hills restaurant on Wilshire Boulevard. Call its FAX number, (213) 278-3798, before 9:00 A.M. with your order and lunch will be ready for pickup at a specified time.

A favorite brandy of European royalty, *eau de vie de poire* has debuted in Oregon at Clear Creek Distillery. The brandy begins with Bartlett pears from a family orchard and is distilled by means of European equipment and techniques. Its fragrant, fiery taste delights devotees and compares favorably with *poire Williams* from France. Presently available in major cities across the country. For more information, contact Clear Creek Distillery, 1430 Northwest 23rd Avenue, Portland, OR 97210; (503) 248-9470.

Celebrating its centenary, Bahlsen, the famous German cookie house, is offering two new collector's tins featuring reproductions of original Bahlsen artwork from turn-of-the-century packaging. In addition, the renowned sweets have found their own niche at New York's Bloomingdale's department store. The Bahlsen cookie boutique offers everything from paper-thin wafers to fruit tartlets with marzipan. For more information, contact Bahlsen, One Quality Lane, Cary, NC 27512; (919) 677-3200.

It's not just banks that are becoming automated. In Paris, fresh baguettes are now available 24 hours a day at streetside dispensers citywide. If the bakery is closed by the time you get off work, just insert eight francs and out pops a baguette—baked that day.

🍎 Foods & Info by Mail

Fran's chocolates are among Seattle's best exports. The most discerning chocoholics applaud her rich sauces and hand-dipped confections, which include caramel- and nut-filled Gold-Bars and Nuggets, truffles, creams and more. But the most favored of the collection are the Bites, which have layers of semisweet and white Belgian chocolate with a thin chocolate coating. Send for a catalog or try the Bites. A 20-ounce box includes 24 candies and costs $20, plus shipping, from Fran's, 2805 East Madison, Seattle, WA 98112; (206) 322-6511.

Even English muffins have gone haute. Available in seven varieties, Joyce's Gourmet English muffins are moist, chewy as crumpets, crunchy when toasted and incredibly habit forming. Best bought in an assorted dozen of four flavors—plain, honey wheat raisin, cinnamon raisin and cheese. Or choose one dozen of any single variety. Also available are oat bran and onion. A dozen costs $13 plus $6.50 for second-day air outside New England ($3.50 for delivery in New England). From Joyce's Gourmet English Muffin Company, 4 Lake Street, Arlington, MA 02174; (800) 234-6836 or, in Massachusetts, call (617) 641-1900.

Miss Grace's baked goods have been enjoyed by West Coast cognoscenti for more than a decade. Such tasty cakes as chocolate fudge, macadamia nut, apple, and an assortment of cookies are the celebrated offerings. But perhaps the biggest star in Miss Grace's cast is her lemon cake. Prepared from a family heritage recipe, it incorporates fresh juice and rind from lemons that grow in local groves. With a crisp lemon-sugar glaze, the bundt-shaped dessert has a taste of sunny California. The 25-ounce cake costs about $24 plus shipping—just call (800) 367-2253.

What's a steak without sauce? Now, with the barbecue season approaching, it's time to find a top-quality condiment for the grill. Try the steak sauce from Manhattan's Ben Benson's Steak House, which happens to be terrific on all meats, and chicken, too. It's a zesty blend of tomatoes, vinegar, prunes, lime, onion, garlic, paprika and other spices. According to Ernie Halpern, chef at Ben Benson's, meats are twice as tasty when brushed with a good sauce just five minutes before being removed from the grill. Available for $3.50 plus $2.90 shipping per 5-ounce bottle from Manny Wolf's Gourmet Shop, 145 East 49th Street, New York, NY 10017; (212) 751-0351.

Mrs. Prindable and her sinful apples came long after the Garden of Eden, but today's chocoholics find her offerings more than tempting. Giant apples are hand dipped in caramel, chocolate and pecans; or coffee almonds and fudge; or caramel, toffee brickle, chocolate and walnuts. They can also be decorated to fit your party theme. Serve one sliced with coffee after dinner, send one to your favorite valentine or get one to eat all by yourself. Available nationwide at selected department stores, or by mail—the cost is $12 to $15 plus shipping—from Mrs. Prindable, Inc., 7323 North Monticello Avenue, Skokie, IL 60076; (800) 441-4489 or, in Illinois (708) 674-4490.

If you're looking for good, flavorful smoked meats, poultry and fish, Nodine's Smokehouse is the place for you. Wild game, Cajun specialties and cheeses are featured treats offered in their catalog. These delicious savory products come in a variety of gift baskets ideal for weekend hosts. For additional information, contact Nodine's Smokehouse, Retail Mail Order Department, P.O. Box 1787, Torrington, CT 06790; (203) 489-3213.

It's not out of the question when you enjoy one of the cleverest ideas to come our way in a long time. A big sweet pizza—complete with the toppings of your choice—is delivered to your door in a regulation pizza box adorned with a festive straw bow. The treat begins with delicious crusts (we recommend the brownie fudge). Then they're spread with a thick layer of bittersweet chocolate or peanut cream. Add any 2 of 52 toppings (peanut brittle, M&M candies, crushed cookies, toffee, caramels, etc.) and you're all set. Available in medium (serves up to 10) for $39 and large (serves up to 20) for $69. For more information, contact Judi Kaufman & Company, 400 South Beverly Drive, Suite 214, Beverly Hills, CA 90212; (213) 858-7787.

French Meadow Bakery's breads are all made from organically grown grains and in the same careful way the Egyptians, Greeks and Romans made their loaves thousands of years ago. There are a number of varieties of bread available, with favorites like Minnesota wild rice, Anaheim pepper, seven-grain prairie, ginger carrot and sourdough French. The four-pound loaves range in price from about $7 to $11 plus shipping. These chewy, long-lasting loaves can be frozen whole or in part. Contact French Meadow Bakery, 2610 Lyndale Avenue South, Minneapolis, MN 55408; (612) 870-4740.

The award-winning Mozzarella Company in Dallas produces about a ton of cheese a week under the well-trained eye of owner Paula Lambert. Her quality products are the result of long and intensive study with cheese experts in Italy, and include fine *caciotta*, *scamorza* and mozzarella. Gift baskets are a specialty. One favorite is a collection of two mozzarella rolls, two Texas goat cheeses and one smoked scamorza for $45 including overnight refrigerated shipping. Contact Mozzarella Company, 2944 Elm Street, Dallas, TX 75226; (214) 741-4072.

Questions about pairing wine and food are answered by David Rosengarten and Joshua Wesson in their bimonthly newsletter, *The Wine & Food Companion*. Vineyards, plus restaurant wine lists and regional varieties are also discussed. One year is $36; call (800) 888-1961.

Different slices for different folks. Really. That's what Sugar Spoon's wheel of sampler cheesecake offers with its 12 slices of different kinds of creamy cheesecake. Perfect for a dinner party of mixed tastes, the paper-divided slices range from simple strawberry to double chocolate amaretto. The stunning selection is $21.95 plus shipping. Contact Lu Clinton's Sugar Spoon, 1855 West A Street, North Platte, NE 69101; (800) 228-0052.

If you can't make it to Martha's Vineyard, you can still savor its indigenous products by mail. A Taste of the Island offers a collection of vineyard victuals, packed in old-fashioned wooden clam baskets. Such homemade goodies as beachplum jelly, cranberry wine vinegar and Spanish peanut brittle plus a cookbook of regional specialties make up the $65 package. Individual items can also be ordered. Contact A Taste of the Island, P.O. Box 623, Martha's Vineyard, MA 02568; (508) 693-5305.

Your guests will "ooh" and "ah" once they get a mouthful of the walnut caramel creme torte from Two Chefs on a Roll. The dessert is made with two layers of butter cookies filled with walnut caramel creme and iced with a generous amount of white chocolate. It's decorated with a dark chocolate design and a border of chopped walnuts. The candy bar-like confection is packed in a gift tin. It's $25 including shipping from Two Chefs on a Roll, 1821 213th Street, Unit E, Torrance, CA 90501; (800) 842-3025.

When chocoholics (or anyone with a sweet tooth) taste the rich, creamy fudges being produced by the Brigittine monks in Oregon, the consensus is always unanimous—the best. The Brigittine order, founded in 1370 and completely self-supporting, owes the superb quality of its candies to fresh dairy butter, pure cream and extremely rich chocolates. They are packed in boxes of one pound each for $7.95 plus shipping, and there are four different flavors to choose from. Order the candy directly from the monastery: The Brigittine Monks Gourmet Confections, 23300 Walker Lane, Amity, OR 97101; (503) 835-8080.

At Rowena's & Captain Jaap's Jam and Jelly Factory, they're stirring up some wonderful flavor sensations. There's a carrot jam that is great on cream-cheesed bagels. And their lemon curd is terrific in tarts and over ice cream. Nine-ounce jars of lemon curd (or 9.5-ounce jars of jam) are $5. There's a $2.75 shipping charge for orders up to $19.99. Available from Rowena's & Captain Jaap's Jam and Jelly Factory, 758 West 22nd St., Norfolk, VA 23517; (800) 627-8699.

Remember rocky road sundaes when you were a kid? Now you can relive that favorite taste sensation, with Prlain's rocky road cheesecake. Complete with bits of marshmallow, creamy cream cheese, chocolate and almonds, it can be yours in a day—all three pounds four ounces of it. Order for $29.50 from Prlain's Foods, Inc., P.O. Box 5802, Aloha, OR 97006; (503) 649-1878.

Prettily packaged for giving, the Moon Shine Trading Company's honeys and nut butters are simply delicious. A sampling of six assorted 2- and 2½-ounce jars is about $15, and a box of one 12-ounce jar of nut butter and one 16-ounce jar of honey costs about $12. Individual large jars cost between $4 and $8.50. Some of the intriguing flavors are eucalyptus honey, Hawaiian Christmas berry honey, yellow star thistle honey, California almond butter and white chocolate almond dream. All are available in specialty stores nationwide; for mail order information contact Moon Shine Trading Company, P.O. Box 896, Winters, CA 95694; (916) 753-0601.

In Parma, Idaho, on a family farm owned by Karen and Charles Evans, some of the finest goat cheese outside France is being produced under the label of Rollingstone Chèvre. There are more than 20 varieties, including a creamy blue cheese, one nipped with jalapeño chilies, a fresh herbed one and delicious globes of *chèvre* marinated in olive oil and bay leaves. Prices vary. For more information, contact Rollingstone Chèvre, 27349 Shelton Road, Parma, ID 83660; (208) 722-6460.

A bite of Caleb's Confections "Pie in the Sky" can indeed be out of this world. This sinfully rich pecan pie blessed with chunks of bittersweet chocolate will capture the fancy of nut and chocolate lovers alike. A nine-inch pie costs $15.95 plus shipping from Caleb's Confections, 5229 Anchorage Drive, Nashville, TN 37220; (615) 833-7751.

Transplanted New Yorkers who are used to their morning bagels with coffee will welcome the service provided by the Manhattan Bagel Co. Fresh, vacuum-packed bagels are available by mail for $5.99 per dozen, plus $4.95 shipping. Call Manhattan Bagel Co., (212) 691-3041.

If you love chocolate (doesn't everyone?), The Chocolate Lady has something for you—her devastatingly, decadently and divinely rich one-pound Silver Spoon Truffle. It comes in three guises: Classic Chocolate Cream, Heavenly White Chocolate (laced with raspberry or praline sauce) and Marble Swirl. Eat it all by yourself if you dare, or share it with guests as an after-dinner treat with espresso. Packaged as a gift, it costs $29.50 including overnight shipping. Contact The Chocolate Lady, 9783 Clayton Rd. in the Market Place, St. Louis, MO 63124; (800) 242-5283.

🍎 *Books*

Julia Child's first book in nine years, *The Way to Cook* (Alfred A. Knopf, 1989), is a winner all around. With more than eight hundred color photos in 511 pages, it is the first cookbook in The-Book-of-the-Month-Club's history to be its main selection. Her editor dubs it Ms. Child's "masterwork—the distillation of a lifetime of cooking . . . a clarion call for good sense in our approach to food."

There is a new and intriguing cookbook for the French sector of your kitchen library. Richard Grausman's *At Home with the French Classics* (Workman Publishing, 1989) is a thorough book with sensible how-to illustrations, wine and serving suggestions and the clear instructions that only a fine cooking teacher such as Mr. Grausman can offer.

A Toast to Wines & Spirits (Harry Abrams, 1989) is a big book—big in scope, concept and size. It pays tribute to an earlier era of poster design that celebrated wines and spirits. Reproduced from the collection of Nicolas Bailly, the curator of collections at the Musée de la Presse Française in Paris, the book features works by such masters as Chéret, Mucha, Cappiello, Carlu and Cassandre. The publishers refer to some pages as suitable for framing, and with 25 full-color illustrations measuring 11½x16 inches, indeed they may be. But then you'll want to get a second copy for Clifton Fadiman's nostalgic introduction.

Melanie Barnard and Brooke Dojny have produced a collection of old favorites and some new in *Sunday Suppers* (Prentice Hall Press, 1989). Here are comfort foods of high order that will chase away the winter chill.

In celebration of its one-hundredth anniversary, Lenox has issued a book that offers advice for the party giver. *The Lenox Book of Home Entertaining and Etiquette* (Crown, 1989) by Elizabeth K. Lawrence is a beautiful handbook that covers celebrations and holidays, weddings and anniversaries, and casual and formal events.

If you don't have time to visit the Caribbean this summer, sample the innovative island cuisine anyhow, but in your own kitchen. *The Sugar Mill Hotel Cookbook* comes courtesy of *Bon Appétit* columnists Jinx and Jeff Morgan, who own the hotel in Tortola in the British Virgin Islands. It's only $12.95 from The Morgan Corporation, Ltd., P.O. Box 425, Tortola, British Virgin Islands.

Our favorite East/West cook and correspondent Ken Hom has done it again with *Fragrant Harbor Taste: The New Chinese Cooking of Hong Kong* (Simon & Schuster, 1989). A plump book with a title that really tells it all, it includes light, easy and nutritious fare that blends old-world flavors with Western innovations.

If you're not sure about what wine to order or serve with certain foods, then the compact handbook *Wine & Food Directory* is exactly what you need. It will tell you the proper wine to serve with courses from appetizers to desserts. The major vineyards of France and the United States are represented and all wines mentioned are widely available. There are 126 wine-food combinations and 558 cross-referenced wines, plus tips on service and storage. It comes in a leather and brass binder, and it costs $36 from the Wine and Food Directory, Shipping and Customer Service, P.O. Box 515, Clarkston, WA 99403; (800) 453-4848.

❦ Restaurants & People

Take two chefs formerly of Spago fame, add a renovated Italianesque building onced owned by Charlie Chaplin and you've definitely got a restaurant designed to keep Los Angeles happy. It's called Campanile (Italian for bell tower), and since Mark Peel is at the stove and wife Nancy Silverton is making the breads and desserts, the food is nothing short of perfect. Enter the two-story atrium courtyard and enjoy the view. There's an attractive bar on your left, Nancy's La Brea Bakery on your right and a lovely tile fountain greeting you in front. The dining rooms are simply furnished to enhance the relaxed feeling—is it L.A. or a palazzo in Venice? It doesn't really matter, because you'll find yourself concentrating on the all-too-tempting Italian-inspired menu. (Campanile, 624 S. La Brea Ave., Los Angeles, CA 90036; (213) 938-1447.)

L'Ecole, the dining room of The French Culinary Institute in New York, offers lunches and dinners prepared and served by the students. It's a real treat to see the young chefs at work, and prices are reasonable. Call (212) 219-3300 for reservations.

If you're hitting the Tuscan trail on your next trip to Italy, there are two fine restaurants not to be missed. First is the sedate and sophisticated Al Ristoro dei Vecchi Macelli by the Arno River in Pisa. Stefano Vanni, a serious young restaurateur, is an outstanding host and will gladly help you select a wine from his excellent list and order from his exciting menu, which is divided into "sea" and "earth" categories.

The second restaurant, Gambero Rosso, is located in the small but chic coastal town of San Vincenzo (known for one of the loveliest stretches of beach in the region) on the Ligurian Sea. There, talented chef-owner Fulvio Pierangelini practices his artistry, most evident in the inspired fish dishes. The food is modern—light and refined, yet brimming with the intense flavors of Tuscany. (Al Ristoro dei Vecchi Macelli, Via Volturno, 49, Pisa, Italy, telephone 050/20-424; Ristorante Gambero Rosso, Piazza della Vittoria, 13, 57027, San Vincenzo, Livorno, Italy, telephone 0565/70-10-21.)

Gone public: Chicago's Whitehall Club is no longer a strictly private affair. Now everyone can enjoy the quiet, comfortable dining room and chef Charles Hayes's delicious dishes. (The Whitehall Club, The Whitehall, 105 E. Delaware Pl., Chicago, IL 60611; 312/280-3096.)

For the diehard meat-and-potatoes set, nothing beats Nashville's Stock-Yard restaurant. Owner Buddy Killen serves up 16 cuts of the most flavorful beef in dinners that include beef and vegetable soup, salad, vegetable and fresh bread. If there's room for more, try the fabulous hot cheesecake. The meals are classically American and enormously satisfying. After dinner, visit the Bull Pen Lounge downstairs for an evening of entertainment, Nashville style. (The Stock-Yard, Second Avenue North and Stockyard Boulevard, Nashville, TN 37201; 615/255-6464.)

The restaurant Odéon, named for the Paris *métro* stop on the Left Bank, is Philadelphia's newest, most exciting bistro. Partners Gary Bachman (the talented chef) and Steve Ledbetter (the knowledgeable sommelier) renovated a two-level flower shop with etched windows and a stylish center staircase. A young and friendly staff serves sophisticated, but never pretentious, fare, such as red bell pepper mousse, sautéed crab in citrus sauce and rack of lamb with caramelized garlic. (Odéon Bistrot à Vin, 114 South 12th Street, Philadelphia, PA 19107; 215/922-5875.)

Curious about what the rich and famous serve on their yachts? According to Ridgewells Caterer, which handles food preparation for parties on Donald Trump's yacht, *Trump Princess*, Dom Pérignon is served at every port of call, and guests enjoy such appetizers as Scotch eggs, tiny beef Wellingtons and crab cakes.

None other than Ken Hom, celebrated cookbook author, has put his seal of approval on the Emperor's Choice, a Cantonese restaurant in the heart of Chicago's Chinatown. He calls it "truly fit for an emperor" and a forerunner in the deserved revival of Cantonese food.

Housed in a historical 1928 building, the spacious restaurant is decorated with antique paintings of some of China's most famous emperors, and an eighteenth-century imperial robe from the Ching dynasty is the room's stunning focal point. The extensive seafood menu offers such delicate dishes as steamed oysters with black bean sauce, lobster baked with ginger and onions, and stir-fried scallops and shrimp in a deep-fried taro root basket. (Emperor's Choice Restaurant, 2238 South Wentworth Ave., Chicago, Il. 60616; 312/225-8800.)

Indelibly French from the strategically placed flowers to the sparkling crystal, impeccable napery and exquisitely silent service, the Duquesnoy is where Parisians go for a classic meal. Here, foie gras marries with Margaux, and the feast begins and ends with fine Champagne. Chef-owner Jean-Paul Duquesnoy's *menu dégustation*, which offers four specialties of the season, matches the room's elegance beautifully. (Duquesnoy, 6 avenue Bosquet, 75007 Paris, France; 47.05.96.78.)

For the first time in the restaurant's 60-year history, the wine cellar of '21' is now open to private dining. Unchanged since the speakeasy days of the twenties and thirties, the world-famous club has a cellar steeped in atmosphere. You enter the labyrinth of bin rooms through a five-thousand-pound, three-foot-thick door and dine cozily in candlelit splendor from chef Michael Lomonaco's menu. To be sure, the wines are quite suitable. Maximum capacity is ten at $350 per person ('21' Club, 21 West 52nd Street, New York, NY 10019; 212/582-7200.)

The City of the Angels's hottest new restaurants celebrate the flavors of the Mediterranean. The most sophisticated of them is Pazzia, a recent venture from the owner of Rex Il Ristorante's Mauro Vincenti. Set in a dramatic modern dining room, Pazzia offers refined rustic Italian fare—very pristine, yet with peasant roots.

On the other hand, Locanda Veneta is everything a casual Italian trattoria should be, and more. Co-owner Jean Louis De Mori and co-owner/chef Antonio Tommasi have created a relaxed and friendly place with some of the most deliciously simple food in town. Everything on the menu is a winner—from the refreshing artichoke salad to the irresistible *crème caramel*.

If it weren't for the view of the Santa Monica Pier, diners at the new pan-Mediterranean bistro, Opera, just might believe they were at a chic seaside restaurant in the south of France. Co-managers Jerry Singer and Doug Delfeld serve California-Mediterranean dishes. It's a beautiful room in a beautiful setting—perfect for the beautiful people of L.A. (Pazzia, 213/657-9271; Locanda Veneta, 213/274-1893; Opera, 213/393-9224.)

Elegant dining—with a view that glides past your window—is what you'll get aboard a Scenic Rail Dining excursion. The dinner train with its grand lounge rolls smoothly from Milwaukee to Iron Ridge to Horicon and returns to Milwaukee four hours later. The domed dining cars are richly appointed in the manner of classic European trains, with soft lights and sparkling table settings. The service moves as expertly as the 76-mile run, and dinner is superb. The experience is a trip back in time, a wonderful way to celebrate a special event with friends. For more information, contact Scenic Rail Dining Depot, 11340 West Brown Deer Road, Milwaukee, WI 53224; (414) 354-5544.

On a smart little mall in the Detroit suburb of Royal Oak, an American bistro called Les Auteurs serves some pretty delicious food. It's got the locals queuing up for the products of its open kitchen. The long and narrow restaurant has a striking black bar, and walls throughout are decorated with pictures of famous chefs and menus from great restaurants around the world. Owner-chef Keith Famie is packing them in for lunch and dinner with his black bean cakes, wild mushroom pizza, rotisserie chicken and southwestern chili. (Les Auteurs, 222 Sherman Drive, Washington Square Plaza, Royal Oak, MI 48067; call 313/544-2887.)

Situated in the beautifully restored Park Central Hotel in the art deco district of south Miami Beach, Lucky's restaurant is one of the leaders in that area's revival. The glass-enclosed Florida Room, which features Gleason Romer hand-colored photo transparencies of 1930s bathing beauties and a glorious view of palm-studded beaches, is the talk of the town. Vying with all this luxury is a stunning American regional menu, which features raspberry duck *confit,* crab sausage and garlic custard with oyster mushrooms. (Lucky's, 640 Ocean Drive, Miami Beach, FL 33139; call 305/538-7700 for reservations.)

Right up to Thanksgiving, The Water's Edge restaurant in New York offers shuttle service that whisks diners across the East River from the 23rd Street Marina in Manhattan to Long Island City. The glass-enclosed restaurant has a panoramic view of the city skyline, sailboats, sunsets and stars. It's the perfect setting for one of executive chef Mark French's candlelit dinners. Try the grouper baked in banana leaves with rum-lime butter or the foie gras sautéed with citrus fruits. The boat leaves Tuesdays through Saturdays on the hour from 6:00 to 10:00 P.M. and returns on the half hour until 10:30 P.M. Of course, you can always just drive over the bridge for your dinner. (The Water's Edge, 44th Drive at the East River Yacht Club, Long Island City, NY 11101; call 718/482-0033 for reservations.)

When in the twelfth-century city of Bern, Switzerland's capital, it's easy to become immersed in medieval grandeur. Even some of its dining rooms date back hundreds of years. The Restaurant Kornhauskeller, a former grain warehouse and wine cellar, is a lively, cavernous place that shouldn't be missed. The large wine barrel at one end and pillars and arches of centuries past are impressive backdrops for such local foods as a bubbling cheese fondue or a Bernese platter heaped with sausage, smoked pork ribs, bacon, potatoes and sauerkraut. At night a group of colorfully dressed musicians provides alpine melodies. (Restaurant Kornhauskeller, Kornhausplatz 18, CH-3011, Bern 7, Switzerland; telephone 22.11.33.)

The much-heralded redo of The Grill Room at Manhattan's celebrated Four Seasons restaurant marks the thirtieth year of this consistently great dining establishment. The remodel, which was directed by original architect Philip Johnson, is subtle, with new upholstery and carpeting, and handsome Villeroy & Boch tableware. The latter is porcelain, bordered in a granite-like treatment flecked with burgundy, green, peach and gray. The redesign should prove to be dynamic but low-key enough to lure the publishing world's power brokers back to their favorite haunt. (The Four Seasons, 99 East 52nd Street, New York, NY 10152; 212/754-9494.)

Looking for the perfect stop for supper after a long day on the ski slopes? Krabloonik (Eskimo for "big eyebrows"), a retreat in the Colorado Rockies in Snowmass, is just the answer. A log building with picture windows overlooking Mt. Daly and Capitol Peak houses this homespun restaurant where robust wild game dishes are the specialty. But the star attraction here is a daytime event—guests can take a sled trip, led by a team of huskies, through the White River National Forest. The half-day trip is $140, with lunch back in the dining room. (Krabloonik, P.O. Box 5517, Snowmass Village, CO 81615; call 303/923-4342.)

🍎 *Getaways*

Like a Federal-period manor house with European fittings and service, the Morrison House in Alexandria, Virginia, is an oasis of serenity and graciousness. English afternoon tea is offered in the parlor and evening Cognac and coffee are served daily in a mahogany-paneled library. The inn's restaurant, Le Chardon d'Or, offers a finely tuned French menu in a setting that boasts Louis XVI-style chairs and a Baccarat chandelier and sconces. All this just a stone's throw from Washington, D.C. (Morrison House, 116 South Alfred Street, Alexandria, VA 22314; 800/367-0800 or, in Virginia, 800/533-1808.)

Built in 1966 in the style of a classic eighteenth-century mansion, Paris's Hôtel Le Colbert is just steps from Notre-Dame and the Latin Quarter. The hotel was remodeled about four years ago, so it offers modern conveniences in a storybook setting. (Hôtel Le Colbert, 7 rue de l'Hôtel-Colbert, 75005 Paris, France; 43.25.85.65.)

The Ritz-Carlton, Atlanta, Culinary Arts School has started a four-week series of cooking classes conducted by executive chef Josef Lageder. Students work right in the hotel's kitchen, meeting every Saturday from 9 A.M. to 2 P.M., with each session based on one area of food: seafood, poultry, meats, and pastries and dessert sauces. Because classes are limited to ten students, everyone gets a chance to participate in hands-on cooking. Sommelier Bill Harris then conducts a tasting of the wine selected to accompany each dish. After the final day's session in the pastry kitchen, an evening graduation dinner is held for students and their guests, incorporating various dishes mastered during the course. For more information, contact Donna Laurent-Gregg at The Ritz-Carlton, Atlanta, (404) 659-0400.

Bon Appétit joins the Royal Viking Line for their "Grand Crus" event aboard a five-star luxury cruise ship. Participants include *Bon Appétit* wine editor Anthony Dias Blue and eight California winemakers featured in Blue's column, "The Year's Best from California," last January. The trip—which begins in San Francisco and concludes in Vancouver—includes wine seminars and tastings, private suppers with the winemakers, and other programs. Contact Larry Martin at HMS Tours, (800) 367-5348.

The Bluffs, a restored vintage shore retreat in Bay Head, New Jersey, offers the lure of the sea—and then some. The century-old charm of this historic landmark has been lightened, brightened and restored to its Victorian gracefulness; it's also furnished with many of the original antiques. Fresh seafood and simply prepared meats are served in the lovely white-on-white dining room, which has a magnificent view of the ocean and sand dunes. It's the perfect spot for a weekend getaway, or just a romantic dinner à deux—and it's only about one hour from downtown Manhattan. (The Bluffs, 575 East Avenue, Bay Head, NJ 08742; telephone 201/892-1114 for the hotel, 201/892-1710 for the restaurant.)

The grand and gracious Goodwood Park Hotel on the island of Singapore offers weary travelers more than a break from the hot climate of the city-state. This English colonial hotel, once a posh German club around the turn of the century, has resplendent gardens with palms and tropical flora where wild birds sing to guests lounging on balconies. The hotel also houses one of the finest Szechwan restaurants in Singapore as well as a Japanese dining spot. Proper English tea is served, too. (Goodwood Park Hotel, 22 Scoots Road, Singapore 0922; toll free 800/323-7500.)

Planning a tour of Burgundy soon? Make the recently remodeled Hôtel Le Cep in Beaune your base. Its 46 rooms, each named for a *grand cru* wine from the Côte d'Or vineyards, are decorated in the traditional French style. Among its charms is a breakfast room located in a former wine cellar. And the adjacent Restaurant Bernard Morillon (entered through a doorway in the hotel) offers some of the most superbly prepared food in the entire area. (Hôtel Le Cep, 27 rue Maufoux, F-21200, Beaune, France; telephone 80.22.35.48. Or make your reservations through Jacques de Larsay, 622 Broadway, New York, NY 10012; 800/366-1510 or, in New York, call 212/477-1600.)

Feel the need to get away from it all? The Carmel Valley Ranch Resort could be an ideal spot for you. Sitting on 1,700 sloping acres, this quiet retreat has one hundred suites with wood-burning fireplaces and Jacuzzis; a championship golf course; tennis courts; swimming pool; and spa. The restaurant, under executive chef Peter d'Andrea, presents a menu of fresh, contemporary dishes. It's just the place to rejuvenate yourself. (Carmel Valley Ranch Resort, One Old Ranch Road, Carmel, CA 93923; 800/422-7635.)

Hong Kong's beloved Peninsula hotel, darling of travelers since 1928, has recently completed a stupendous renovation. Rooms, suites and the famous lobby restaurant have been refurbished without disturbance to the hotel's inherent charm. The next step is the addition of a pair of 17-story towers, to be completed by 1992.

For the ideal retreat from city life, try the Home Hill Country Inn, just minutes from Hanover, on the Connecticut River bordering Vermont. This dreamy restored 1818 Federal mansion stands on 25 acres of lush grounds, complete with tennis court and swimming pool for summertime activities and, for the winter, several cross-country ski trails.

Each of the five large bedrooms in the white brick house is handsomely furnished. Innkeeper Roger Nicolas offers a four-course prix fixe dinner that changes nightly. A typical supper might include sweetbreads with locally grown morels in Port sauce, or red mullet and spinach in a light saffron sauce. In the morning, relax over coffee and croissants in the kitchen. How's that for a weekend getaway? (Home Hill Country Inn & French Restaurant, River Road, Plainfield, NH 03781; 603/675-6165.)

With a visit to the Hotel Bristol and its spectacular Restaurant Korso, you'll see Vienna in all its glory—the sparkle of the city's golden age and the dazzle of its cuisine. Located on the edge of the old city on the Ring Strasse, this fin de siècle hotel provides a taste of *Altes Wien* with its beautiful art nouveau antique furnishings. Restaurant Korso boasts the same elegance, with beveled glass panels, carved chairs, crystal chandeliers and a marble fireplace. The menu offers traditional Austrian ingredients prepared in a light style influenced by modern French cuisine. Of course, dinner comes *after* a most necessary visit to the Opera across the street: The Viennese may dine gloriously, but they also dine late. (Hotel Bristol, Kärntner Ring 1, A-1015 Vienna, Austria; 0222/51516; Restaurant Korso bei der Oper, 51516, extension 546.)

The Beverly Hills hotel that was the home-away-from-home for stars of all wattage, and once belonged to the courtly Hernando Courtwright, has reopened its doors with more glitter than ever before. Now called the Regent Beverly Wilshire, it has been renovated and beautified in a two-year transformation that cost $250 million. It's glamorous and glorious.

Take a visit to the châteaux and cathedrals of northern France, the museums of Belgium and the windmills and old towns of Holland. They're the focus of a series of 7- and 14-day canal cruises aboard the luxurious *Etoile de Champagne*. For details, contact Raymond & Whitcomb, (800) 356-8846.

🍎 *For the Kitchen & Table*

Cooking fresh-caught salmon on a plank was the Pacific Northwest Indian way of preparing their bounty. The ancient cooking method is now introduced to the modern kitchen with the Original Chinook Cedar Baking Plank. Just place salmon—or any other fish—on the Western Red cedar plank and cook. It goes nicely from oven to table. The delicate flavors of the fish are richly enhanced by the sweet tang of the wood. A neat gift for the fisherman-cook, it costs $48 plus $4 shipping (item no. 6643) from Eddie Bauer, Fifth and Union, P.O. Box 3700, Seattle, WA 98124; or telephone (800) 426-7020.

How can you avoid wasting that half-consumed bottle of Chateau Margaux? A new device for preserving opened wines by stopping oxidation comes from Encore and lets you enjoy a glass days later. A cork of lightweight plastic is engineered to absorb oxygen in one 750-ml bottle. Simply pull a tab and an "air cathode" automatically removes oxygen from the empty space in the bottle. No foreign objects touch the wine. Available by mail for about $2 singly, and about $12 for a six-pack. Contact MATSI, 1321 61st Street, Emeryville, CA 94608; (415) 654-1960.

Milk-can-style canisters in blue or clear glass are a brand new old-fashioned design by Libbey. Great to display in a kitchen's sunlit window, they are available in department stores nationwide in 48-ounce, 64-ounce and 80-ounce sizes for about $6, $7 and $8, respectively.

Homemade *pommes frites* can be yours without fuss, fumes, spatters or spills with the Tefal Super Deep Fryer. This French import has a filtered cleaning system that clears the oil after each frying, a charcoal-filtered locking lid and a thermostatic control

to maintain temperature. It's also great for onion rings, fritters, fried chicken and tempura. Find it in white and gray in department stores for about $100.

When the bash is a big one, catering-size platters are in order. JMO Custom Ceramics, which makes serving pieces for fancy delis and caterers, now offers a line of porcelain pieces that can handle your most ambitious buffet creations. There is a wide selection of sizes and shapes, and prices range from about $60 to $100. Contact Dean & DeLuca, 560 Broadway, New York, NY 10012; telephone (212) 431-1691.

Old or new, glass paperweights are prime collectors' items. In the clear globes you may find anything from abstract mosaics and swirls of color to seashells and leaves. One talented craftsman is Ken Rosenfeld, a California artist whose appealing designs incorporate flowers and miniature vegetables. Our favorite—for a special gift for a special cook—has carrots, radishes, turnips and asparagus. The colors dazzle, the crystal sparkles. Get it (item no. KR20A) for $250 plus shipping charge from L.H. Selman Ltd., 761 Chestnut St., Santa Cruz, CA 95060; (800) 538-0766.

Look like a professional cake decorator with the help of Frostability, a nifty little kit created by food consultant-writer Jim Fobel. Aside from its simplicity, its best feature is the flower makers, which, with a single twist, produce whole flowers with every petal in place. The kit also includes a leaf maker, plain round metal tip, pastry bag, plastic coupler, recipes and instructions. It costs $10.95 from Frostability, Dept. BA, 6 West 83rd Street, New York, NY 10024.

Jacquelynn's China Matching Service in Milwaukee has an inventory of more than 20,000 pieces of discontinued patterns from Lenox, Wedgwood, Royal Worcester, Spode and others. They just might have the piece to complete your heirloom pattern. For more information call (414) 272-8880.

Now you can have soft ice cream at home, just like the local parlor serves. But with the Cream 'n Serve machine, you can choose your own fresh ingredients to make sherbets, frozen yogurt, iced drinks and ice cream to your taste. Make a full liter at a time in about 25 minutes, without the mess of salt and without having to turn any heavy handles. The compact machine costs about $130, and is available in specialty foods stores and department stores nationwide.

Does someone at home prefer decaffeinated coffee, while you like regular java? Mr. Coffee's Brewmates solves the problem. Its twin automatic brewing system can make two four-cup pots of whatever type you choose—simultaneously. And there are color-coded buttons for identification of the contents to simplify it all. It's available for about $60 at department stores throughout the country.

Seiko Instruments' little Kitchen Whiz will dazzle you with its versatility. It can convert recipes by increasing or decreasing measurements, reduce portion sizes and change metric quantities back over to the U.S. system and vice versa. The Kitchen Whiz also has a clock, calendar, calculator and kitchen timer. A wonderful gift for any cook. It's available for under $50 at department stores nationwide.

One of the great silver houses of the world, Puiforcat, known for its art deco style, has chosen Manhattan as the site of its first American boutique. China, flatware and holloware are all available in a handsome showcase designed to reflect the milieu in which Jean Puiforcat worked—Europe of the 1930s. A departure for this famous house is the introduction of a silverplate version of one art deco flatware pattern known as Chantaco. A five-piece place setting sells for $198, as opposed to the sterling silver place setting (known under a different name, Biarritz), which costs $1,250. (Puiforcat, 811 Madison Ave. at 68th St., New York, NY 10021.)

When you send a message to friends and family across the miles, make it an edible one. The rolling Typeface Cookie Cutter lets you punch out all letters of the alphabet in your favorite cookie dough. Compose your greeting, then bake and send. It's also a neat way for your kids to have fun while learning to spell. Order for $5.99 plus $3.15 shipping from Williams-Sonoma, Mail Order Department, P.O. Box 7456, San Francisco, CA 94120; (415) 421-4242.

There's a long-needed tool—known as a fish and asparagus cradle—now available for cooks. Designed to hold such foods as fish fillets, whole trout or asparagus, it is slightly rounded with a white plastic handle and stainless steel body. Get it for $19.95 plus $3.95 for shipping (no. 3-3286) from Community Kitchens, P.O. Box 2311, Department FY01, Baton Rouge, LA 70821; (800) 535-9901 or, in Baton Rouge, (504) 381-3900.

From Villeroy & Boch's most popular dinnerware patterns comes a series of nine wall clocks to complement country or contemporary room designs. For kitchen to nursery, patio to playroom, there's a compatible design. The clocks have a Swiss movement that is battery operated. An attractive wedding gift, each costs about $75 in department stores nationwide, or order by mail from Villeroy & Boch Creation, 974 Madison Avenue, New York, NY 10021; toll free (800) 228-1404.

Diet News

Edible flowers—nasturtiums, squash flowers, daylily buds, rose petals and calendula—are more than just pretty. They're rich in vitamin C, have no calories and are tasty additions to soups and salads. Make sure that you buy them at your greengrocer, where they are sold pesticide free.

Jacques Pépin takes the ho-hum out of diet recipes with the Cleveland Clinic Foundation video and cookbook, *A Fare for the Heart*. The 67 recipes range from casual to elegant and are for low-sodium, lowfat and low-cholesterol dishes. The 60-minute video and cookbook cost $39.95. The book is $9.95 if purchased separately. Write The Cleveland Clinic Foundation, 10465 Carnegie Avenue, Cleveland, OH 44106, or call (800) 258-8787, ext. 240.

Le Slim Cow is France's answer to lowfat butter and margarine. Made with buttermilk, milk fat and vegetable oils, it is low in sodium and high in calcium, and has half the fat of regular butter or margarine. It's good for baking and nice on your morning toast. Look for it in specialty foods stores.

Said to be the world's first mail order catalog for low-calorie and sugar-free confections, *Delicious Products for the Diet Conscious* provides a source for peanut brittle, chocolates, caramels and more. Send $1 to receive the catalog and assorted samples (specify low-calorie or sugar-free) to Lescal, Sweete & Sauer, 9215-A Skokie Boulevard, Skokie, IL 60077.

Looking for something more healthful than the standard potato chip? The Bean Chip, a no-cholesterol high-protein snack, is deliciously addictive salted or plain. Made from black-eyed peas (which are really beans), stone-ground corn, rice flour, safflower oil and sesame seeds, it is available in six-ounce packages in natural foods stores. Or telephone Johnson Ranches, (916) 824-4537, for a store near you.

Crabtree & Evelyn offers fruit conserves with no added sugar. Six flavors—apricot, blueberry, raspberry, black currant, strawberry and orange marmalade—are available in 7.1-ounce jars for $5.75 at specialty foods stores nationwide. Sorrell Ridge also has a collection of 20 pure fruit spreads for about $2 per 10-ounce jar. They're in supermarkets nationwide. Both are great for diabetics and dieters.

Coming to the rescue of the 50 million Americans who suffer from lactose intolerance are the makers of Lactaid products. They've instituted a hot line for questions regarding the disorder. Call (800) 257-8650 between 9:00 A.M. and 4:00 P.M. EST.

Hot on the dessert track is another new diet sweetener called Sweet One. Its secret ingredient is Sunette, the brand name for acesulfame-K, which was approved by the FDA after six years of testing.

Craig Claiborne has masterminded a delicious little collection of recipes for the diabetic, including Armenian rice pilaf, salmon with asparagus sauce and shrimp with rosemary vinaigrette. Get it free from B-D Micro-Fine IV Recipe Booklet, P.O. Box 2147, Young America, MN 55399.

Credits and Acknowledgments

The following people contributed the recipes included in this book:

Bruce Aidells
Marlene Andrews-Gilboy
Deborah Bernstein
Anthony Dias and Kathryn K. Blue
Jan Buckingham
Café des Artistes, New York, New York
Lane S. Crowther
Cuistot Restaurant, Palm Desert, California
Dakota's, Dallas, Texas
Dino's, St. Croix, U.S. Virgin Islands
Melanie Barnard
Brooke Dojny
Dorothy Dworsky
Janet Fletcher
Jim Fobel
Steven Froman
Gordon, Chicago, Illinois
Tracey Greenwald
Barbara Griff
The Grill, Beverly Hills, California
Nao Hauser
Janet Hazen

Beth Hensperger
Michael Hutchings
Jerome's, Tucson, Arizona
Karen Kaplan
Lynne Rossetto Kasper
Jeanne Thiel Kelley
Kristine Kidd
La Nouvelle Patisserie, San Francisco,
    California
Silvia Lehrer
Abby Mandel
The Mansion on Turtle Creek
Michael McLaughlin
Mark Miller
Jefferson and Jinx Morgan
Pamela Morgan
Selma Brown Morrow
Carolyn Myers
Rebecca Naccarato
Norbert's, Santa Barbara, California
Cola Parker
Harlan Peterson

Prairie, Chicago, Illinois
Rao's Italian Restaurant, Houston, Texas
The Rattlesnake Club, Detroit, Michigan
Betty Rosbottom
David Rosengarten
Julie Sahni
Irene Sax
Richard Sax
Kimberly Scharf
David Schmidt
Marie Simmons
Nina Simonds
Dorothy Smith
Katy Sparks
Sarah Tenaglia
Judy Tuckerman
The Vintage Press, Visalia, California
Water's Edge, Long Island City, New York
Beverly Yorke
Zarela, New York, New York

"News '89" text supplied by Zack Hanle

Foreword and chapter introductions written by Nancy D. Roberts

Editorial Staff:
    William J. Garry
    Barbara Fairchild
    MaryJane Bescoby

Copy Editors:
    Brenda Koplin
    Marilyn Novell

Graphics Staff:
    Bernard Rotondo
    Gloriane Harris
    Juri Koll

Rights and Permissions:
    Catherine Lawson-McNeil
    Stephanie Mack

Indexer:
    Rose Grant

The Knapp Press
is a wholly owned subsidiary of
KNAPP COMMUNICATIONS CORPORATION

Composition by Andresen Typographics, Tucson, Arizona

This book is set in Sabon, a face designed by Jan Teischold in 1967
and based on early fonts engraved by Garamond and Granjon.